To Dorothy.
for her smiling
face + sunny disposition
and faithfulness as
a teacher.
love Pilley
Joan

God Bless!
Karl Pilley

Presented to

_____

By

_____

On the Occasion of

_____

Date

_____

GREAT IS THY
Faithfulness

365 DAILY DEVOTIONS

Larry Burkett

PROMISE
PRESS
An Imprint of Barbour Publishing

Published by Promise Press, an imprint of Barbour Publishing, Inc., P.O. Box 719, Uhrichsville, Ohio 44683, http://www.barbourbooks.com

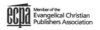
Member of the
Evangelical Christian
Publishers Association

Printed in the United States of America.

Dedicated to

the memory of Dr. Larry Hyde,
the kindest man I've ever known.

INTRODUCTION

WITHOUT a doubt, most Christians could benefit from a regular, systematic study of God's Word. In modern terms that's called a devotional study.

Ideally, it would be best to dedicate at least one hour per day exclusively to getting to know God better by studying his guidebook, the Bible. But, sadly, few Christians actually dedicate sixty minutes a day to studying the Bible, including me. Oh, some days I do; sometimes even more. But *not* every single day.

I will always be grateful for the wise counsel of my first pastor, Reverend Peter Lord, who, observing that I tended to make overly zealous time commitments, advised me to follow a simple plan. He called it his 959 plan: nine minutes and fifty-nine seconds a day dedicated to a systematic devotional study. I argued that I could give God much more time than that. "Great," he responded, "and some days, you will be able to dedicate hours to the study of God's Word. But you can *always* give Him ten minutes a day, no matter what, and in ten minutes a day you'll be able to cover any topic you choose in one year."

Over the years his wisdom has proved to be true. Some days, because of travel, illness, tiredness, or just laziness, I fail to dedicate an hour to Bible study. But I have stayed true to the 959 commitment. Anyone can commit to ten minutes a day.

This daily devotional is dedicated to that simple concept: Some days you will have more available time, in which case you can expand your study time. But you can always complete one of these devotional studies in ten minutes. Do this devotional every day for a year and you will have a good, basic understanding of God's Word. And if you'll read the suggested Scripture reading at the bottom of each page, you will have read through the Bible by the end of the year.

I pray you'll be as blessed by reading these pages as I was by writing them.

LARRY

NEW YEAR'S COMMITMENT

*"You shall love the Lord your God with all your heart,
and with all your soul, and with all your mind. . . .
You shall love your neighbor as yourself"*
(Matthew 22:37, 39).

As the new year opens, I'd like to challenge you to make one commitment (you'll notice I didn't say resolution). I believe the most important issue in this New Year is to set priorities for your life. It is imperative that you stay focused on the things that are really important.

We find out what is important by reading God's Word. In Matthew, when someone asked Jesus, "Which is the great commandment in the Law?" Jesus answered with what is in our Scripture passage for today. Read that again.

What does that have to with setting priorities? Those are the priorities: love God and love people. If you do, everything else will fall into place.

Decide today what your priorities will be for the coming year, write them down, and ask for God's help in setting those priorities in your everyday life this year.

DAILY SCRIPTURE READING: Genesis 1, 2, 3

WE ARE THE LORD'S

"Not one of us lives for himself, and not one dies for himself;
for if we live, we live for the Lord;
therefore whether we live or die, we are the Lord's"
(Romans 14:7-8).

I GREW up in a non-Christian atmosphere. I never saw Christianity manifested in my parents, so I didn't know anything about Christianity; nor did I have any interest in it.

My wife Judy was saved through door-to-door evangelism by Campus Crusade for Christ. In all honesty, at that time I thought, "That's okay. If it helps her, it keeps her off my back and lets me do what I want to do."

A lot of people shared Christ with me after that; I was pulled into Christian circles because of Judy. It didn't matter. I only wanted to have success, which to me meant buying the houses and cars I wanted.

Happiness doesn't come from material things. So, I started attending a Bible study with Judy, but I went looking for error, not for truth. I argued every point that was made, until the teacher finally asked to meet with me privately. He asked me to do two things: "Read the Bible, ask God if it is the truth, and if it is accept it; if not, put it down because it isn't for you. And two, don't come back to my Bible study. You are a disruptive influence."

Well, I picked up the Bible and read it with a different attitude and I accepted the Lord at age 32. My life changed from that moment. I became a different person, which is what the Lord asks of all of us.

What a joy it is to serve our God!
Father, am I the person You want me to be?

DAILY SCRIPTURE READING: Genesis 4:1-6:8

At What Price?

*"He who loves money will not be satisfied with money,
nor he who loves abundance with its income"*
(Ecclesiastes 5:10).

I OFTEN think of people, like Howard Hughes, who made tremendous successes of their lives financially and materially. These people did what they thought was best, but when they got to the end of life they asked, "What is life all about?" "What good is money now that I'm going to die?"

If I hadn't received Christ, that's exactly where I would be. There is no question. I would never have been happy and would have died thinking, "What is this all worth? What a worthless effort this has been!"

But, in Christ, life is totally different. I made a promise to God that, to the best of my ability, to this day I have not violated. I said, "God, if You will make it clear, I'll do whatever You say. You'll have to deal with my ignorance, because I am really ignorant about You, God, but I will never be rebellious or disobedient again. So, if You'll make it clear, I'll do it."

God's Word is really clear about what He wants us to do. We just aren't very obedient about following it. And, I'm not just talking about money (although that's what I teach about). That's true in the area of loving other people and putting the right priorities in our lives. It's putting God first.

It doesn't cost anything to say "I believe in God; I put God first." But, if you live it, it will cost something.

Have you put God first in your life? Is there some area of your life that you are holding back? Ask God to show you what that is and then surrender it to Him.

DAILY SCRIPTURE READING: Genesis 6:9-9:29

January 4

Lifesaving

"The ministry of this service is not only fully supplying the needs of the saints, but is also overflowing through many thanksgivings to God"
(2 Corinthians 9:12).

IMAGINE you are walking along a beach and you see a woman flailing in the water. As you draw closer and peer toward the churning waves, you see her head go under. You stand there transfixed, wondering if you just imagined it all. But then she surfaces, gasps for air, and the agony on her face is apparent.

She tries to call for help but the undercurrent attacks, and before you see her again she sinks below the surface. Finally she disappears.

On a daily basis, the number of single parents continues to grow to staggering numbers. Many of them find it difficult, even impossible, to keep their heads above water and are drowning in the cares that are associated with being single parents.

Until we have walked in someone else's shoes, we cannot possibly understand the needs of that person. Does that mean we simply do nothing to help single parents?

The church (and this means you if you know Christ as Savior) can make a difference in the lives of single parents and in the lives of their children.

Think of the single parents you know and ask God to show you what you can do to help them.

If you are a single parent, let your needs be made known in your church. No one can help unless your needs are known.*

*Adapted from *The Financial Guide for the Single Parent* workbook (Moody Press).

DAILY SCRIPTURE READING: Genesis 10, 11

TRUSTING TOTALLY

"Trust in the Lord forever, for in God the Lord,
we have an everlasting Rock"
(Isaiah 26:4).

IF I could wake up tomorrow, having gained one ability I don't have, I would want it to be the ability to absolutely trust God in everything I do—to have no doubts and no fears.

I believe there have been people in the past who had that ability and I admire them greatly. (The apostle Paul is one great example.)

From a human perspective, I could be perfectly content if I had really turned everything over to God and was trusting in Him completely.

My personality is such that I think too much sometimes. Then I remember the passage from God's Word in which Jesus asked, *"Why do you worry so much? No matter how much you worry, you can't add even a moment to your life. Each day has enough trouble of its own; therefore, trust in Me"* (paraphrased from Matthew 6:19-34).

How would you measure the amount of trust you have in God? Is it total, complete, unconditional, or is it limited by your circumstances?

God's Word says, *"Trust in the Lord with all your heart, and do not lean on your own understanding. In all your ways acknowledge Him, and He will make your paths straight"* (Proverbs 3:5-6).

DAILY SCRIPTURE READING: Genesis 12, 13, 14

January 6

Dealing with Pride

"Everyone who is proud in heart is an abomination to the Lord"
(Proverbs 16:5).

In order to cure a disease, we must first be able to recognize its symptoms.

Once we are trapped by our pride, we are of no service to God. Without a change and a commitment to accountability, we will not even be aware of our attitude of pride.

God will give us plenty of opportunity to recognize and correct the attitude of pride. The difficulty most times is admitting we have a problem.

It is vital for us to stay open to criticism, particularly from those who are spiritually discerning. Those most consistent in discerning our faults are usually our spouses. God has placed them in our lives as a balance, and they will help to offset our extremes if we will listen.

When we find that we only want to associate with the "right" people and look down at others because they're less educated, less intelligent, or less successful, then we are no longer useful to God and His work.

We must actually demonstrate that no one person is more or less important than another.

Who do you think is most important in God's sight?

The apostle Paul wrote, *"With humility of mind let each of you regard one another as more important than himself"* (Philippians 2:3).

How do you break out of the pride trap? Vow to serve God and God's people, and then make yourself accountable to others.

Is pride a problem in your life?

Daily Scripture Reading: Genesis 15, 16, 17

LETTING YOUR LIGHT SHINE

"We are ambassadors for Christ, as though God were entreating through us" (2 Corinthians 5:20).

IF you are a business owner or manager, you may want to start witnessing to your employees, creditors, and customers. But, first, be sure that you treat employees with love, pay your creditors on time, and provide a good product to your customers.

Once you demonstrate that Christianity works in your own life, you may want to consider trying some of the more overt ways of sharing that others have found effective. Not every idea for witnessing will fit every situation.

The Edwards Baking Company in Atlanta stamps Bible verses into the aluminum pie pans holding their delicious products. I met a businessman who was saved after reading one such pie pan. His Christian wife had just died after a long illness. The day of her passing she had ordered an Edwards pie and left it in the refrigerator for her husband. Just before she died she told him, "I left a surprise for you in the refrigerator, Honey. Read it carefully." The verse stamped into the pan was Romans 8:28.

A national trucking company in the Midwest painted signs on all their trucks that said, "Truckin' for Jesus!" They get between 500 and 600 letters a year from Christians and non-Christians, asking for more information.

No one can apply all the techniques that others have used in taking their stand for Jesus Christ. Find the plan that God has for your life and your business and it will work. If you aren't a business owner or manager, pass these ideas along.

If even 10 percent of Christian companies were used as tools to expand the Gospel, what a difference there could be!

DAILY SCRIPTURE READING: Genesis 18, 19

ONLY PART OF GOD'S PLAN

*"You do not know what your life will be like tomorrow. You are just a
vapor that appears for a little while and then vanishes away"*
(James 4:14).

SOMETHING happened to me while I was in charge of an experiments ground station on the first unmanned launch of Apollo. As we were about to launch our first spacecraft, I got called for jury duty.

I showed up at the courthouse with a letter from the head of NASA and the head of the Air Force, saying that I had to be there and asking that I be released from jury duty.

The judge, who wasn't impressed, looked at me and said, "Young man, let me ask you: if you died today, would they cancel that launch?"

I answered, "No, Sir. I don't guess they would."

He said, "Then you aren't all that necessary, are you?"

That's something we should remember as Christians. God uses us but we're just a part of God's plan. We should never think more highly of ourselves than we are.

God was getting along fine before we were born and will continue to function after we are gone.

He has a different plan for everyone. I happen to teach and write because God gave me a gift to be able to do that. Whatever gifts He has given you, they are just as important.

Think of what your gifts are. Perhaps you might even list them. Then ask God if there is anything else in His plan for you that you are missing. Trust Him to give you any abilities you feel you lack.

He is the God of the possible!

DAILY SCRIPTURE READING: Genesis 20, 21, 22

KEEPING COMMANDMENTS

"Whatever we ask we receive from Him, because we keep His commandments and do the things that are pleasing in His sight" (1 John 3:22).

FEW of us willfully violate the Ten Commandments. The spiritual and emotional consequences are devastating.

Most committed Christians exercise a godly motivated self-discipline to avoid overt disobedience. Externally, most Christians appear basically moral. Internally, however, many earnest believers struggle with doubts, temptations, and failure. They have fallen for one of Satan's most subtle ploys: Don't let religion interfere with pleasures.

Violating many of God's commandments involves attitudes more than actions: lustful thoughts, selfishness, anger, pride. These attitudes arise over a period of time and are difficult to avoid. Most of us develop them without realizing how or when they started.

God's minimum acceptable attitudes are to love God totally and to love others as ourselves. Christ said that loving God foremost is a prerequisite to receiving God's best (reread today's Scripture verse).

We are fully responsible and accountable for our actions, regardless of what anyone else does. Often we desire to obey and trust God but are unwilling to stand without compromise in all situations.

As Nehemiah did when he refused to compromise God's way, even to save his own life, we must precondition all responses to temptations and problems on the basis of what God says. God promises He will prosper and protect us, so He may receive the glory.

"Call upon Me in the day of trouble; I shall rescue you, and you will honor Me" (Psalm 50:15).

DAILY SCRIPTURE READING: Genesis 23, 24

January 10

A Reflection of Values

"Whatever you do, work at it with all your heart, as working for the Lord, not for men. . . . It is the Lord Christ you are serving"
(Colossians 3:23-24 NIV).

IT is enlightening to reflect on what the Bible has to say about business. Many Christians say they have a Christian business, but what does that mean? In order to understand business from a biblical perspective, it is necessary to first define what is meant by "Christian business."

Obviously, the actual business entity is neither Christian nor non-Christian. A Christian business, therefore, is one that is controlled by a Christian. The more control this Christian has, the more the business can reflect his or her spiritual values.

It is interesting how many Christians would like for God to make them successes so they can be witnesses for the Lord and how few really are once God does.

Clearly, Christians in business can be used by the Lord but only if the correct priorities have been preestablished.

One key to being useful to the Lord is to make decisions on the basis of God's Word and not on circumstances, feelings, or what is acceptable to society. To do this without compromise requires unwavering obedience.

If you know people who either own or manage a business, pray that God will help them not to compromise their beliefs.

DAILY SCRIPTURE READING: Genesis 25, 26

WHAT NOBODY WANTS

"Where there is no guidance, the people fall,
but in abundance of counselors there is victory"
(Proverbs 11:14).

SOME years ago a Christian friend was caught in immorality. He was a dynamic teacher, an avid witness for Jesus Christ, and had led many people to the Lord. However, as facts surfaced, the man was found guilty of numerous immoral acts and dishonest business dealings, and he was sentenced to prison.

He was a typical example of what can happen to a Christian who has virtually no accountability. He was president and chairman of the board of directors of his own company and ran his daily life as he saw fit, with no real input from anyone around him. By the time he had begun to stray from God's path, he was insulated from any accountability to his peers or to his family.

Unfortunately, many of God's servants in business today also are leaders without true accountability. Without the input of godly advisors, these Christians run the risk of doing what is right in their own eyes.

Ultimately everyone is accountable to God. To voluntarily accept God's system, we must first willingly accept His absolute authority over each of our lives. To say we accept God's authority but reject His direction to be accountable to each other is a contradiction.

Read Matthew 18:15–17 to see some basic accountability guidelines. It points out that failure to repent in light of biblical evidence amounts to rebellion against the Church.

To whom are you accountable? your spouse? your business associates? your church? your Lord? Don't let pride keep you from being accountable for your actions.

DAILY SCRIPTURE READING: Genesis 27, 28

GOD TOLD ME TO

"Brethren, I do not regard myself as having laid hold of it yet;
but one thing I do: forgetting what lies behind and
reaching forward to what lies ahead"
(Philippians 3:13).

HAVE you ever witnessed a Christian who was obviously doing something rather questionable but rationalizing it to all dissenters by saying, "God told me to do it"?

That's a hard argument to overcome, because by merely challenging it you feel like you're doubting God.

No one has a perfect insight into God's will. The soundest, most mature believers can and do make mistakes about God's will. Usually, when confronted by either a loving, but firm, challenge from another Christian, or the resulting problems, they will change direction.

Some believers refuse to believe they could be wrong and cloak themselves in spiritual pride by saying, "I know God wants me to do this."

God has given us the opportunity to fail. A brief review of Adam's life will attest to that. Our attitude should be to thank God for showing us what doesn't work and then get back to the task of discovering what does.

There is ample direction in God's Word to avert most of these errors. A sure way to step out of God's will is to compromise His Word and justify it by the obvious "success" it brings.

"The world is passing away, and also its lusts; but the one who does the will of God abides forever" (1 John 2:17).

DAILY SCRIPTURE READING: Genesis 29, 30

January 13

Individual Responsibility

"Do not be conformed to the former lusts which were yours in your ignorance, but like the Holy One who called you, be holy yourselves also in all your behavior"
(1 Peter 1:14–15).

IN October 1994 Judy and I celebrated our 36th wedding anniversary. What makes that day stand out as an event we won't forget is because on that day I had eye surgery to correct a longtime problem.

As I lay there, two things struck me: I knew I could count on Judy being there, even though I had inadvertently scheduled the surgery on our anniversary date. And, second, I was glad we still have a health care system that provides the best care in the world. I wonder what kind of care will be available once the government controls medicine.

I also wonder, given the current trend in our society, how many young couples will still be married to each other 36 years from now. Not many if we don't stop the destruction of basic values in America.

The real problem eating away at the foundation of our society is the lack of individual responsibility. The human tendency to avoid individual responsibility has always been around; however, rejecting individual responsibility has become a way of life in America. It's a direct result of rejecting God's sovereignty over our lives.

When God's rules are followed, individuals are held accountable for their actions, and it doesn't matter that they were born poor or that their mothers didn't love them enough.

Pray about ways that you can recommit to your individual responsibility and bring honor and glory to the Lord.

DAILY SCRIPTURE READING: Genesis 31, 32

January 14

Stealing

*"Not to steal from them, but to show that they can be fully trusted,
so that in every way they will make the teaching
about God our Savior attractive"*
(Titus 2:10 NIV).

DEXTER was guilty of stealing, caught in the act by his Christian employer. As a company salesman, Dexter had been asked to call on a prospective customer, who represented a very sizable profit. Dexter decided to keep this account for himself, which was not an option.

It wasn't the company's policy to follow up on sales calls, so Dexter was surprised when his employer called him in to talk about that particular sales call. In answer to the questions, he said the call was a waste, and after further questions he still stuck to his story.

The employer then revealed that the customer was a personal friend and had called to say that Dexter was planning to steal the account for himself.

Dexter's employer could have fired him, but as a Christian he was truly concerned about his employee's salvation and his personal success. So, instead, he offered him an opportunity to admit the truth, make amends, and begin again.

The employer believed an important biblical principle: All decisions concerning justice should be administered in mercy (see James 2:13). It was his desire to be Christlike in his business that helped Dexter become responsible in his career.

Today's verse speaks of being "fully trusted." Have you ever been tempted to steal anything? What was the outcome? Pray about this particular aspect of stewardship today and determine to use fidelity (faithfulness, allegiance) in your walk with Christ.

DAILY SCRIPTURE READING: Genesis 33, 34, 35

PLANNING GOD'S WAY

"Commit your works to the Lord, and your plans will be established"
(Proverbs 16:3).

OFTEN Christians question whether they should do any planning. The question I'm often asked is, "Shouldn't a Christian depend totally on God?" Yes, but that doesn't mean that we are to sit back and do nothing. Our faith requires action.

Planning is essential in any life but especially in the lives of Christians. God is an orderly provider and He expects us to have an attitude of doing our best in our everyday decisions.

Don't try to develop plans with no flexibility. Remember that God's wisdom may be exercised by redirecting our paths.

Patience and caution are necessary in any venture—particularly if it is a financial decision.

The Christian home should be characterized by orderliness and excellence. Neither is possible without good planning. Family discussions allow each member of the family to have an active part.

Written goals provide visible objectives toward which to work.

Any plans that are made should be compatible with God's will. You should be able to find Scripture to back anything you plan to do. Don't make decisions based on what others are doing.

If you need counsel, be willing to ask for it. Many Christians are willing to help others but are never willing to ask for help themselves. That's just ego. All of us need counsel and advice.

Pray together about every decision. Prayer brings God directly into our lives and strengthens our faith so we can trust Him in even greater things.

RESPONDING TO THE TESTING PROCESS

"Consider it all joy, my brethren,
when you encounter various trials,
knowing that the testing of your faith produces endurance"
(James 1:2–3).

IN His great wisdom, God has ordained that the perfecting of our faith and walk with Him should come by way of testing. God allows problems and circumstances to occur that will break our stubbornness, keep us dependent upon Him, and make us profitable for His service.

So often our first reaction to the pressures that accompany the testing process is to question God or try to escape, but should we?

Of course, there are times in all our lives when we feel defeated and would like to get away from it all. If that happens to 40- to 50-year-olds, we usually blame it on midlife crisis. In reality, such crises come at every stage of life.

The great preacher, Charles Spurgeon, said, "Many men owe the grandeur of their lives to their tremendous difficulties."

Until we come to the point of total dependence on God, in good times or bad, we are not really useful in His plan.

God, what is Your plan for me this day? I know You will be with me, no matter what happens.

DAILY SCRIPTURE READING: Genesis 38, 39, 40

BROKENNESS

*"Therefore I ask you not to lose heart at my
tribulations on your behalf, for they are your glory"*
(Ephesians 3:13).

BROKENNESS, whether it is financial, physical, or emotional, has at its center the purpose of teaching us to trust in God. Paul knew that his tribulations were the result of his persistent battle against Satan. They were neither pleasant nor enjoyable to Paul, but he knew they were necessary in order to build his character.

Remember, our loving Father's goal throughout our lives is to conform us to the image of His Son. But to that end, our ego and pride, which naturally oppose God and His purposes, must be broken.

"The Lord is near to the brokenhearted, and saves those who are crushed in spirit" (Psalm 34:18).

Is there anything in your life that might result in brokenness? Pray about it today. Do you see brokenness in someone else's life? Pray for that person now.

DAILY SCRIPTURE READING: Genesis 41, 42

GOD'S FAITHFULNESS THROUGH TRIALS

"The steadfast of mind Thou wilt keep in perfect peace,
because he trusts in Thee"
(Isaiah 26:3).

MY first reaction to the doctor's diagnosis was one of total shock. Cancer? No way! Impossible! The MRI dispelled all doubts. Embedded in my left shoulder blade and within my right kidney were two tumors. The biopsy results: renal cell carcinoma, a particularly virulent form of cancer. There were no "ifs" about it.

There was no way around this problem and I was concerned. Not about death; that was settled a long time ago. I didn't like the prospect of dying young—especially from cancer.

My doctor scheduled two surgeries in short order. In spite of the relentless pain and the ever-present specter of cancer, God was always with me—just as He promises. He has taught and is teaching me some important lessons.

Suffering is an integral part of the Christian experience. When God chooses to support His child through a trial rather than immediately snatching him or her out of it, has His goodness or love or power changed? Of course not.

The support and encouragement of fellow believers is indispensable. I can't imagine going through this kind of ordeal without the sweet ministry of God's people. The prayers and strong support of my family and the church carried me through.

I've gained a clearer perspective of what is important in life. How much simpler it is to prioritize demands on my time and resources when they are put to the ultimate test: Will this be of enduring value in the eternal kingdom of God?

DAILY SCRIPTURE READING: Genesis 43, 44, 45

God Is in Control

"For the sorrow that is according to the will of God produces a
repentance without regret, leading to salvation [deliverance];
but the sorrow of the world produces death"
(2 Corinthians 7:10).

SINCE I had to face the ordeal of cancer, in spite of the initial periods of questions, doubt, pain, and anxiety, I can honestly say that I've experienced the gracious presence of the Lord in my life as never before.

Obviously cancer is something that I never would have chosen to be a part of my life. Yet God, in His infinite wisdom, has allowed this for a special purpose. Of that fact I am confident.

We all can take comfort in the absolute truth that God is in control. If we are serving Him, then nothing can befall us except what He allows. Rarely do troubles seem beneficial at the time, but if we believe God's Word then we must believe He will ultimately receive the glory.

One verse that has meant a lot to me is, *"Call upon Me in the day of trouble; I shall rescue you, and you will honor Me"* (Psalm 50:15).

If you are going through a period of trial, don't become discouraged. Share your struggle honestly with those around you. Garner the prayers and emotional support of God's people.

Draw strength from the promises of His Word, and recall the many past instances when God has delivered you.

Think about one of those times and look up the verse or verses of Scripture that gave you assurance during that time. As you reread them, think of God's goodness and give Him praise.

DAILY SCRIPTURE READING: Genesis 46, 47

January 20

Alone with the Lord

"Now when Jesus heard [about the death of John the Baptist], *He withdrew from there in a boat, to a lonely place by Himself"* (Matthew 14:13).

FIVE days after my second cancer surgery—when my left shoulder blade and surrounding tissue was removed—I was released from the hospital. Everything was an effort: to sit up, to move, to sleep. I found myself getting depressed as I viewed the future. But, precisely when things seemed to be dimmer than ever, I began to sense a new work of God's Spirit in my life.

When all the visitors left and family members had fallen asleep, the house was completely quiet. I was alone with the Lord. It was enough for me to be alone with Him—to discover new depths of His love and grace.

During these times I would read my Bible, studying familiar passages but discovering new meaning in them.

Particularly encouraging were passages that spoke of God's desire to draw near to me for fellowship, along with verses that talked about life after death and the fact that our eternal reward is with the Lord.

Being stripped of personal wants, wishes, and desires, I began to sense the nearness of His presence in a deeper, richer way.

One of the passages that meant special comfort to me is one I want to leave with you: *"Draw near to God and He will draw near to you"* (James 4:8).

DAILY SCRIPTURE READING: Genesis 48, 49, 50

FRIENDS

"The Lord is the portion of my inheritance and my cup;
Thou dost support my lot. The lines have fallen to me in pleasant
places; indeed, my heritage is beautiful to me"
(Psalm 16:5–6).

FRIENDS are so important. I praise God for the friends He's given me through the years. Strength, peace, and encouragement are mine because of praying friends.

Within days of my first cancer surgery, cards, letters, faxes, calls, and flowers began to flow into the CFC ministry office. Perhaps you never know how many friends and well-wishers you have until you're down. Certainly that's how it was for me.

In the days, weeks, and months following my surgeries, Judy and I read every card and letter. I obviously couldn't read them all myself, so Judy read many of them to me. I was so moved by the faithfulness and compassion of God's people.

Perhaps the thing I remember most about these cards and letters was the compassion that God's people demonstrate for one another.

I was startled by the numbers of people who testified that they had met the Lord while listening to our radio program, which deals with personal finances.

It truly convicted me that God uses His Word in a mighty way if we'll simply be a transmitter of God's Word and not an interference.

Share His Word with someone today.

DAILY SCRIPTURE READING: Job 1, 2, 3

January 22

The Mind of Christ

"Have this attitude in yourselves which was also in Christ Jesus."
(Philippians 2:5).

WHAT does it mean to have the mind of Christ? Even though Jesus was God, He humbled Himself, became a servant, and obeyed even to death.

It's important to see that Scripture instructs us to have the mind of Christ and the humble attitude of a servant. God's grace is given to those who exhibit humility through their attitudes, words, and actions.

The Lord Jesus experienced humility in rank, because He left the heavens and came to Earth as a man. He remained humble throughout the disbelief, accusations, and physical pain associated with His trial and crucifixion.

Most of us have been humbled in specific circumstances; however, being humble is an act of our own will and occurs when we voluntarily serve others. Usually we prefer to be served and may even feel deserving, but this is when we don't have the mind of Christ.

Just as Jesus humbled Himself to do the will of the Father, we are to humble ourselves in obedience to God's will.

Having the mind of Christ is not a mystical experience; it is the humble act of an obedient servant.

Think of times when you definitely have not had the mind of Christ. You might want to list them. Then ask for forgiveness for those times.

DAILY SCRIPTURE READING: Job 4, 5, 6, 7

January 23

Indulgence

*"Like a city that is broken into and without walls
is a man who has no control over his spirit"*
(Proverbs 25:28).

MOST people don't get up in the morning and say "I'm going to indulge myself today." No, this attitude is much more subtle. An indulgence is almost always rationalized as being a need, but in reality it is something that has little or no long-term utility.

Consider how many expensive pieces of exercise equipment have been purchased with the best of intentions, only to be relegated to the closet or basement, unused and forgotten. And while we go to sleep disturbed over whether to buy a big screen TV, over half the world's children go to bed hungry or cold.

If you are constantly seeking to indulge whimsical desires, the results will be frustration and bondage.

I've found that before you buy something it's best to identify the need for the item, allocate the money for it, find the best buy, and pray about the purchase.

God often allows us to have more than our basic necessities, of course, but leave the door open for Him to bless you. Don't run ahead of Him and miss God's best.

DAILY SCRIPTURE READING: Job 8, 9, 10, 11

Greed

"Do not let immorality or any impurity or greed even be named among you, as is proper among saints"
(Ephesians 5:3).

GREED means "I want more. I want the best. I'll not be satisfied with anything less." Greed can separate families and friendships, and it breeds dishonesty and guilt. Greed is evident in our society in everything from bigger homes to flashier cars to obsession over hoarding money.

Many Christians are going to be ashamed to face the Lord and explain why they hoarded money while others went hungry.

Once commitment has been made to a disciplined lifestyle, regardless of the abundance of income, the danger of greed and its by-products is significantly reduced.

It's only when we discern the true needs in our lives, based on God's principles and values, that we can control greed.

Jesus warned us, *"Be on your guard against every form of greed; for not even when one has an abundance does his life consist of his possessions"* (Luke 12:15).

DAILY SCRIPTURE READING: Job 12, 13, 14, 15

The Slothful Person

"The hand of the diligent will rule,
but the slack [slothful] hand will be put to forced labor"
(Proverbs 12:24).

To be slothful means to be apathetic or inactive.

William had been out of work for nearly a year. He had little money left in his checking account and was worried about the financial situation of his family. He had some investments but didn't know their value.

William was surprised to find out the investments were valued at over $20,000. The fact that he didn't know about this detail might be indicative of why he hadn't worked in nearly a year. He had been fired from his last job, possibly because he didn't pay attention to the needs of his employer either.

This kind of action is the slothfulness warned about in the Scripture. Being slothful in one area usually translates into other areas. His home was in disrepair—not a surprise.

William's failure to take care of the things God had placed in his care was due to slothfulness. He confessed this attitude and asked for God's help.

The best way to keep what you have is to take care of it. As Proverbs 27:23 says: *"Know well the condition of your flocks, and pay attention to your herds."*

Ask God to show you what you need to do to take better care of what He has entrusted to you.

MAKING THE GRADE

*"No one can serve two masters;
for either he will hate the one and love the other,
or he will hold to one and despise the other.
You cannot serve God and mammon"*
(Matthew 6:24).

SINCE finances is a topic frequently discussed in the New Testament, it's obvious that God can and will use that area to test our obedience to Him.

In our society we have a value-rating system that is based on material worth. Sadly, that's just as true within Christianity as it is in the unbelieving world.

Fortunately, God's value system is based on spiritual worth and is measured by our willingness to accept His direction. This struggle between materialism and spirituality is addressed directly by the Lord in today's Scripture verse.

God desires that we use financial difficulties as an opportunity to trust Him more fully and to demonstrate to others that we are God's servants.

As was said of Job, *"Through all this Job did not sin nor did he blame God"* (Job 1:22).

Have you ever blamed God for your problems? Confess it to Him and ask for His forgiveness.

DAILY SCRIPTURE READING: Job 20, 21, 22

HUMILITY

"[If] My people who are called by My name
humble themselves and pray, and seek My face
and turn from their wicked ways,
then I will hear from heaven, will forgive their sin,
and will heal their land"
(2 Chronicles 7:14).

EVEN though Christ is the most exalted being in the eternal kingdom of God, He assumed the lowliest, most humbling position possible during His lifetime.

God wants us to question the condition of our hearts. Do we really consider ourselves higher than someone else, simply because we may have special talents that give us the ability to earn more money or have more advantages? Did you "earn" your looks or your size or your intelligence?

Having humility means we can accept our unique differences without feeling superior to any other individual. It is more than just an attitude, though. It is living a life of servanthood.

DAILY SCRIPTURE READING: Job 23, 24, 25, 26, 27, 28

COMMITMENT

"Delight yourself in the Lord; and He will give you the desires of your heart. Commit your way to the Lord, trust also in Him, and He will do it. And He will bring forth your righteousness as the light, and your judgment as the noonday"
(Psalm 37:4–6).

GOD calls each of us to a radical lifestyle: total commitment to Him. You can discern a great deal about spiritual commitment by what Christians treasure. God's Word says that our treasures will be wherever our hearts are.

All that truly matters is what we can do for the kingdom of God. Certainly, the things we accumulate are not important. They are simply tools for us to use in accomplishing God's work.

Sometimes commitment to God's way breaks down when a sacrifice is required. We must make a choice about commitment, and there are only two options: God or the world.

Which takes first place in your commitment?

DAILY SCRIPTURE READING: Job 29, 30, 31

JANUARY 29

CONTENTMENT

"Godliness actually is a means of great gain,
when accompanied by contentment. . . .
If we have food and covering,
with these we shall be content"
(1 Timothy 6:6, 8).

CONTENTMENT does not mean complacency. Complacency means that I have a problem that I could change, but I don't put forth the effort.

Contentment means that I know that I'm in the center of God's will. I change the things I can. The things I can't change I am willing to accept and be content with because I know the One who is in control.

The secret of a happy life is to learn how to deal with both the good times and the bad and, like the apostle Paul, to know how to be content with either.

If anything is standing between you and contentment, pray about that right now and turn it over to the Lord.

DAILY SCRIPTURE READING: Job 32, 33, 34

January 30

The Work Ethic

"Whatever you do, do your work heartily, as for the Lord rather than for men; knowing that from the Lord you will receive the reward of the inheritance. It is the Lord Christ whom you serve"
(Colossians 3:23–24).

In addition to supplying our physical needs, work plays a very important role in our spiritual lives. It provides the opportunity to put into practice spiritual principles that would otherwise be mere academics.

A Christian can study every passage in the Bible dealing with serving others and read every biography of those who were noted servants, such as George Mueller, and still not really understand the principle of surrendering rights.

The way we do our work provides the best exterior reflection of our commitment to serve the Lord in a real, physical way. It doesn't matter whether that work is in the home, on an assembly line, or in a corporate office.

Our true Christian beliefs will be reflected in our work situation, as we interface with others, more than in any other environment outside the immediate family relationships.

In his second inaugural address, Abraham Lincoln said, "With malice toward none; with charity for all; with firmness in the right, as God gives us to see the right, let us strive on to finish the work we are in."

Do you do all your work heartily and "as unto the Lord"? If not, what changes could you make?

Daily Scripture Reading: Job 35, 36, 37

January 31

Biblical Admonition in Work

*"He said to them, 'You are those who justify yourselves in the sight
of men, but God knows your hearts; for that which is
highly esteemed among men is detestable in the sight of God' "*
(Luke 16:15).

IT is fortunate for all of us that God's Word is both simple and complete. No subject affecting our lives is left to our own resources. Those who are resentful about the success of others, whose feelings are hurt because of the lack of recognition, or who use jobs as their alter egos all suffer from the spiritual malady: They are in service to self instead of to God.

Unfortunately, people will always fail; fortunately, God never will. If we approach our jobs with the attitude that some person must recognize us as the best, there will almost always be disappointment, because the first time the boss forgets to show appreciation or your spouse takes your hard work for granted, resentment creeps in.

We should look to the Lord for our rewards and, in doing so, find that His standards of conduct are much higher than any person's.

Satan's number one weapon is pride. God's number one defense is humility.

DAILY SCRIPTURE READING: Job 38, 39, 40, 41, 42

February 1

Work Attitudes

"Do you see a man skilled in his work?
He will stand before kings; he will not stand before obscure men"
(Proverbs 22:29).

FOR too many people work is a necessary evil; for others it's an obsession. Obviously, both are extremes and represent a spiritual imbalance.

Many Christians view their jobs as drudgery. For these people, jobs are literally just a means to earn money so they can entertain and recreate. They are dissatisfied with their vocation, disgruntled on the job, and resentful of others' successes.

A by-product of all this mental anxiety is quite often fatigue on the job and restlessness at home. To compensate, they fill their lives with endless outside activities. For nonbelievers, these are usually hunting, fishing, boating, skiing, golfing, and so on. For the Christian, they may be church activities and civic functions.

None of these activities is bad in itself; in fact, they can be quite good, unless the activities are a substitute for the lack of fulfillment at work.

Somehow Christians have been duped into believing that work is a secular activity and, therefore, they shouldn't expect to feel spiritual about a job.

That attitude destroys your greatest area of outreach and witness. If you view your work as a chore, you won't have much of a witness on or off the job. This is true whether your work is done in a factory, in an office, out-of-doors, or in the home. You can honor God in everything you do if you maintain the right attitude.

DAILY SCRIPTURE READING: Exodus 1, 2, 3, 4

FEBRUARY 2

TOO BUSY TO SERVE

"What sort of people ought you to be in holy conduct and godliness"
(2 Peter 3:11).

NOTHING interferes with our ability to serve God more than our need to earn a living. The simple truth is, most Americans are too busy to serve God.

We have grown complacent and comfortable in God's material blessings and have forgotten the first commandment. In the meantime, immorality and cults have grown to alarming proportions because their advocates are more zealous in their dedication.

Since God asks for obedience rather than demanding it, many Christians simply ignore the very reason for their existence: to glorify God.

Without exception, God has a unique and meaningful plan for every believer, and it does not depend on age, income, or ability.

God calls each of us to fulfill His plan and we have to decide either to be used by Him or to be bypassed. What a loss if we allow temporary comforts and laziness to rob us of true riches, both now and for all eternity.

Ask God to reveal to you if you have been "too busy to serve."

DAILY SCRIPTURE READING: Exodus 5, 6, 7, 8

CONSIDER THE COST

"No one, after putting his hand to the plow and looking back, is fit for the kingdom of God"
(Luke 9:62).

SERVICE to Jesus Christ is demanding. It may actually mean that we will have to work as hard for God's kingdom as we do for earthly riches or, perish the thought, even harder.

Few salespeople consider it an imposition on their time to talk about their product line. Being a success at anything requires dedication, training, and perseverance.

It would be a very foolish company that trained its sales force to expect success on every call. Just one turndown and they would give up, considering themselves failures.

Jesus knew that not everybody would serve God, and most might not even want to. Some would like to have a foot in both worlds. They are willing to be called Christians, provided they can pick the times and places to serve.

However, Jesus Christ said that only total service to God would yield peace and blessings within His will.

"What will a man be profited, if he gains the whole world, and forfeits his soul?" (Matthew 16:26).

DAILY SCRIPTURE READING: Exodus 9, 10, 11

TIME OUT

"You will be blessed, since they do not have the means to repay you;
for you will be repaid at the resurrection of the righteous"
(Luke 14:14).

MOST Christians would never refuse to do God's will; it's just that the timing is not right.

When God calls us, He wants obedience first and excuses last. We have allowed the urgent things of this society in which we live to overshadow the important things.

That fact is neither new nor unique to our generation. In fact, Christ witnessed it in His walk and predicted it for us. He gave a parable of God's calling to follow Him. People were invited to a dinner, but most were far too busy to attend right then. They wanted to be a part of what was happening but had a great many responsibilities. The result was that others were chosen in their places.

We all, to a greater or lesser degree, suffer from being too busy to serve God. Some are so busy doing things for God they fail to do the things of God.

Does this description fit you? Ask God to help you set your priorities in the right order.

DAILY SCRIPTURE READING: Exodus 12, 13

SOWING AND REAPING

"Do not be deceived, God is not mocked;
for whatever a man sows, this he will also reap"
(Galatians 6:7).

MOST Christians are familiar with the principle of sowing and reaping as it applies to giving—though few really believe it.

That same principle applies to sharing time in the Lord's work. Just as God can multiply the fruits of our labor, He can also multiply the use of our time. Any good administrator knows that ten minutes spent in productive planning is more valuable than two hours spent in confusion and frustration.

Therefore, one of the first things a busy, frustrated, over-worked Christian needs to do is to dedicate the best part of the day, week, month, and year to the Lord.

To do so will mean reordering priorities at work and at home to allow for time alone with God.

No other goals are going to be meaningful until the first and most important one is settled: your relationship with God.

DAILY SCRIPTURE READING: Exodus 14, 15

STANDING BY

"The Lord restored the fortunes of Job when he prayed for his friends"
(Job 42:10).

THOUGH it may seem strange to some, the book of Job is one of my favorites in the Bible. The way Job was able to pray for his friends, even though they had already shown their true colors to him, is an indication of what kind of man he was. And, because of that, God blessed him.

I would never avoid a friend if he or she had a disease, even if it was AIDS or any other contagious disease. I believe that a friend is a friend at all times (just as it says in Proverbs 17:17).

I had a good friend with AIDS, and before his death I tried to love him just as much as I would have any other person. He had been in a homosexual lifestyle and had come out of it. Unfortunately, the disease was a consequence of his sin, and he accepted that.

If you know someone with AIDS, contracted through homosexuality or promiscuousness, you should still try to help that person. It isn't up to us to condemn anyone. We can point out to that person that sinful lifestyles aren't in accordance with God's plan or the teaching from His Word. But without love, that counsel is callous.

I believe God expects us to treat others the way we would want to be treated in similar circumstances.

Father, lead me to someone who needs my help and encouragement, and give me the wisdom I need.

DAILY SCRIPTURE READING: Exodus 16, 17, 18

THE CALL OF GOD

"Whoever serves, let him do so as by the strength which God supplies;
so that in all things God may be glorified through Jesus Christ, to
whom belongs the glory and dominion forever and ever"
(1 Peter 4:11).

SOME have been called by God to go into full-time Christian service, but they weighed the call against the cost and rationalized that they could serve God best where they were.

Others clutter their lives with so much materialism that they never have time to listen to God. The desire for more "things" overwhelms them and the call to Christian service is shelved until "a better time."

We can all give thanks to those committed saints, from the apostles forward, who did not feel that fame and success in the eyes of the world were as important as God's blessings.

Without fear of contradiction, I can say that one day each of us will grade 100 percent of our success or failure on the basis of our service to Jesus Christ and nothing else.

I trust that each of us will hear Him say, "Well done, My good and faithful servant."

RESTITUTION

"He shall confess his sins which he has committed, and he shall make restitution in full for his wrong, and add to it one-fifth of it, and give it to him whom he has wronged"
(Numbers 5:7).

THE most important relationship you have is between you and God. God's Word clearly states that if you have cheated or deceived someone, you are to make restitution.

To make restitution simply means to right a wrong and to restore. If you will establish an absolute standard that you'll retain no personal benefit as a result of deception, it will precondition your response to any temptation.

This is especially true if you adopt the same restitution policy Zaccheus did—to repay 400 percent. It then becomes economically unprofitable to cheat or to deceive because you know that, ultimately, even more must be repaid.

We all have weaknesses. For some it is lying, for others spending, for others stealing, and so on. The way to handle personal weaknesses is to turn them over to God, confess them, and make restitution.

Remember the story of Zaccheus, the rich tax-gatherer. When the Lord visited his house, Zaccheus repented and said, *"If I have defrauded anyone of anything, I will give back four times as much"* (Luke 19:8). He chose the honorable way.

DAILY SCRIPTURE READING: Exodus 22, 23, 24

LONG LIFE

"Hear, my son, and accept my sayings,
and the years of your life will be many"
(Proverbs 4:10).

GOD gave us a promise: if we would put into practice the principles He teaches, we would have a long life.

I believe that the illnesses we have are a result of violating many of the dietary rules. And many of the problems we encounter are the result of not living by His Word.

I would say, without hesitation, biblical ethics and long life go together. For instance, when you give your word, you keep it. When you marry, you commit yourself to your spouse for a lifetime. When you have a job to do, you do your absolute best.

God's Word says, *"As for the days of our life, they contain seventy years, or if due to strength, eighty years"* (Psalm 90:10).

DAILY SCRIPTURE READING: Exodus 25, 26, 27

SEEK HIS KINGDOM

"Seek first His kingdom and His righteousness;
and all these things shall be added to you"
(Matthew 6:33).

THE admonition to seek first the kingdom of God is given by the Lord as a contrast to worrying about material possessions. I believe there never has been a generation of Christians so caught up in worry about possessions as we are.

We have a greater abundance available on a day-by-day basis than any previous generation. Most of us have machines that reduce the daily household labor required, our children are well-clothed and well-educated, and life expectancy is more than God's promise of threescore and ten.

We have insurance plans, retirement plans, unemployment plans, and disability plans. Yet, we are so caught up in making more money and buying bigger and better things that we have lost most of our thrust to reach the unsaved world.

As I read through God's Word, it keeps asking the same fundamental question: "Are we seeking first the kingdom of God?"

If we are going to spend an eternity in God's presence and only seventy or so years on earth, we should be more concerned about what we will receive than what we are getting now.

DAILY SCRIPTURE READING: Exodus 28, 29

WHAT DO YOU STAND FOR?

"Where your treasure is, there will your heart be also"
(Matthew 6:21).

THE question often is asked, "What do Christians stand for?" The answer the world would give is, "Not much other than what we do."

The sad part about it is that most people really want to know a personal God, but because of their desires they make gods out of material possessions and worship them instead. Time, energy, and money all are spent on the wrong things.

We have the only hope to offer a generation that is without hope, and yet we're spending the majority of our time pursuing vain things.

Our energies are so depleted in accumulating bigger homes, businesses, cars, computers, and retirement plans that we don't have much time to see that our priorities are out of order.

We can stand for accumulating things, or we can stand for building the kingdom of God.

A SPIRITUAL GIFT

"You will be enriched in everything for all liberality,
which through us is producing thanksgiving to God"
(2 Corinthians 9:11).

THERE'S only one reason God supplies a surplus of wealth to a Christian: so that he or she will have enough to provide for the needs of others. True wealth comes with the gift of giving. God promises His blessings to all who freely give and promises His curse on those who hoard, steal, covet, or idolize.

The apostle Paul defines the reason for having wealth as meeting the needs of the saints. In today's Scripture verse, the gift of giving is defined as the foundation for a life of selfless devotion to others.

Being a wealthy Christian establishes a greater responsibility than being a poor Christian. Being rich or being poor is a matter of providence in God's will, and He will give us only what we are capable of handling.

But the duties and responsibilities of wealth are very heavy because of the temptations. You can step outside of God's plan simply by attitude.

Becoming content without God in our abundance is a much more subtle sin than stealing. We just slip outside of God's will and never realize it until calamity hits.

The Christian's responsibility is awesome and sobering. God, in His eternal plan, has decided to use us to supply His work. One day we must all stand before God and give an account of what we have done with His resources.

God allows an accumulation of wealth so His people can exercise the spiritual gift of giving.

DAILY SCRIPTURE READING: Exodus 32, 33, 34

SHARING OUT OF OBEDIENCE

"He has given freely to the poor; his righteousness endures forever;
his horn will be exalted in honor"
(Psalm 112:9).

MANY of the decisions we make in our Christian lives don't make sense to the world. Therefore, we make them because of a commitment to God's Word—in other words, out of obedience. We must predetermine that if God defines a course of action in Scripture, we will follow it.

Attitudes play an important part in sharing with others. Have you ever given to someone resentfully? I have and almost immediately realized I had given up more than money.

Anyone who gives willingly receives a blessing that comes only with true love. God will honor your attitude more than the amount.

Remember, when you give to meet the needs of others, you give to God. He does not need the money. He is allowing us to share in His work.

When God places the needs of others on your heart and you supply those needs, that is obedience. But I'd like to emphasize that sharing from obedience differs from giving the tithe.

The tithe is given in recognition of God's ownership; obedience is sharing with those in need, out of a conviction that they should not be deprived.

I read somewhere that when you give of your possessions you give little, but the real gift is giving of yourself.

Pray for direction in your giving.

DAILY SCRIPTURE READING: Exodus 35, 36

SACRIFICIAL GIVING

"He said, 'Truly I say to you,
this poor widow put in more than all of them; . . .
she out of her poverty put in all that she had to live on' "
(Luke 21:3–4).

SACRIFICIAL giving with a right attitude is possible only for Christians submitted to God. In the United States, giving sacrificially is almost unknown. Worldly attitudes have clouded our thinking and dulled our sensitivity to others.

God will not allow His work to tarry for lack of funds. He will redistribute the necessary funds to Christians who have the correct attitudes—primarily those who are seeking His will and are willing to sacrifice their luxuries for the needs of others.

The use of our money is a very objective measure of our commitment to Jesus Christ and to His work. Christians who bypass God's work because they refuse to experience even a slight discomfort have missed the mark.

Sacrificial giving is possible for those who have a little as well as those who have much. All Christians can give sacrificially.

Begin to sacrifice a small portion from your wants or desires for the needs of others. Ask God to lay their needs on your heart and then put your commitment to sacrificial giving into action.

SELF-DISCIPLINE

"Poverty and shame will come to him who neglects discipline,
but he who regards reproof will be honored"
(Proverbs 13:18).

IN the natural order of things, God designed us to be disciplined people. The lack of self-discipline usually leads to all kinds of problems: debt, obesity, bad health—to name a few.

Self-discipline can't be limited to one's "self" or even to standards of society. If the majority of people are self-indulgent, instead of self-disciplined, does that make the lack of discipline acceptable? God's Word says it does not.

True self-discipline is not self-oriented at all; it is God-oriented. *"Cease listening, my son, to discipline, and you will stray from the words of knowledge"* (Proverbs 19:27).

Only by knowing and applying God's self-discipline can a Christian be free and, therefore, receptive to God's direction.

LEARNING SELF-DISCIPLINE

*"The waywardness of the naive shall kill them,
and the complacency of fools shall destroy them"*
(Proverbs 1:32).

BEING legalistic and rigid is surely not a cure for the lack of self-discipline. Both conditions are extremes and are beyond scriptural boundaries.

Self-sacrifice does not ensure spirituality and often is the indicator of self-centeredness. For instance, if the time you spend watching television is robbing you of time in God's Word, set a realistic time limit. Determine to watch television only between certain hours and no more.

In financial decisions, self-discipline should be the norm, but they must be balanced by reason. Overreacting will result in frustration and failure. It also will create conflict in the home. Instead, create the goals of a budget and a balanced bank account.

Whether your lack of self-discipline is in spending, entertainment, gossiping, eating, or some other area, correcting the problem can free your mind of doubts, frustrations, and bondage.

Only by knowing and applying self-discipline can you have self-respect and develop a godly self-image.

DAILY SCRIPTURE READING: Leviticus 1:1-5:13

WHAT IF?

"The Lord is my light and my salvation; whom shall I fear?
The Lord is the defense of my life; whom shall I dread?"
(Psalm 27:1).

OUR anxieties and worries usually are not related to the lack of things but, rather, to the loss of things. One of Satan's favorite tools is the question, "What if?"

Dedicated Christians get trapped in fear: the "what if" of extended illness, retirement, disability, unemployment, economic collapse. God wants us to consider these things and even plan for them, within reason; but, a Christian must consciously reject the attitude of fear.

Fear is the antithesis of trust; therefore, if we live in fear of the future, we suffer from the problem of not putting our trust in God. That doesn't mean that we shouldn't plan for the future, but if we live in fear it means that we have taken on a responsibility that belongs to God.

If other people see us living lives of fear, we lose our witness. Don't get trapped in fear.

Father, help to remember that You are my light and my salvation—my deliverance.

FEAR OF THE FUTURE

*"I am the Lord your God who upholds your right hand,
who says to you, 'Do not fear, I will help you' "*
(Isaiah 41:13).

CHRISTIANS cannot truly serve God and live in fear of the future. Many of the decisions God's people make on a day-by-day basis are motivated by fear of the future, not by trust in God.

For instance, many people stay with jobs they dislike because they fear change. This is particularly true with those who are 40 and older. Society has convinced us to a large degree that those over 40 are past their prime. What nonsense this is! It runs totally contrary to God's intention.

Fear of the future causes Christian families to scrimp and sacrifice for the elusive day known as retirement.

Often the total focus of the earlier years is toward the eventual day when "we can relax and enjoy ourselves." Unfortunately, the same fear that necessitated the hoarding for the retirement years forces further sacrifices—"just in case."

I don't mean to imply that planning is not God's will; obviously, it is. But when a Christian looks inside and finds primary attitudes of fear and worry, bondage has occurred. Ask God to deliver you from that bondage.

FAITH CONQUERS FEAR

*"In the fear of the Lord there is strong confidence,
and his children will have refuge"*
(Proverbs 14:26).

THE opposite of fear is faith. Therefore, when dealing with fear, one must first understand faith. In Hebrews it is described as "things we hope for and things that we do not presently have." So, if we have no needs, we have no need of faith.

Martin Luther said, "Faith is a living, daring confidence in God's grace."

It is God's plan that we have some needs in order that we may develop faith in Him, and it is vital that we view these future needs as opportunities to exercise and develop our faith.

We are told in God's Word that He is a rewarder of those who diligently serve Him. We must decide if we believe that or if those are just words.

F. B. Meyer said, "God incarnate is the end of fear; and the heart that realizes He is in the midst will be quiet in the middle of alarm."

No Christian can truly serve God and live in fear. It's a choice.

WOULD YOU ROB GOD?

"Do not be anxious for tomorrow; for tomorrow will care for itself.
Each day has enough trouble of its own"
(Matthew 6:34).

MANY families literally rob God and their families because of this underlying fear. They start a savings or insurance plan, initially with an eye toward family provision, but then more and more contingencies must be provided for.

Finally, there are so many contingencies that no amount of protection is adequate, and fear pervades all decisions about money. Some are willing to give a tithe from regular income, but any invasion of their surplus is viewed with resentment and alarm.

The net results of this lifestyle are bitterness, conflict within the family, and growing separation from God.

My heartfelt concern for this spiritual illness is that it is increasing among dedicated believers and is being rationalized as good planning for the future. That is an absolute lie. Any action that is not done from faith is done from sin.

The mania we have in the United States about buffering ourselves from any possible future event is straight from the deceiver. When our "sand castle" of affluence comes tumbling down—and it shall—our faith had better be founded in the person of Jesus Christ and not in material security.

God's Word says it better than I can: *"Everyone who hears these words of Mine, and does not act upon them, will be like a foolish man, who built his house upon the sand. And the rain descended, and the floods came, and the winds blew, and burst against the house; and it fell, and great was its fall"* (Matthew 7:26–27).

DAILY SCRIPTURE READING: Leviticus 13, 14

THE NEED FOR QUALITY

"Be sincere and blameless until the day of Christ;
having been filled with the fruit of righteousness which
comes through Jesus Christ, to the glory and praise of God"
(Philippians 1:10-11).

WE live in a society in which average is exceptional and slothful is normal. The trend today is to seek the path of least resistance and when the going gets difficult, give up.

In school, when the total grades are averaged, it's called "grading on the curve." As Christians we have allowed our standards to be graded by the curve of the world.

To avoid the trap of "curve grading," each of us must establish some minimum, godly goals. It means that we cannot be content to just "get by."

God's Word requires believers to make quality products and make them available at a fair price. Quality really means putting the best possible effort into whatever we are doing—whether it be products or services—because, by doing so, it reflects our value systems.

There's nothing more honoring to God than quality service or a quality product from a professing Christian. And there's probably nothing more dishonoring to God than poor service or a poor quality product from a professing Christian.

DAILY SCRIPTURE READING: Leviticus 15, 16, 17

GEORGE WASHINGTON

"The Lord is the defense of my life. . . .
Though a host encamp against me, my heart will not fear;
though war arise against me, in spite of this I shall be confident"
(Psalm 27:1, 3).

IN 1776 King George was not about to concede a very successful and prosperous part of his empire. England had the greatest military force on Earth and its navy truly ruled the seas.

When George Washington and the others committed themselves to open rebellion, they all knew the ultimate decision would either be freedom or the gallows. In the winter of 1777 the Continental Army was all but defeated. Washington warned that the prospect of defeat was all but certain, except for the intervention of the Almighty.

The ragtag army of 8,000 was trapped in Yorktown, with its back to the river and its front to 21,000 crack British troops. Although the circumstances were desperate, two things drove them as they retreated to their last stand along the river: their burning desire for freedom and their hope for better lives for their children.

Washington rallied his men with the cry: "If God be for us, who then can stand against us." He was convinced that God would not bring them so far to let them fail.

In the midst of a heavy fog, Washington's troops made their escape to the other shore, and the American dream was born—the dream that our founders gave us.

Washington was right: With God's providence we all can "reach the other shore" if we place ourselves in His hands.

DAILY SCRIPTURE READING: Leviticus 18, 19, 20

EXCELLENCE IN A MEDIOCRE WORLD

"Do you see a man skilled in his work?
He will stand before kings;
he will not stand before obscure men"
(Proverbs 22:29).

THERE'S an old saying: "If you want someone to do a good job, find a busy person." The precept is that a person who is not busy probably doesn't want to be.

Obviously that's not always true, but in the long run I have found a great deal of truth in it.

Many (or even most) people do no more than is necessary to meet the minimum standards set for them. They will continually belittle others who work to capacity and will demand more and more "protection" for their positions.

Solomon described these people well: *"Poor is he who works with a negligent hand, but the hand of the diligent makes rich"* (Proverbs 10:4).

DAILY SCRIPTURE READING: Leviticus 21, 22, 23

HOW TO BE A SUCCESS

"You ask and do not receive,
because you ask with wrong motives,
so that you may spend it on your pleasures"
(James 4:3).

THE world's view of success does not agree with God's view. What are you willing to sacrifice to achieve success according to God's way?

In many national magazines, there are ads promising to reveal the secrets of being a "success" today. Naturally, the ads are obscure enough that they don't reveal these "secrets" unless you respond. But the implication is clear enough: Success today is related to money, power, and position.

It's really not much different today than it has been. We first look at the material accumulation to determine if someone is successful. The admiration of society is carried one step further because even those who earn their wealth by deceit, extortion, or pornography are elevated to a platform of success today.

Most of those we call successful people today are frustrated and miserable, with terrible family lives; and, quite often they terminate their lives because they have nothing left to live for. The worst thing that can happen to those without Christ is to accomplish their goals, because then there is the potential that they may turn out to be worthless.

A successful person is one who accomplishes goals and is able to enjoy the benefits that result.

THE CHRISTIAN VIEW OF SUCCESS

"For all these things the Gentiles eagerly seek;
for your heavenly Father knows that you need all these things"
(Matthew 6:32).

As Christians we have to be careful not to fall into Satan's traps. We must have our guard up so thoroughly that we recognize the dangers.

If you spend too much time building security, the family grows up without proper guidance. When material priorities are substituted for spiritual priorities, children are spoiled by things and, thus, have an indifferent attitude.

Unfortunately, Christians do fall into traps. Why? Because the lies are so convincing we believe they have to be true. From one perspective, big homes, new cars, and private schools seem great. However, what had to be surrendered in the pursuit of them may have been greater: family relationships.

Remarkably, God's Word says that things are not the problem; in fact, God promises us that we will be blessed.

However, if we have the same desires as unbelievers do, our priorities probably are misplaced.

Father, show me a true picture of my own priorities.

THE POVERTY SYNDROME

"If I give all my possessions to feed the poor,
and if I deliver my body to be burned,
but do not have love, it profits me nothing"
(1 Corinthians 13:3).

SINCE the world puts so much store in material success, many Christians have naturally concluded that the opposite extreme is God's way and Christians should be poor. Or, if they aren't poor, at least they ought to look that way.

Satan is very tricky. Those he can't trap into his plan he tries to drive through and out the other side. So he naturally perverts one of God's blessings so that God's people will be careful to avoid it.

Poverty is a reality in Scripture, but it certainly is not a promise. God said there always would be poor in the land, but He never said they would be His people. The norm taught in God's Word is either "enough" or an "abundance" for those who believe and follow.

Many Christians believe that giving up something makes them spiritual. Although they may not believe they earned their salvation, they now believe that by self-sacrifice they must earn God's acceptance.

Surely the apostle Paul laid this deception to rest once and for all in his letter to the Corinthians (see today's Scripture verse above).

God is not looking for martyrs; He's looking for believers (literally, doers). We are to be doers of the Word and not hearers only.

DAILY SCRIPTURE READING: Numbers 1, 2

THE RICHES SYNDROME

"Who are you, O man, who answers back to God?
The thing molded will not say to the molder,
'Why did you make me like this,' will it?"
(Romans 9:20).

MANY Christians have concluded that since poverty isn't normal, riches must be. Therefore, they have assumed that God must make them wealthy to protect His image.

Then most of them set about in a totally secular way to accumulate what is supposed to be a Christian testimony. If God doesn't provide according to their preconceived plan, they rationalize that the end justifies the means and "help Him out."

So what if they don't have a personal prayer or study life? After all, just think what a witness God will get from their "success"! And even though their children don't get much parental direction, they do get the best possible "advantages."

Others try to manipulate God to work for them. They give, but usually to get. They continually demand "more" and "the best," while fervently trying to convince others that it is normal. Rarely, if ever, do they stop to consider God's plan, for fear it won't coincide with their concept of prosperity.

There is a great danger is seeing God only through worldly eyes, because then all riches and all blessings are measured in terms of what God can do for us, rather than what we can do for God.

To be a spiritual success, a Christian must be willing to relinquish all rights and accept God's plan. Of necessity, God will place believers at every tier (or income level) in society to minister to those around them.

DAILY SCRIPTURE READING: Numbers 3, 4

GOD'S VIEW OF SUCCESS

*"So then it does not depend on the man who wills or
the man who runs, but on God who has mercy"*
(Romans 9:16).

A LOOK into God's Word quickly reveals that material blessings
were given because God loved His people, not because they
deserved the blessings. They were withdrawn from those who used
them foolishly and were transferred to more faithful stewards.

To be a success from a biblical perspective, some prerequisites must be met.

Surrender: To be a successful servant of the Lord and to be
entrusted with material and spiritual rewards, we must first demonstrate an acceptance of God's leadership.

Obedience: To be truly blessed by God, we must demonstrate
a willingness to use our material resources for God. The more we
"let go and let God," the more God is able to glorify Himself
through us.

Persistency: To be successful we must be persistent in the face
of problems. We cannot give up easily. If all the doors were supposed
to be open and waiting, there would not be so many Scriptures
directing us to "knock."

Nothing and no one can shake a true believer from doing
God's will once it is understood. The evidence of this can be
observed in the lives of every servant who ever was used by God.
God's Word is full of examples.

DAILY SCRIPTURE READING: Numbers 5

Movies

"Beloved, let us cleanse ourselves from all defilement
of flesh and spirit, perfecting holiness in the fear of God"
(2 Corinthians 7:1).

I GREW up in a movie era and enjoy movies very much. But they've gotten so bad—not only the language, sex, and violence, but the general intent of the movies. They are commercials for secular humanism.

Recently I was watching a PG-rated movie with friends and it was so bad I got up and left. It had four-letter words, sex, and violence all through it. I thought, *Something's wrong with this picture.* A PG rating means you should be able to bring children to it without it being demoralizing.

I decided if this was rated PG I'd go see what an R-rated film was like. It was worse, and the theater was full of young people! No wonder so many kids don't have any values in their lives.

It's a shame that Christians don't involve themselves anymore. If your kids are going to be exposed to such trash, you not only need to teach them that it's bad but why it doesn't fit with what we believe and the way we live as Christians.

I hear Christians complain about the language and violence in movies, but they continue to go to them. We have to decide what our values are and then live by them.

"Our old self was crucified with Him, that our body of sin might be done away with, that we should no longer be slaves to sin" (Romans 6:6).

RECOGNIZING GOD'S WILL

"Because of the proof given by this ministry they will glorify
God for your obedience to your confession of the gospel of Christ"
(2 Corinthians 9:13).

IT seems evident that many Christians fall victim to worldly success motivation. They have a lot of drive and ambition, but they fail to recognize God's will for them and, thus, they submit to the world's will.

Often they spend too much time asking someone else about God's will for their lives, when it is God they should be asking. Ask those who are truly living God's plan how they found it, and usually they will say "God just revealed it to me."

Many times other people helped to point them in the right direction, but just as many tried to talk them out of doing God's will. God will reveal His plan to those who seek Him diligently.

The difficulty is that although Christians sense God's will for them it may not agree with what they had in mind, particularly in regard to income and ego, so they rationalize their way out of it.

For a while there will be a feeling of loss, but with time it passes. The next time, the direction is not quite as strong and it's easier to ignore. Eventually, God's call just fades away and the thorns choke out any further direction.

Once a Christian examines his or her life and discovers that the fruitfulness is gone (regardless of income), it is certain that God's will has been bypassed and another master has become Lord.

There are no quick, simple solutions to resolving this condition. Only earnest, honest prayer and petition will restore that sensitivity to the Holy Spirit's guidance.

DAILY SCRIPTURE READING: Numbers 7

CHRISTIAN CONCERN

"For the despairing man there should be kindness from his friend;
lest he forsake the fear of the Almighty"
(Job 6:14).

PERHAPS the number one cause of discouragement for those with problems is the lack of support on the part of other Christians.

Often children are cruel to those who are different, and in this matter I often wonder if some Christians have reverted to childhood.

What most troubled people don't need is for someone else to point out their problems or to counsel them about the sins in their lives that are causing the problems.

The majority of people who are discouraged already recognize they have erred (if they have) and have more than adequately condemned themselves. What they need is love and support.

The lack of loyalty to Christians undergoing problems is not new. All through the apostle Paul's letters there is evidence that his problems caused others to doubt his calling and to avoid him. Looking back further in time, the record of Job's friends stands as a testimony to disloyalty.

Outwardly, treat your troubled friends with patience, kindness, and love. And lift them up in intercessory prayers.

BE AN OVERCOMER

"Who is the one who overcomes the world,
but he who believes that Jesus is the Son of God?"
(1 John 5:5).

I HAVE counseled many people who are discouraged about their problems—many to the point of suicide. Satan knows where we're vulnerable, and in America it's usually in our self-esteem concerning material things.

In a land of plenty like ours, even those who are poor are better off than the majority of the world. So why do we see despair and discouragement? Because we have adjusted our expectations and made them relative to everyone else around us. It's the same symptom that causes despair in a multimillionaire whose assets have shrunk to a few hundred thousand dollars.

Discouragement abounds today because of unemployment or underemployment. When everyone is poor, it seems that most people can adjust to that. But when someone has lost a job and others still have theirs, it's hard to handle. High debt loads and creditor pressures simply add to the feelings of inadequacy and failure.

Discouragement, depression, and self-pity are the result of problems and adversity for some. For others, problems are a challenge and help bring about faith, trust, and victory.

As Christians we are admonished to be overcomers.

Think about something in your life that you need to overcome and ask the Lord to help you.

DAILY SCRIPTURE READING: Numbers 11, 12, 13

EXPECTATIONS

"Consider it all joy, my brethren,
when you encounter various trials"
(James 1:2).

MOST of us suffer from unrealistic expectations of what God promised. In Christians it is sometimes worse, because we fear that others will think of us as being less spiritual.

We actually have come full circle from the Christians of the first and second century who believed that problems were the evidence of spiritual depth.

Actually neither extreme is scripturally correct, but the case for Christians undergoing trials is more scriptural.

The trials James is addressing in today's Scripture verse are a consequence of serving God without compromise. However, most of our current problems are the result of violating biblical principles.

If we follow the teachings of God's Word, we will have realistic expectations of what He has promised. There's a promise in His Word for every circumstance or happening in our lives. All you have to do is to learn those verses and apply them to your life.

UNREASONABLE EXPECTATIONS

*"The overseer must be above reproach as God's steward,
not self-willed, not quick-tempered. . .not fond of sordid gain. . .
hospitable, loving what is good, sensible, just, devout,
self-controlled, holding fast the faithful word"*
(Titus 1:7–9).

UNREASONABLE expectations often create discouragement, particularly in the lives of our church leaders. The pastor obviously should be a Christian of very high character, but where in that description does it imply that a pastor is to be perfect?

Unfortunately, according to the "Book of Christian Opinions," pastors don't have the right to have problems. So those who have trouble communicating with their spouses or who are trying to live on much less than what others live on often get discouraged.

One of Satan's favorite weapons is discouragement. He knows that if he can get you to doubt God there's a chance you will give up.

It would shock many Christians to find out that their pastors even doubt God from time to time and that their problems get so overwhelming that they suffer depression.

Some collapse into despair and self-pity, but others grow stronger. Those who grow stronger can be categorized, as James said, as doers of the Word and not hearers only who delude themselves (see James 1:22).

Examples of doers are Abraham, Nehemiah, Daniel, and Paul. It's pretty clear they weren't perfect, but they were obedient. In their times of difficulty they did not panic or get depressed; they turned to the Lord. They were a good example for all of us.

Lord, are my expectations unreasonable?

DAILY SCRIPTURE READING: Numbers 16, 17, 18

EXPECTATIONS ABOUT CHILDREN

*"Like apples of gold in settings of silver is
a word spoken in right circumstances"*
(Proverbs 25:11).

EVEN the most humble Christians are quick to brag about achievements by their children, particularly if it's something in the Lord's work.

It's as if we want to validate our commitments through our children. If we are elevated spiritually by the achievements of our children, then we also are demoralized by their failures.

It's probably time for us to realize that God doesn't have grandchildren or stepchildren—only children. Everyone decides individually to follow or not to follow the Lord. This doesn't mean that we shouldn't lead our children, correct them, or encourage them, but we must recognize their right to choose, just as we did.

Share failures you've had with your children and allow them to observe that Christians haven't totally arrived—we're still on the way. I experienced such an event when one of my sons came home from college to ask me for help in clearing up his checking account.

He had eight checks overdrawn and $70 in overdraft charges. Needless to say, I was discouraged. The only thing worse for a Christian financial counselor would be for my own account to be overdrawn (which happened once when I forgot to make a deposit).

God used my son's problem to help me realize that just because I teach financial discipline doesn't mean my children understand it. I was able to share why financial principles are in God's Word.

First, set an example; then, lead and encourage your children.

DAILY SCRIPTURE READING: Numbers 19, 20, 21

FINANCIAL DISCOURAGEMENT

*"No one can serve two masters; for either he will hate the one
and love the other, or he will hold to one and despise the other.
You cannot serve God and mammon"*
(Matthew 6:24).

PERHAPS the most consistent area of discouragement for most
people is financial failure. Not only are our egos involved with our
ability to provide, but our security also is threatened.

Quite often the demonstration of our stewardship is not
how much we give but how we react when there isn't much to give.

With many, if not most Christians, their faith at any given
time seems proportional to their material resources. Obviously this
is not true for everyone. Some Christians find that in the midst of
their most difficult times their faith grows and matures, which is
exactly what James says it will do if we abide in Christ (see James
1:2–3).

God's Word teaches that it is impossible for a Christian to
divide loyalties. We can serve but one God. We must decide where
our hearts are.

Sometimes God will allow financial crises to come into our
lives to give us the opportunity to decide where our loyalties are.

How to Defeat Discouragement

*"But in all these things we overwhelmingly
conquer through Him who loved us"*
(Romans 8:37).

THERE is a cliché that summarizes this subject: "Keep on keeping on." You must decide what you believe and trust God, regardless of the outside circumstances.

Also, your response to any situation should be determined in advance. If anyone, Christian or otherwise, waits until a problem occurs to decide how he or she will handle it, that person will be controlled by the events—not God's Word.

If all we are looking for is what we can have in this world, then we're only slightly better off than the lost.

Be ready at all times to "overwhelmingly conquer" whatever comes into your life. You can do it with God's help.

God wants to bless us with peace in this life and eternal rewards in the next.

DAILY SCRIPTURE READING: Numbers 25, 26

HOW DECEIT DESTROYS

*"A worthless person, a wicked man,
is the one who walks with a false mouth,
who winks with his eyes, who signals with his feet,
who points with his fingers"*
(Proverbs 6:12–13).

DECEIT is an external, visible expression of inner spiritual flaws. The most devastating loss associated with deceit is the dulling of our spiritual awareness.

Guilt associated with a known deception will cause us to withdraw from God's presence. Once withdrawn, subsequent deceptions (lies) become easier, and we feel less conviction.

Often the pretense of spirituality remains (church, conferences, Bible studies), but the sensitivity and fellowship are gone. Literally, we no longer feel worthy and believe that we have failed God. If we allow this to continue, the result can easily be a life of defeat and frustration.

Fortunately, God knew we wouldn't be perfect and made allowances for our weaknesses by a principle called confession. Confession is often more difficult than honesty would have been originally, but it is absolutely necessary to restore fellowship with God.

Since confession is so painful, total honesty will look more attractive the next time.

DAILY SCRIPTURE READING: Numbers 27, 28, 29

TEMPTATION TO DECEIVE

"He who conceals his transgressions will not prosper,
but he who confesses and forsakes them will find compassion"
(Proverbs 28:13).

NO one is immune to the temptation to deceive, particularly when money is concerned. Some people establish their responses prior to the situation and are able to resist, not on the basis of their own strength but on God's.

When I was an unsaved businessman, the temptation to deceive was a constantly nagging problem. Quite often it was not a desire to lie but, rather, to just simply omit a few pertinent facts about a product to potential buyers. *After all,* I would tell myself, *what they don't know won't hurt them.*

Sometimes that old cliché is right and sometimes it's wrong, but invariably I found the one it did hurt was me. I felt guilt and a loss of honor each time. As a Christian, I naturally assumed such weaknesses would never tempt me again, especially as I became more familiar with God's Word.

The one way to fail is to deceive yourself into believing you're too strong to fail. Many times in our lives there are situations in which an undetected compromise to God's way could be made; in fact, many times it is.

Fortunately, when Jesus went to the cross He opened the way of repentance. All we have to do to restore fellowship with God is to repent and ask for forgiveness.

Forgiveness follows genuine repentance.

DAILY SCRIPTURE READING: Numbers 30, 31

HYPOCRISY

"Put away from you a deceitful mouth,
and put devious lips far from you"
(Proverbs 4:24).

THERE is nothing more devastating to a believer's life than to look spiritual but live in defeat. The immediate consequence is the loss of esteem in the eyes of loved ones, close friends, and business associates.

Children are rarely attracted to a weak, watered-down version of Christianity that says one thing and does another. If they see mom and dad put on their "church" faces only on Sunday, they will believe that's what being a Christian is all about.

When we live lifestyles that are contrary to God's way, the step from hypocrisy to a critical spirit is a short one. It is the desire to cut others down to our level that brings about the critical or judgmental attitudes. Every small flaw in others will be amplified and expounded on in an effort to justify the flaws in our own attitudes.

Instead of accomplishing the desired result of hiding the deceptive spirit, usually the opposite occurs, and others who normally would not notice are even more aware.

I'm sure you've heard it before, but you may be the only "Gospel" that someone near you will "read." It may be a loved one, a friend, or a business associate. If unbelievers see hypocrisy in your life, they'll have no desire to be Christians.

Is someone "reading" your life? What does that person see?

DAILY SCRIPTURE READING: Numbers 32, 33

BOUND WITH UNBELIEVERS

"Do not be bound together with unbelievers;
for what partnership have righteousness with
unrighteousness or light with darkness"
(2 Corinthians 6:14).

WAS the apostle Paul saying that we should never have anything to do with nonbelievers? Absolutely not! We are to comingle with nonbelievers so they can see Christ being manifested through our lives.

The admonition is not to be bound with them. This means being in business, being married, or being yoked with an unbeliever in any other way.

My recommendation to any Christian is to diligently avoid all yokes with unbelievers. However, if you are married to an unbeliever, read Paul's teachings from 1 Corinthians 7:12.

The same principle can be applied to business partnership with an unbeliever. Let the partnership remain, provided you are allowed to exercise your faith in that business. If your partner wants out, it's time to dissolve the partnership.

Your commitment to serve the Lord has to be greater than any business or family tie.

Think of anything or anyone you are yoked with in any way that would be displeasing to the Lord, and ask Him to show you the way out of that situation. He wants what is best for you.

"If the Son shall make you free, you shall be free indeed" (John 8:36).

CORRECTING DECEPTION

"He who conceals his transgressions will not prosper,
but he who confesses and forsakes them will find compassion"
(Proverbs 28:13).

LORD Denman wrote that "deception is a delusion, a mockery, and a snare."

Whenever you detect a deception in your own life, large or small, stop what you're doing and confess it immediately. This means to confess not only to God but also to the others who are involved.

There are many rationalizations for not doing this, but there really is only one reason: pride. You must resolve not to be deceptive before the situation presents itself or it will be impossible for you to do the right thing when you are faced with a decision.

You can't assume that the victims of your act of deception will understand or accept an apology either. But, the apology is not for them; it's for you, because if you don't confess your transgression (deception) you will not prosper.

However, just as today's Scripture verse says, when you confess your sins you will find compassion.

DAILY SCRIPTURE READING: Deuteronomy 1, 2

March 14

Be Accountable

"Without consultation, plans are frustrated,
but with many counselors they succeed"
(Proverbs 15:22).

WE need to be accountable to others, so that when we stray off the path they will correct us. Unfortunately, many Christians are accountable to no one because they don't have to be. This is particularly true of those who are materially successful; they isolate themselves behind a wall of ego and pride.

The best accountability comes from the home between husband and wife. With rare exception, one spouse is acutely aware of the other's strengths and weaknesses. If a couple has an open and honest relationship, one will detect the other's deceptions quickly.

Correcting must be done gently and in love, or the result may be bitterness. Always remember that the purpose is to restore a loved one to the right relationship with God, not to accuse.

Children can participate wholeheartedly in the detection and correction process. (Mine never failed to detect when I exceeded the posted speed limit.)

In addition to family, every Christian should become accountable to one or more other Christians who care enough to admonish and correct. Sometimes it's painful for both parties, but it is absolutely necessary for spiritual growth.

God's Word says it better than I can. *"With gentleness correcting those who are in opposition, if perhaps God may grant them repentance leading to the knowledge of the truth, and they may come to their senses and escape from the snare of the devil, having been held captive by him to do his will"* (2 Timothy 2:25–26).

RECOGNIZING PRIDE

*"Everyone who is proud in heart is an abomination
to the Lord; assuredly, he will not be unpunished"*
(Proverbs 16:5).

PRIDE is what caused Satan's eternal ruin and it is also what led Saul astray. When we take things into our own hands, it becomes easier to disobey God.

Once we are trapped by pride, we are not of service to God. Without a change and a commitment to accountability, we will not be aware of our attitude of pride.

Dr. Samuel Johnson wrote, "Pride is a vice, which pride itself inclines every man to find in others, and to overlook in himself."

God will give plenty of opportunities to recognize and correct this attitude. The difficulty most times is admitting that the problem exists.

Pride is deceptive because it's so normal today. We are told to achieve and to be the best we can be so we can be effective witnesses. Then, somewhere along the way, the goal of achieving takes a higher priority than witnessing—the result of pride.

It's good to remember what we read in God's Word: *"Everyone who exalts himself shall be humbled, but he who humbles himself shall be exalted"* (Luke 18:14).

HARD WORK:
REWARD ENOUGH?

"Do you see a man skilled in his work?
He will stand before kings;
He will not stand before obscure men"
(Proverbs 22:29).

WORK plays a very important role in our lives as believers. It provides the opportunity to put into practice spiritual principles that otherwise would be mere academics.

We can read every passage in the Bible dealing with noted servants and still not really understand the principle of surrendering rights. On the job, however, the opportunity to yield our rights presents itself every day.

The way we do our work day by day provides the best exterior reflection of our commitment to serve the Lord in a real, physical way. It doesn't matter whether that work is in the home, on an assembly line, or in a corporate office. Our true Christian beliefs will be reflected more clearly there than in any other environment outside of the immediate family relationships.

Somehow we've been duped into believing that work is a secular activity and, therefore, we shouldn't expect to feel spiritual about our jobs. This attitude destroys our greatest area of outreach and witness. Few Christians, if any, who view their work as a "chore" have much of a witness on or off the job.

What is your attitude toward your job? Do your coworkers and your employer know that you are a Christian by your attitudes and work habits?

DAILY SCRIPTURE READING: Deuteronomy 8, 9, 10

ESCAPING THE PRIDE TRAP

*"Before destruction the heart of man is haughty,
but humility goes before honor"*
(Proverbs 18:12).

I THINK Robert Burton said it best when he wrote, "They are proud in humility, proud in that they are not proud." Does that sound like anyone you know?

How do you break out of the pride trap? First, vow to serve God and then make yourself accountable to others.

Too often Christian leaders are not accountable to anyone. Consequently, they have little or no feedback from those who can recognize the symptoms associated with pride.

First and foremost, a husband and wife must be accountable to each other. Major decisions should be discussed together and opinions and insights exchanged. If a wife has the liberty to be honest, she usually will detect (and expose) his pride (and vice versa).

Second, Christian businesspeople should be accountable to peers or people they respect who are strong enough to be totally honest. Those I know who practice accountability find they must meet regularly and learn each other's basic flaws. They both must be studying God's Word and be seeking to truly serve God or it won't work.

One rule I use for those I have helped to get started: the criticism must be honest and based on God's Word. Also, the person pointing out the problem must suggest a way to change the attitude and must testify how the change helped in his or her life.

Sophocles wrote, "Pride, when puffed up, vainly, with many things unseasonable, unfitting, mounts the wall, only to hurry to that fatal fall."

DAILY SCRIPTURE READING: Deuteronomy 11, 12, 13

THE DANGER OF AFFLUENCE

"Where your treasure is, there will your heart be also"
(Matthew 6:21).

IT is not necessary to live poorly to serve the Lord. The only people who think poverty is spiritual are those who haven't tried it.

But, just as certainly, it is clear from God's Word that affluence presents the greatest threat to our walk with the Lord.

Poverty is not God's norm; but, neither is lavishness.

It is a rare individual who can actually handle much wealth and keep his or her priorities straight.

While we are laying awake wondering whether to buy a new car or a boat, over half the world's children are going to bed hungry and cold.

Everything starts with a first step and that is to get involved with the needs of others. This will help us focus more clearly on what our actual needs are.

Perhaps you think you don't have much, but compared to someone else you are very affluent.

Lord, please show me someone that I can help—someone who really needs what I can give.

DAILY SCRIPTURE READING: Deuteronomy 14, 15, 16, 17

FAILING GRACEFULLY

"Without faith it is impossible to please Him,
for he who comes to God must believe that He is,
and that He is a rewarder of those who seek Him"
(Hebrews 11:6).

THERE are many Christians who are "graceful failures." They don't demand anything of God and, in fact, expect nothing. Usually, they get what they expect: nothing. Many people accept failure as God's will when it isn't.

The Scripture says God wants to bless us and wants us to ask of Him. We must believe that God wants to bless us.

And, until God individually convicts someone that His plan is otherwise, we are not to accept failure. If you believe you should accept failure, you should read Christ's parables in Luke 11:5–13 and Luke 18:1–8. One of God's principles is persistence in the face of discouragement.

Satan wants you to fail. He will plant a dark thought in your mind and then "fertilize" it daily. But you don't have to listen to him. God's Word says plainly to resist Satan and his tricks. The Bible is full of encouragement.

Do you trust God, or do you just say you trust God?

DAILY SCRIPTURE READING: Deuteronomy 18, 19, 20, 21

BEING IN GOD'S WILL

"Forgetting what lies behind and reaching forward
to what lies ahead, I press on toward the goal for
the prize of the upward call of God in Christ Jesus"
(Philippians 3:13–14).

EVEN with the best discernment, it's possible, and even probable, that we will do things that are out of God's will.

How can you know God's will for your life? God's Word, the Bible, tells us what His will is. *"If anyone is God-fearing, and does His will, He hears him"* (John 9:31).

One sure way to step out of God's path is to compromise His Word or His will for us and justify it by the obvious success it brings. Satan is quite willing and able to bless any plan that serves his purpose rather than God's. Only by staying in God's Word, praying, and seeking godly counsel can we avoid Satan's traps.

Thomas Guthrie wrote, "If you find yourself loving any pleasure better than your prayers, any book better than the Bible, any persons better than Christ, or any indulgence better than the hope of heaven—take alarm."

If you find yourself outside of God's will and are experiencing a lack of peace (spiritual deadness), you must be willing to abandon everything and seek God's path again—reaching toward the "goal for the prize of the upward call of God."

DAILY SCRIPTURE READING: Deuteronomy 22, 23, 24, 25

MARCH 21

IS IT GOD'S WILL?

*"When Cephas came to Antioch, I opposed him to his face,
because he stood condemned"*
(Galatians 2:11).

HAVE you ever witnessed to a Christian who was obviously doing something rather dumb but rationalized it by saying, "God told me to do it"?

You found that hard to argue with, because by challenging it you felt like you were doubting God. But later the whole thing fell apart, and you found yourself wishing you had had the courage to speak up.

Why don't we speak up when we see another Christian who is obviously wrong? Because most of us are timid about applying biblical truth to a real-life situation.

The soundest and most mature believers can and do make mistakes about God's will. Usually, when confronted by either a loving but firm challenge from another Christian (or the resulting problems), they will change direction.

In today's Scripture verse we find that the apostle Paul knew the truth—Peter's actions didn't conform to the truth—so Paul confronted the leader of the Christian church.

Of course, some Christians simply refuse to believe they could be wrong and cloak themselves in spirituality by saying "I know God wants me to do this." Those are the ones who confirm the cliché: "Often wrong, but never in doubt."

Lord, show me Your will for me in everything I do today, and, as I read in Your Word, *"Give me understanding, that I may know Thy testimonies"* (Psalm 119:125).

DAILY SCRIPTURE READING: Deuteronomy 26, 27, 28

DEVOTED ASSISTANCE

*"Be devoted to one another in brotherly love; . . .
contributing to the needs of the saints,
practicing hospitality"*
(Romans 12:10, 13).

ONE Sunday after church, Paige, a single mother, was leaving the sanctuary, dragging her two-year-old beside her. Paige was exhausted. She'd been working 11-hour days and had worked all day Saturday. Her toddler needed her but she had nothing left to give. She needed rest and time to regroup, so during the service she had silently asked for God's help.

One of the ladies in the church noticed her as she walked by and said, "Paige, would you let me take Rachel for the afternoon? You look like you could use a break."

It was the best thing anyone could have done for this young mother. It was an answer to prayer.

As the body of Christ, or as individuals, we can be the answer to a single parent's prayer. God will be honored by our service and we will be blessed.

Do you have someone in your church (or your neighborhood) who needs your help for an afternoon now and then? Sometimes we think the only way to help others is to give money, but time is a valuable commodity in situations like this one.

Ask God to show you someone you can be a blessing to by giving of your time and resources. Single parents are in a daily tug-of-war and they need to know that there's hope.

CONFIRMED BY SUCCESS

"The faith which you have,
have as your own conviction before God.
Happy is he who does not condemn
himself in what he approves"
(Romans 14:22).

MATERIAL success does not necessarily constitute God's endorsement of our actions. This applies to businesses and ministries alike. Every action must meet two criteria for a Christian.

First, it must be in accordance with God's written Word. Some decisions are objective enough to be eliminated on the basis of direct contradiction to the Bible.

The second criterion that must be met is personal conviction. The Christian life is not just a set of rules that can be obeyed to the letter and thus satisfy our commitment. We are held to an even higher standard that requires constant input from the Holy Spirit to keep us going in the right direction.

It means we are accountable if we defile our consciences by doing something we feel is wrong. This feeling must be based on a firm conviction from God.

How do you know? You will lack the feeling of inner peace that comes from being in God's will.

"From Thy precepts I get understanding; therefore I hate every false way" (Psalm 119:104).

DAILY SCRIPTURE READING: Deuteronomy 31:30-34:12

CHRISTIAN COMMITMENT

*"Prove yourselves doers of the word,
and not merely hearers who delude themselves"*
(James 1:22).

IF most Christians in America were as dedicated to Christian activities (Bible study, prayer, evangelism) as they are to sports, we would truly have a spiritual revival today. Christians often are confronted with a conflict between God's way and the world's attractions.

One pastor of a large dynamic church confided that he had come under severe criticism for allowing the Sunday morning services to go beyond noon when the local professional football team had home games.

Obviously, it is not sports, recreation, or other activities that are the problems; it is a lack of vital, dynamic commitment to God's way.

The non-Christian world will try to test our commitment to see if it's real. If it's not, they will reject our message as just another philosophy. Quite often, the testing ground will be on the job or in our own neighborhoods.

Many Christians have lost their witness because they weren't "doers of the Word."

COMMITTING TO LORDSHIP

*"Whoever does not carry his own cross and
come after Me cannot be My disciple"*
(Luke 14:27).

THERE are many dedicated Christians who are willing to accept God's direction at any moment and surrender their jobs, homes, and comforts to accomplish their assigned tasks. However, they do not represent a majority within the Christian community.

We have an Americanized standard for Christian service that requires very little of us. It yields a sizable body of believers who never mature.

It seems in God's discipleship plan that some adversity and self-denial are necessary ingredients for spiritual maturity. One has to wonder what Bible some Christians read that promises them perfect health, unlimited success, and permanent residence at the location of their choice. Certainly it's not the one that gave us the Scripture verse for today.

A commitment to the lordship of Christ means that we must be willing to go where and when God determines we can best be utilized. There's a hymn that goes something like this: "I'll go where You want me to go, Dear Lord; I'll do what You want me to do."

The apostle Paul describes us as soldiers in God's army, and we are admonished not to get so caught up in the everyday affairs of this life that we take ourselves out of the battle.

Remember that in Psalm 91 we read, *"He will give His angels charge concerning you, to guard you in all your ways."*

DAILY SCRIPTURE READING: Joshua 5, 6, 7, 8

GOD, FAMILY, WORK

"Seek for His kingdom, and these things shall be added to you"
(Luke 12:31).

MOST Christians know that in God's priority system He must come first, family second, and work and recreation third.

However, it is possible to confuse this priority system and step out of God's will. Putting God first means the active, daily process of knowing and being known by God.

It starts with a thorough understanding of God's handbook for life, the Bible. It requires a heartfelt desire to please God and a willingness to accept God's authority over us.

Many times in the pursuit of this first priority, conflicts will arise in the lower priorities. For instance, what happens when a husband is called by God to serve Him and it requires relocating, which causes family conflicts? Usually, it's a conflict because of family ties to a particular area.

It seems that those who are willing to be used by God through the years are faced with the same conflicts, but determining the first priority—seeking God first—will last for eternity. All other priorities cease at death.

Can you say with the psalmist, *"I will give thanks to Thee, O Lord my God, with all my heart, and will glorify Thy name forever"* (Psalm 86:12)?

DAILY SCRIPTURE READING: Joshua 9, 10, 11

MARCH 27

SERVING THE MASTER

*"No one, after putting his hand to the plow and looking back,
is fit for the kingdom of God"*
(Luke 9:62).

OUR motives about earning a living are encompassed within our service to the Lord.

Many times our commitments will break down when they require sacrifices that may include a career change.

I met a Christian who was a hotel chain executive. The company he worked for had made a decision to include a pornographic cable system in its guests' rooms. After complaining as loudly as he could about it, he determined that as a Christian he could no longer be associated with them.

At almost 60 years of age, he knew his decision was clearly one of deciding which master he must serve. He went on to be a successful real estate salesman who sought to put the Lord first in everything.

The decision of choosing which master to follow is one that each of us must make every day. Are we willing to weigh every decision against God's Word and follow the narrow path God requires?

CHRIST'S REQUIRED COMMITMENT

"No servant can serve two masters; for either he will hate the one,
and love the other, or else he will hold to one, and despise the other"
(Luke 16:13).

A REVIEW of Christ's commitment on earth demonstrates pretty clearly that He was seeking those who would commit everything to the service of God's kingdom.

Even as he walked and taught, because of the miracles He was performing, many people were attracted to Him. When others asked Him if they could join His disciples, He directed them to lay aside their own desires and follow Him unreservedly.

With few exceptions, they turned back to whatever they had been doing before; the price was simply too high for them.

The lesson for Christians today should be overwhelmingly clear: All of those who were too busy for Christ will spend an eternity regretting it. So, all that truly matters is what we can do for the kingdom of God.

The things we accumulate are not important. They are tools for us to use in accomplishing God's work. Some will need great resources and some only a little. God owns it all anyway.

Christ said we must make a choice about our commitment, and there are only two choices. These are given in today's Scripture verse.

Whom do you choose?

CHOICES IN A CHRISTIAN BUSINESS

"The Lord gives wisdom, and from his mouth
come knowledge and understanding. . . .
for he guards the course of the just and
protects the way of his faithful ones"
(Proverbs 2:6,8 NIV).

BEING a Christian businessperson is not easy. Many choices that are highly acceptable in most business groups are expressly forbid den to anyone seeking to serve the Lord.

I was talking with the owner of a large importing company who boasted that he regularly paid customs officials to "expedite" his goods. When I asked if he thought it was wrong, his reply was "Only if I get caught."

He professed to being a Christian but said he didn't usually tell anyone because some of the things he had to do in business wouldn't look good if people knew he was a Christian.

When I challenged him on his dual ethics, he said that God must approve because He was blessing the business. His sole basis for this analysis was the abundant profit he was making. Such an analysis could just as easily apply to the Mafia.

The purpose of any Christian, in business or otherwise, is to glorify God—not just to make a profit.

"By this is My Father glorified, that you bear much fruit, and so prove to be My disciples" (John 15:8).

PRIORITIES IN BUSINESS

*"Be strong in the grace that is in Christ Jesus. And the things you
have heard me say in the presence of many witnesses entrust to reliable
men who will also be qualified to teach others"*
(2 Timothy 2:1–2 NIV).

As in any other area of Christian service, it is important to establish priorities. We can quickly become so involved with the "urgent" things of this world that we neglect the important things.

Early in a business career, the urgent thing is to make payroll. Later it becomes urgent to make a greater profit or build a bigger company.

There will always be a reason to neglect the important areas, most of which will seem pretty trivial one second after death. Therefore, it is always important to strive for balance in business.

This is as true in a spiritual sense as it is in a material sense. For example, sales are important to any business, but if a manufacturing company applies 100 percent of its labor force to sales, the imbalance will be readily apparent.

One of the priorities of a business should be to lead others to a saving knowledge of Jesus. But if all other functions are ignored in pursuit of evangelism, the work will be short-lived.

Therefore, the priorities of a business boil down to this: "What are my goals and can my goals be balanced to achieve the overall objectives of serving God while meeting material needs?"

Compared to eternity, the profile of a business is rather trivial and a lifetime of work rather insignificant. If used wisely, though, a business can be used to change the lives of countless lost people.

DAILY SCRIPTURE READING: Joshua 20, 21, 22

KEEPING A VOW

*"A good name is more desirable than great riches; to be esteemed is
better than silver or gold. Rich and poor have this in common:
The Lord is the Maker of them all"*
(Proverbs 22:1–2 NIV).

IT is clear in God's Word that a vow (promise) of any kind is not
to be taken lightly. Once someone has given his or her word, it
becomes a binding contract to be fulfilled. Thus before agreeing to
any terms, it is assumed that an individual has carefully considered
the consequences.

For the current generation, this concept is rarely taught and
seldom applied. Often a vow is deemed something made under
one set of circumstances that may be broken under another—
whether it be a financial agreement or a marriage. The original
conditions may change and one begins to think he or she should
have negotiated a better "deal."

The reason that most Christians aren't able to claim God's
promises is because they are not willing to meet His prerequisites. We read in 1 John 3:21–22 that God will answer our prayers
when we do the things that are pleasing in His sight and keep His
commandments.

Few scriptural principles are clearer than that of keeping our
vows—literally keeping our word—both to God and to others.

"Make vows to the Lord your God and fulfill them" (Psalm
76:11).

DAILY SCRIPTURE READING: Joshua 23, 24; Judges 1

RIGHTS OR RESPONSIBILITIES

*"Everything is permissible—but not everything is beneficial.
Everything is permissible—but not everything is constructive.
Nobody should seek his own good, but the good of others"*
(1 Corinthians 10:23–24 NIV).

I BELIEVE that we are so conscious of our rights today that our "rights" will ultimately cost us our freedom.

To be responsible means to be accountable for our actions. Christ said His followers must be willing to surrender their rights and become His stand-ins.

We can be truly thankful that God's contract with us is binding and firm. Otherwise, He might really give us what we deserve.

We read in Matthew 20 about various workers who were hired during the day at an agreed sum. At the end of the day, those who had worked all day got paid the same wage as those who had worked only one hour, and they were grumbling at the landowner because they thought it wasn't fair. The issue wasn't whether the wage was sufficient—it was that someone else got a better deal, and that wasn't "right."

It is inconceivable to think that our Lord would have made an agreement with someone and then changed His mind and tried to negotiate a better deal.

We must decide to fulfill our responsibilities—regardless of "rights."

Say with the psalmist, *"The Lord is my portion; I have promised to keep Thy words"* (Psalm 119:57).

DAILY SCRIPTURE READING: Judges 2, 3, 4, 5

"MATERIAL" WITNESS

*"If anyone would come after me,
he must deny himself and take up his cross daily and follow me"*
(Luke 9:23 NIV).

GOD has placed us in a materialistic world, not only to witness to the unsaved but also for the purpose of examining our relationship to Him.

There can be no clearer reflection of the true value system of a Christian than the way he or she handles money and the way others are treated when a profit or loss is concerned.

Can Christians be honest in our society? To experience the fullness of God's power and love, we must be honest. There will be times when it will seem that others take advantage of that honesty. The Lord knew that would happen; that's why He admonished us to take up our crosses daily and follow Him.

There is often a price to be paid for following in the path of Christ, but there also is a great reward as a result of doing so.

We must decide whether to build on the solid rock of God's Word or on the shifting sands of society.

The decision to behave by the world's normal standards is a decision to deny Christ.

What is your decision?

DAILY SCRIPTURE READING: Judges 6, 7, 8

WHOM WILL YOU CHOOSE?

*"You did not choose me, but I chose you and appointed you
to go and bear fruit—fruit that will last.
Then the Father will give you whatever you ask in my name"*
(John 15:16 NIV).

IN our society, most people are looking for guidance and unwavering commitment to principles.

Unfortunately, when these can't be found, many people believe the humanists' argument that "values are established by society." The end result of this lie can be seen in the use of drugs to escape reality, sexual immorality, a high rate of divorce and, ultimately, in the collapse of society itself.

Why do people turn to enslavement through a form of government like communism? It is because it offers an uncompromising set of principles that seem to represent stability. In reality, only Christ assures both stability and love.

It is the responsibility of every believer to adhere uncompromisingly to the set of values presented in God's Word. These values encompass every area of life.

We must decide either to follow Christ or to follow Satan; there is no middle road.

Jesus told the disciples, *"You did not choose Me, but I chose you, and appointed you, that you should go and bear fruit, and that your fruit should remain"* (John 15:16).

DAILY SCRIPTURE READING: Judges 9

THE COST OF COMPROMISE

"Since they did not think it worthwhile
to retain the knowledge of God,
he gave them over to a depraved mind,
to do what ought not to be done"
(Romans 1:28 NIV).

THERE'S a cost to be paid for every compromise, especially to God's Word. That price is the loss of peace from God.

Compromise at any level results in further compromise—until finally the conscience is seared and right and wrong are no longer distinguishable.

Sometimes an inner conviction about sin decreases and the sins begin to increase. Why? Because fellowship with God was broken at the earliest stage, and from that point selfishness and self-control took over.

Have you allowed yourself to compromise in any area of your life?

Our greatest advantage is that God will restore anyone who will acknowledge sin and return to His way.

"Bless the Lord, O my soul, and forget none of His benefits; Who pardons all your iniquities. . . Who redeems your life from the pit; Who crowns you with lovingkindness and compassion" (Psalm 103:2–4).

DAILY SCRIPTURE READING: Judges 10, 11, 12

GETTING OUT THE MESSAGE

"Christ in you, the hope of glory.
We proclaim him, admonishing and teaching everyone
with all wisdom, so that we may present everyone perfect in Christ"
(Colossians 1:27–28 NIV).

NOTHING interferes more with our ability to serve God than our need to earn a living. An observer from 100 years ago would be awestruck by the improvement in our living standards and by the amount of leisure time our technology has provided.

Few Americans regularly work more than a 50-hour week; most work 44 hours or less. In addition, we now live an average of 18 years longer than we did 100 years ago.

When all these factors are weighed together with the fact that in America alone we have perhaps 30 million Christians, it would seem clear that we ought to be getting out the message of Jesus Christ much better than we are.

The simple truth is that most Americans are too busy to serve God. We have grown complacent and comfortable in God's blessings and have forgotten the first commandment.

In the meantime, immorality and cults have grown to alarming proportions, because their advocates are more zealous in their support.

Since God asks for obedience rather than demanding it, we must be sure not to ignore the very reasons for our existence: to glorify God and get out the message.

"Obey My voice, and I will be your God, and you will be My people; and you will walk in all the way which I command you, that it may be well with you" (Jeremiah 7:23).

DAILY SCRIPTURE READING: Judges 13, 14, 15, 16

CONSIDER THE COST

*"No one who puts his hand to the plow and
looks back is fit for service in the kingdom of God"*
(Luke 9:62 NIV).

SERVICE to Jesus Christ is demanding. It may actually be that we will have to work as hard for God's kingdom as we do for earthly riches.

Few salespeople consider it a great imposition on their time to tell about their product line. Being a success at anything requires dedication, training, and perseverance.

A good sales manager knows that not everyone can be good at sales, and many don't even want to be. Christ knew that not everyone would serve God, and some might not even want to.

Some would even like to have a foot in both worlds. They are willing to be called Christians, provided they can pick the times and places to serve.

These poor souls are actually worse off in this life than they were before. They are content to know about God but are fruitless fakers who must generate false blessings. They are poorly nourished spiritually and quickly waste away until there is real doubt in their minds about their salvation. These are the ones who fall prey to every wind of doctrine because they are too "busy" to grow firm roots.

What a loss that we will allow temporary comforts and laziness to rob us of true riches both now and for all eternity.

"I shall not die, but live, and tell of the works of the Lord" (Psalm 118:17).

EXCUSE ME PLEASE

"What kind of people ought you to be?
You ought to live holy and godly lives as you
look forward to the day of God and speed its coming"
(2 Peter 3:11 NIV).

WITHOUT exception, God has a unique and meaningful plan for every believer, and it does not depend on age, income, or ability.

It is also clear that God calls each of us to fill in our gap. The story of Esther, in the Old Testament, shows us that every believer must decide either to be used by God or to be bypassed and another chosen instead.

Most Christians would never refuse to do God's will; it's just that the timing might not be right. When God calls us, He wants obedience first and worldly wisdom last.

We have allowed the "urgent" things of society to overshadow the "important" things. This fact is neither new nor unique to our generation.

In fact, Christ experienced it during His life and predicted it for us. He told a parable in Luke 14:16–24 of God calling men to follow Him. They were invited to a dinner, but most were far too busy to attend right then. They wanted to be part of what was happening but had to spend their time fulfilling a great many responsibilities.

If we are wise, we will realize that it is God's timetable we want to live by—not our own. This is the only way we will receive the best He has for us.

"My prayer is to Thee, O Lord, at an acceptable time; O God, in the greatness of Thy lovingkindness, answer me with Thy saving truth" (Psalm 69:13).

DAILY SCRIPTURE READING: Judges 20, 21

WORKING AT GOD'S WORK

"You are worried and upset about many things,
but only one thing is needed. Mary has chosen what is better,
and it will not be taken away from her"
(Luke 10:41–42 NIV).

I ONCE heard someone laughingly say, "I'm not physically able to be a Baptist."

Christians who apply themselves to fruitless effort in the name of the Lord busy themselves to the point of exhaustion, going to conferences and countless church activities and serving on many committees. However, they are rarely, if ever, quiet enough for the Lord to direct them. They are irritable and often envious of others. They are truly working at God's work and not in it.

When Jesus was visiting Martha's home, she complained to the Lord that she was stuck doing all the "important" work while Mary was just sitting and listening to Him. We see what Jesus replied in today's Scripture verse.

How many of us have taken on a life of meaningless works to avoid the reality of serving God according to His will?

"Cease striving and know that I am God; I will be exalted among the nations, I will be exalted in the earth" (Psalm 46:10).

DAILY SCRIPTURE READING: Ruth

APRIL 9

THE WORLD'S YARDSTICK

*"In vain you rise early and stay up late, toiling for food to eat—
for he grants sleep to those he loves"*
(Psalm 127:2 NIV).

THERE is nothing wrong with being successful, even when measured by worldly standards, unless you end up being a failure by godly standards.

The rate of divorce and bankruptcy among Christians is an undeniable indicator that Christians have been duped into using the world's yardstick when setting their priorities.

Each Christian must ask, "Am I certain my priorities are in line with God's?" If not, then a change is in order—no matter what the cost in dollars and cents.

It is remarkable that usually those at the highest end of the material scale are the biggest violators of priorities (executives, doctors, attorneys). But equally guilty are many in full-time Christian service, with pastors leading the group.

We can all give thanks to those committed saints, from the apostles on down, who did not feel that fame and success in the eyes of the world were as important as God's blessings.

One day each of us will be measured on the basis of Christ's evaluation and none other.

Father, I pray that some day I will hear you say, "Well done, My good and faithful servant."

DAILY SCRIPTURE READING: 1 Samuel 1, 2, 3

GOD FIRST

"I consider everything a loss compared to the
surpassing greatness of knowing Christ Jesus my Lord,
for whose sake I have lost all things.
I consider them rubbish,
that I may gain Christ and be found in him"
(Philippians 3:8 NIV).

ONE of the most overwhelming characteristics of those who discern God's will for their lives is that they continually seek to put God first.

Most Christians experience doubts and anxieties when faced with major decisions. However, most major decisions are actually a series of minor decisions that converge into a changed direction.

Consistently putting God first eliminates most decisions before they become crises.

God has already endowed each of us Christians with unique abilities, desires, and gifts to accomplish His will.

As you seek to serve God, the Holy Spirit will make known God's perfect plan for your life. What He wants for you will be different from what He wants for your other family members or friends.

Putting God first and living for Him every day—consistently —is difficult. However, if you exercise self-will, He will do the rest.

"If then you have been raised up with Christ, keep seeking the things above, where Christ is, seated at the right hand of God" (Colossians 3:1).

DAILY SCRIPTURE READING: 1 Samuel 4, 5, 6, 7

WHAT'S IT WORTH?

*"When Judas, who had betrayed Him, saw that He had been
condemned, he felt remorse and returned the thirty pieces of silver. . . .
And he went away and hanged himself"*
(Matthew 27:3, 5).

WHEN we celebrate the resurrection of our Lord, we should turn our thoughts to the one who betrayed Him.

How much is your faith worth? I'm convinced that Judas, who sold out the Lord, didn't realize what the outcome would be. Judas was the one Christ had assigned the responsibility of managing all the finances for the disciples. It wasn't that Judas didn't hear the Lord's message—I believe that he even loved Him—he obviously loved money more than he loved Jesus.

When he was approached by the Jews and offered money to betray Jesus, the first thing he should have done was to refuse them and tell the disciples, but he listened to them—much like Eve listened to the serpent in the Garden of Eden. He heard a tempting proposition and was trapped by his own weaknesses.

Judas sold out the Lord for what might have been as little as maybe five weeks of wages—not much when you consider what happened. I really don't know if Judas thought they would kill Jesus or what he would have done if he had known.

What is your faith worth today? Would you sell out the Savior for money? Do you ever sell out your faith to save a little on your income tax? Would you sell it out for the time or things you steal from your employer?

Don't be too critical of Judas until you examine your own life in the light of God's Word. Ask the Lord to help you with a bit of self-examination.

DAILY SCRIPTURE READING: 1 Samuel 8, 9, 10

VOCATIONAL PURPOSE

"What good will it be for a man
if he gains the whole world,
yet forfeits his soul?
(Matthew 16:26 NIV).

So often, at the end of a lifetime, a successful person states, "If only I had known 40 years ago what I know now, I would not have wasted my life pursuing wealth."

As Christians, we have the advantage of knowing the certain future. We have the advantage of being able to see life from God's perspective. We will spend eternity reaping the rewards of faithful service to God. Thus, we have the responsibility to orient our lives accordingly.

Vocational planning for us and for our children is based primarily on how we can serve Him best.

It is vital to seek discernment about God's plan and accept nothing less than the vocation that will complement and extend our ministries.

"Let him labor, performing with his own hands what is good, in order that he may have something to share with him who has need" (Ephesians 4:28).

FAMILY GOALS

"Commit to the Lord whatever you do, and your plans will succeed"
(Proverbs 16:3 NIV).

GOALS should be set individually, but they also must become a part of your partnership with your spouse. If your spouse is not a Christian, you have an excellent goal to establish in your personal prayer life.

Don't give up praying for your unsaved spouse (or any other unbeliever). One Christian lady I know prayed for her husband 22 years before he accepted the Lord. It finally took the shock of three years in prison before he responded.

A minimum family goal, which would be a good start, should be to read a few verses of Scripture and pray together regularly.

As Christian parents, we should teach our children God's principles. With very young children, study and prayer are relatively easy habits to develop in the family. Start with a good children's Bible guide and pray for each other.

With older children, start where you can. Read a brief devotional at the breakfast or dinner table, and set aside a few minutes to pray together. You get to know about God by studying His Word, but you get to know God through prayer.

Set a goal with your family to pray regularly and consistently. Even though it may sound trite, it is true: The family that prays together stays together.

You can get your start from God's Word. *"Father, hallowed be Thy name. Thy kingdom come. Give us each day our daily bread. And forgive us our sins, for we ourselves also forgive everyone who is indebted to us. And lead us not into temptation"* (Luke 11:2–4).

DAILY SCRIPTURE READING: 1 Samuel 14, 15

INHERITANCE

"A good man leaves an inheritance to his children's children,
and the wealth of the sinner is stored up for the righteous"
(Proverbs 13:22).

GOD leaves no subject untouched in His Word and, fortunately, that includes inheritance. Even a brief survey of the Bible reveals that God provided for each generation through inheritance.

In biblical times, the sons inherited their fathers' properties and thus provided for the rest of their families. What is not so obvious is that, in most instances, the sons received their inheritances while their fathers were still living, enabling the fathers to oversee their sons' stewardship.

It would be interesting to see what money management training most children would receive if their parents knew that one day the estate would be in the children's hands and the parents would have to depend on them for their support.

Good stewardship includes providing an inheritance for your family and being sure that every family member knows how to manage it.

If you have not prepared a will, this is the time to do it. Ask God to lead you in your decisions.

DAILY SCRIPTURE READING: 1 Samuel 15, 16, 17

PAY YOUR TAXES

"Render to all what is due them:
tax to whom tax is due; custom to whom custom;
fear to whom fear; honor to whom honor"
(Romans 13:7).

MOST Christians would consider themselves honest, and yet many violate the tax laws regularly. One of the most common examples is stay-at-home moms who are operating a small business, such as a babysitting service or home product sales, but they are not declaring the income for tax purposes.

There is no question that our current tax laws punish married couples and, particularly, stay-at-home moms. For working mothers to have to pay upward of 40 percent of their earnings in taxes is unconscionable.

Moms who babysit at home have to cope with screaming kids to earn precious little income. Then they have to forfeit up to 40 percent of it to some bureaucrat in Washington, who promptly flushes it down the drain called "entitlements."

Yes, it is a problem. But cheating is not the solution. We must get involved personally and do our best to change the system (not to mention the politicians).

God's Word makes it clear that we are to pay taxes. Read today's Scripture verse again.

"Search me, O God, and know my heart; try me and know my anxious thoughts; and see if there be any hurtful way in me, and lead me in the everlasting way" (Psalm 139:23–24).

DAILY SCRIPTURE READING: 1 Samuel 18, 19; Psalm 59

April 16

Ministry Support

*"Let the one who is taught the word
share all good things with him who teaches"*
(Galatians 6:6).

THERE must be a balance in a Christian's attitude toward ministry support. Too often a Christian will read a spectacular biography of how God used a particular individual and he or she will use that as an absolute rule against everyone else.

Personal testimonies are exciting and rewarding and can be of great value in providing alternatives. However, they are not to be used as yardsticks for giving, unless they are confirmed in God's Word.

Many Christians have read the story of George Mueller's life and how he trusted God for everything without asking. They conclude that no Christian should ever let a material need be known. This is noble and admirable—but not scriptural.

Paul admonished the Corinthians because they felt he didn't have the right to ask them for support. And in Exodus 25:1–3 the Lord told Moses to tell the people of Israel to raise a contribution for the tabernacle.

However, just because asking is acceptable, it doesn't mean that it's God's plan for everyone or that every letter sent to supporters should ask for more money.

Balance is the key principle. Nowhere in the Bible is there any indication that God's people went begging. It's evident that many more needs were met by praying than by asking.

It's also clear that once God's people are made aware of their responsibilities to give and support God's work, the need to ask goes down dramatically.

Jesus said, *"The laborer is worthy of his wages"* (Luke 10:7).

DAILY SCRIPTURE READING: 1 Samuel 20, 21; Psalms 34, 56

WHICH GROUP TO SUPPORT

"You are acting faithfully in whatever you accomplish for the brethren. . .and they bear witness to your love before the church; . . . send them on their way in a manner worthy of God"
(3 John 1:5–6).

GOD doesn't intend for every Christian to give to every need. Attempting to do so will quickly result in frustration and perhaps poverty. Therefore, we must be able to sort out those we are to help.

This doesn't mean that the cause or the organization isn't worthy—only that the need is meant for someone else to satisfy. There are some simple biblical principles to follow when you are considering giving to any cause.

Limit your giving to groups who are operating in the name of the Lord. Other organizations are serving the needs of the poor, sick, and elderly but make no pretense of doing it in the name of the Lord. It is abundantly clear throughout the Bible that gifts dedicated to God were to be distributed in His name.

Just because a group has an emotional presentation for a seemingly worthy cause doesn't mean it automatically qualifies for support. Determine that the funds actually will be used for the purpose for which they were given. Be a good steward.

Organizations that have met needs in your life should be high on your support list.

Organizations that manage their funds wisely should be considered first. If you have a desire to support a particular type of ministry, locate the most efficient and productive one.

The most important principle of all: Allow God to direct your giving. Ask for His guidance and lean on His wisdom.

DAILY SCRIPTURE READING: 1 Samuel 22, 23;
1 Chronicles 12:8-18; Psalms 52, 54, 63, 142

KEYS TO THE KINGDOM

"The Lord will deliver me. . .and will bring me safely to His heavenly kingdom; to Him be the glory forever and ever" (2 Timothy 4:18).

OVER the last few years, I have read and reread Paul's letter to the Romans. It is obvious to me that Paul describes a man (himself) who found the keys to God's invisible kingdom. He's a man who accepts God as the absolute authority in his life and is willing to surrender everything, if necessary, to serve Him, even to the point of death.

Several years ago I met a Chinese Christian who was saved as a member of the "Red Brigade" in communist China. He was imprisoned, tortured, starved, and beaten in an effort to get him to renounce his faith. When he refused, his family was executed to teach others a lesson.

He said the thing that sustained him was an ever-deepening relationship with Christ and an unyielding commitment to serving God. When most of our commitments are weighed against his, it's easy to see why the keys to the kingdom elude us.

Perhaps God hasn't called us to the physical sacrifices that many Christian martyrs have suffered. But, the admonition that Christ gives to all of us is absolutely clear. We must do what Jesus told the disciples: *"If anyone wishes to come after Me, let him deny himself, and take up his cross, and follow Me"* (Mark 8:34).

Is this something you are willing to do?

DAILY SCRIPTURE READING: 1 Samuel 24, 25; Psalm 57

Where Am I?

"I gave you an example that you also should do as I did to you"
(John 13:15).

It's always good to have some standard of measure to compare where we are with where God wants us to be.

The evidence in God's Word is clear and simple. All we have to do is eliminate our ego and pride and consistently put the needs of others before our own; then we'll be on the right track. Difficult? No, impossible. But in Romans the apostle Paul gives us God's solution: Let go and trust God.

Christ is the most exalted being in the eternal kingdom of God. Even though this is true, He assumed the lowliest, most humbling position possible during His life. Perhaps to us this will mean giving up pride and ego and giving of ourselves to others, as Christ did when He washed the disciples' feet.

It is a contrast in human logic that by giving up something we can receive even more. But Christ taught this principle frequently; it's called sowing and reaping. It's our choice to take what we want now or store it and receive it in God's eternal kingdom.

God's Word tells us that an evidence of our commitment to His way will be shown in our concern for others.

As we start each day we have a choice: follow God or follow the world. If we totally follow God it may be costly. We may be buffeted by Satan as never before, but on the sole authority of God's Word we can clearly know that our priorities are in order.

"Pursue righteousness, faith, love and peace, with those who call on the Lord from a pure heart" (2 Timothy 2:22).

Daily Scripture Reading:
1 Samuel 26, 27, 28, 29; 1 Chronicles 12:1-7, 19-22

WHAT DOES IT MEAN?

"Give and it will be given to you;
good measure, pressed down, shaken together, running over,
they will pour into your lap.
For by your standard of measure
it will be measured to you in return"
(Luke 6:38).

FEW verses are quoted more than today's Scripture regarding the principle of giving and receiving. When I first read this verse, shortly after committing my life to Christ, I pondered it for many weeks.

Did God really mean what this verse says? To me, there were some seemingly obvious difficulties with the principle that receiving was a matter of having to give first.

After many hours of contemplation and study, my conclusion was that we should give expecting but never demanding. Even if God blesses us far beyond our expectations, both materially and spiritually, our giving must be out of a desire to please God, not to profit from the relationship.

Giving is a material expression of a deeper spiritual obedience to God.

What is your motive for giving? Is it from a heart of love? Do you expect to receive from God? Pray that you will give in the right spirit.

DAILY SCRIPTURE READING:
1 Samuel 30, 31; 2 Samuel 1; 1 Chronicles 10

APRIL 21

PURPOSE OF THE TITHE

"Bring the whole tithe into the storehouse,
so that there may be food in My house, and test Me now in this. . .
if I will not open for you the windows of heaven,
and pour out for you a blessing until it overflows"
(Malachi 3:10).

THE purpose of the tithe has been established as a physical, earthly demonstration of our commitment to God. God understood our greedy, selfish nature and provided a readily identifiable sign of our sincerity.

By the act of surrendering some of our physical resources, we are testifying to our origin, just as a farmer does when he surrenders some of his crop back to the earth from which it came.

The tithe is not a law now; nor was it a law in the Old Testament. Although it appears in Leviticus 27, there is no punishment associated with a failure to tithe. There is a consequence (the loss of blessings), but do not misinterpret this. It is not a punishment from God.

Thus, God said that the tithe is an expression of commitment —or the lack of it—by which we can determine our relationship to Him.

What are your thoughts about tithing—why you do (or don't)? Do you think it is a reflection of your commitment to God?

HOW MUCH IS A TITHE?

*"All the tithe of the land, of the seed of the land or
of the fruit of the tree, is the Lord's; it is holy to the Lord"*
(Leviticus 27:30).

THIS is a difficult question to answer quantitatively. The word tithe in Hebrew literally means "tenth." In Hebrews 7 the tithe is used to describe Abraham's relationship to Christ by drawing a parallel between the tithe and the acknowledgment of authority.

I believe the tithe was meant to be individualized. It was never intended that everyone should give the same amount; each should give according to abundance and conviction. The tenth that we are so familiar with was considered the minimum. You are in no way limited to giving only a tenth.

Anyone unable to make a commitment of a tenth of his or her resources to God should realistically examine all spending and living habits.

The thing to remember is that whatever you give probably is an indicator of your personal relationship with the Lord.

God's Word says to *"Bring the whole tithe into the storehouse, so that there may be food in My house, and test Me now in this. . .if I will not open for you the windows of heaven, and pour out for you a blessing until it overflows"* (Malachi 3:10).

DAILY SCRIPTURE READING: 2 Samuel 5:1-6:11;
1 Chronicles 11:1-9, 12:23-40, 13:1-14:17

APRIL 23

GIVING ABOVE THE TITHE

"Let each one do just as he has purposed in his heart;
not grudgingly or under compulsion;
for God loves a cheerful giver"
(2 Corinthians 9:7).

IN the book of Deuteronomy there are several additional offerings described as the "tithes of your increase." These were special offerings meant to care for the priests, the poor, the sick, and the elderly.

It's not possible to exact an amount except by inference, but I calculate these total "regular" gifts to be about 23 percent per year. Today it would be the equivalent of a family who is totally committed to giving.

Ask God to show you how to share in special needs above your regular giving. What worthwhile organization or ministry should you be helping to support?

The writer of Hebrews said, *"Do not neglect doing good and sharing; for with such sacrifices God is pleased"* (Hebrews 13:16).

SACRIFICE

"Everyone who has left houses or brothers or sisters
or father or mother or children or farms for My name's sake,
shall receive many times as much,
and shall inherit eternal life"
(Matthew 19:29).

THE concept of sacrifice is not popular with most Christians. Most of us like to discuss this subject in generalities, rather than in specifics.

It's all right for the pastor to mention sacrifice when he talks about missionaries or full-time Christian workers, but when he talks about giving up golf or a new car for God's work, suddenly he becomes a radical.

In this country we are not asked to sacrifice our lives, as Christians are doing in other lands.

However, if we will truly surrender ourselves to God and give Him a sacrifice of praise and thanksgiving, we will experience His faithfulness. He loves us and will never give us less than His best as long as we are surrendered to His way of living.

Ask God to reveal to you someone in need and then give sacrificially from what you have. You will be more blessed than you can imagine.

Father, stand ready to help me, because I have chosen to follow Your will.

DAILY SCRIPTURE READING: 2 Samuel 6:12–23;
1 Chronicles 15, 16; Psalm 96

UNMET CHRISTIAN NEEDS

*"If a brother or sister is without clothing and in need
of daily food, and one of you says to them,
'Go in peace, be warmed and be filled,'
and yet you do not give them what is necessary
for their body, what use is that?"*
(James 2:15–16).

UNFORTUNATELY, unmet needs in the church is the norm in today's Christianity. But it is the responsibility of each Christian to supply the needs of others who cannot do so for themselves.

Harry Truman made a famous statement about the presidency: "The buck stops here." And the same is true for each Christian.

If we see a brother or sister in need and we close our hearts to that need, what kind of love is that?

Of course, God will not lay every need on every Christian's heart, but He does lay on our hearts specific needs that we are to meet.

Stephan Grellet said, "I expect to pass through this world but once; any good thing therefore that I can do, or any kindness that I can show to any fellow creature, let me do it now; let me not defer or neglect it, for I shall not pass this way again."

Ralph Waldo Emerson said, "It is one of the most beautiful compensations of this life that no man can sincerely try to help another without helping himself."

And the psalmist said, *"To those who fear Him, there is no want. . . . They who seek the Lord shall not be in want of any good thing"* (Psalm 34:9–10).

DAILY SCRIPTURE READING:
2 Samuel 7; 1 Chronicles 17; Psalm 105

BUDGETING YOUR TIME

"There is an appointed time for everything.
And there is a time for every event under heaven"
(Ecclesiastes 3:1).

MANY people think they're organized and use their time efficiently but, in reality, most of us work according to external pressures, with the most demanding things getting done first. It's called tyranny of the urgent.

Before writing one of my books I did a survey of stay-at-home moms, and one of the questions dealt with time management in their homes. The most common comment was something like, "It seems like I never get everything done now. I don't know how I was able to work and keep a home, but I did."

Not using time wisely usually results from being disorganized. Disorganization is an accumulation of little bad habits all strung together and it is the major enemy of personal success.

Sir John Lubbock said, "In truth, people can generally make time for what they choose to do; it is not really the time but the will that is lacking."

It's important to keep a good balance. As important as good organization of your time is, don't go overboard. When you budget your time, build in some slack as well.

Ask God to help you budget your time so you can keep a good balance in your everyday life. And of course, that includes spending time with Him.

"The steps of a man are established by the Lord; and He delights in his way" (Psalm 37:23).

DAILY SCRIPTURE READING: 2 Samuel 8, 9, 10;
1 Chronicles 18, 19; Psalm 60

DON'T PANIC, PRAY

"He will call upon Me, and I will answer him;
I will be with him in trouble;
I will rescue him, and honor him"
(Psalm 91:15).

ONE day I was traveling in my car and tuned to a Christian radio station that played a song with the lyric, "God said it and I believe it." That should be the standard by which we all live our lives. Unfortunately, all too often we allow doubts and fears to get in our way.

There is no problem too big for God to solve, if we believe. That doesn't mean that God will keep every problem away from us; nor does it mean He must miraculously solve every crisis, although I've seen Him do so many times.

Sometimes the problems are for our growth. Other times they are for discipline. And there are times when we simply don't know why things happen to us. But through it all, God is still there, comforting us.

I have learned that although God never promised to remove every difficulty, He has promised that we can have peace in the midst of them if we continue to serve Him.

Use the following verse as your prayer: *"O Lord, don't hold back your tender mercies from me! My only hope is in your love and faithfulness. . . . Come and help me!"* (Psalm 40:11, 13 TLB).

DAILY SCRIPTURE READING: 2 Samuel 11, 12;
1 Chronicles 20:1-3; Psalm 51

LEARN TO SAY NO

*"God is not a God of confusion but of peace,
as in all the churches of the saints"*
(1 Corinthians 14:33).

WE live in a time-crazy society. When you prioritize your time, be honest about it. There are only so many things you can accomplish realistically in one day. Concentrate on the important ones.

I have found that much of my own unrealistic schedule is a result of my own doing. I hate to say no to people, especially when there are so many good things to do.

Some of this tendency is probably ego: I like to be asked to do things. Some of it is naiveté. There was a time when I thought I could teach full-time, travel full-time, write full-time, and run an organization—all at the same time.

Instead, I found that the busier I was the more behind I got; the more behind I got, the more frustrated I got; and the more frustrated I got, the less productive I became.

Therefore, I have learned to say "No!" And you know what? The world just goes on turning anyway. I have long since discovered that I am not God's plan; I'm just a part of it.

Does this strike a chord in your own life?

The Illegal Underground Economy

"Your iniquities have made a separation between you and your God, and your sins have hidden His face from you, so that He does not hear" (Isaiah 59:2).

You should never participate in the illegal underground economy (I'll go into more detail in a moment). Even though many people don't consciously set out to cheat, it ultimately ends up that way.

Always establish your standards based on what God's Word says—not on what is acceptable in the eyes of society. The illegal underground economy is operating all around us, and it's too easy to get caught up in it when money is tight.

For example, several of the cabinet-level appointments made by President Bill Clinton were withdrawn because the people had hired illegal workers (undocumented) and employed them without paying the proper taxes.

You can get cheaper domestic help that way, but in doing so you break the law. It's not worth it financially and certainly not spiritually.

Another example is paying cash for discounted services. Several years ago a man came to our home and asked if we needed some dead trees removed, which we did. He offered to do the work for far less than any previous estimate we had received, provided we agreed to pay him in cash. The obvious conclusion was that if he didn't have to declare the income he would discount the work. We refused and he left.

This kind of transaction is not abnormal today. A lot of business is done in cash so that taxes can be avoided. If you participate knowingly, it is the same as committing the crime yourself. Nothing is worth blocking God's direction in your life.

Daily Scripture Reading: 2 Samuel 15, 16, 17

A Decision Must Be Made

*"The lovingkindness of the Lord is from everlasting to everlasting
on those who fear Him, and His righteousness to children's children,
to those who keep His covenant, and who remember
His precepts to do them"*
(Psalm 103:17–18).

ALL parents need to ask themselves how they want to be remembered by their children.

If you are a parent, ask yourself whether you want to reinforce your own children, instill in them your beliefs, and bring them up in the way they should go. Or do you want to let someone else do it for you?

Obviously, many mothers have found ways to do this, even while working outside their homes. But, usually, the majority of working mothers sacrifice some or all of their family goals in order to work.

My advice for anyone who is thinking about becoming a stay-at-home mom: When you are sure, do it! When you are in doubt, pray about it!

Positive self-worth and godly character are very important to your children. Maybe they will get this outside the home, but are you willing to take the chance? Your children only have one childhood and you only get one chance.

If you aren't a parent, you may know someone who is struggling with this issue and you can encourage and pray for that parent today.

"Teach me to do Thy will, for Thou art my God; let Thy good Spirit lead me on level ground. For the sake of Thy name, O Lord, revive me. . . . For I am Thy servant" (Psalm 143:10–12).

DAILY SCRIPTURE READING: 2 Samuel 18, 19; Psalm 3

MAY 1

MOTHERS

*"Honor your father and your mother, as the Lord your God
has commanded you, . . .that it may go well with you
in the land which the Lord your God gives you"*
(Deuteronomy 5:16).

GOD commanded us to give honor to our mothers. What is a mother? She's the one person who knows us best and loves us in spite of it.

The most famous mother in the Bible, outside of Mary the mother of Jesus, was a woman by the name of Hannah. She suffered ridicule because she was barren; during her generation that was considered a curse from God.

Hannah made a promise to God that if He would give her a son she would dedicate him totally to God. He answered her prayer and Samuel was born. Hannah was a mother like all mothers, and to give up her son was a sacrifice, but when Samuel was 3 years old she left him with the prophet Eli.

The books of Samuel in the Old Testament are about the life of Samuel: Hannah's love for her son, how she prayed for him regularly, and how she visited him every year to bring him clothing and food. Can you imagine giving birth to a son, having him for only three years, and then only seeing him once a year? But Hannah had made a vow to God and she kept her promise.

If you have children, love them dearly, pray for them regularly, and at some point surrender them to God.

We'll be celebrating Mother's Day soon. If your mother is still living, call her and tell her how much you love and appreciate her—every day.

DAILY SCRIPTURE READING: 2 Samuel 20, 21, 23:8-23;
1 Chronicles 11:10-25, 20:4-8

MAY 2

HASTY DECISIONS

"We are the temple of the living God;
just as God said, 'I will dwell in them and walk among them;
and I will be their God and they shall be My people"
(2 Corinthians 6:16).

OFTEN Christians rationalize hasty, even foolish, decisions on the basis of "God told me to do it."

If God tells someone to do something, He will provide for that person's needs.

The evidence that God hasn't directed everyone who says He has is the fact that sometimes the situations actually get worse.

Kenneth Wuest said, "When we have limitations imposed on us we do our best work for the Lord, for then we are most dependent on Him."

God has an individual plan for everyone. It has been my observation that this sometimes involves allowing us to work our way out of a situation of our own making—because of a hasty decision.

Ask God to show you His plan for you today. Be sure you know He is guiding you before you make any decision.

"I have chosen to do right. I cling to your commands and follow them as closely as I can. Lord, don't let me make a mess of things. Just tell me what to do and I will do it, Lord. As long as I live I'll whole-heartedly obey" (Psalm 119:30–31, 33–34 TLB).

DAILY SCRIPTURE READING: 2 Samuel 23:24-24:25;
1 Chronicles 11:26-47, 21:1-30

MAY 3

A COURAGEOUS DECISION

"I will instruct you and teach you in the way which you should go;
I will counsel you with My eye upon you"
(Psalm 32:8–9).

THE decision a woman makes to leave a paying job and return home is clearly going against the tide of our society. Not only will a stay-at-home mom face discouragement from those who don't agree with her decision, but a single-income family also runs contrary to "official" government policy.

I say that because our government has built the tax system around the need for two incomes per family. In fact, government tax policies often dictate two wage earners per family.

As the marginal tax rates of our country have climbed, they have absorbed more and more of the primary wage earner's income. Today, median-income wage earners pay an effective state and federal tax rate of almost 30 percent. With two wage earners, the percentage is even higher.

The family actually nets less today than they would have 30 years ago; thus, the pressure for a wife to go to work is applied through income dilution.

If a woman intends to buck the trend and return home from the workplace, in most cases it will require a great deal of discipline and sacrifice. However, in our Scripture verse for today, the Lord promises to instruct, teach, and counsel.

Make this your prayer: *"Teach me good judgment as well as knowledge. . . . I have sense enough to follow you"* (Psalm 119:66, 70 TLB).

DAILY SCRIPTURE READING: 1 Chronicles 22, 23, 24

NECESSITY OR LUXURY?

"Rest in the Lord and wait patiently for Him;
do not fret because of him who prospers in his way"
(Psalm 37:7).

THERE are more "things" to buy and do than ever before. Once two cars were a luxury; now they are a necessity for most families.

I grew up in the generation of the fifties and started a family in the sixties. I remember well that there were not all the distractions (attractions) that are available to families today. Few couples we knew took their kids to Disneyland or on skiing trips. Although credit was available for housing or cars, credit cards were nonexistent and school loans not a consideration.

Nowadays, though, it is a different story; luxuries have become necessities. We "need" newer cars, more advanced computers, designer clothes.

E. S. Fields says, "The man or woman who concentrates on 'things' can hardly be trusted to use those things for the good of mankind. Only those who have guided the development of their spirit as well as their mind are really. . .qualified to use wisely the things that man's reason has enabled him to fashion out of nature's raw materials."

Regardless of what others have or do, before you spend money, decide whether it is a necessity or a luxury. God doesn't mind if you have luxuries; He wants you to have the best, but He wants you to have it in His timing.

"The Father sets those dates. . .and they are not for you to know"
(Acts 1:7 TLB).

DAILY SCRIPTURE READING: 1 Chronicles 25, 26; Psalm 30

DEPRESSION

*"You are from God, little children, and have overcome. . .
because greater is He who is in you than he who is in the world"*
(1 John 4:4).

ONLY once in my life was I genuinely depressed. It was due to what I would call burnout. I was traveling, doing 50 to 60 seminars a year, and I had let my spiritual life run down. I got so busy for the Lord I didn't have time to spend with the Lord.

Ironically enough, this is something many full-time Christian workers experience; they are so busy serving God there's no time to spend with Him.

I didn't have time to study, to pray, to read the Bible. Everywhere I went I was giving, giving, giving, because that's what people expected.

Everyone gets down from time to time, but this time it really frightened me to realize I didn't have any control over it. I was in a downward spiral and couldn't eat, couldn't sleep, couldn't think straight, couldn't work anymore.

I had lost my direction, so I stopped, confessed it to the Lord, canceled everything, and determined to reestablish my relationship with the Lord.

I stayed with a friend until I regained my focus. I decided to resign as manager of the universe. God made it abundantly clear to me that He didn't give me that job in the first place.

Don't get so busy serving God that you don't have any time for Him. Spend time in prayer and meditate on His Word. And when you lack peace in your life, stop!

DAILY SCRIPTURE READING: 1 Chronicles 27, 28, 29

STRONG OR WEAK

*"Behold the eye of the Lord is on those who fear Him,
on those who hope for His lovingkindness"*
(Psalm 33:18).

ONE thing I've found after many years of counseling is that even the strongest of Christians have their weaknesses; and there is nothing unspiritual about admitting them. In fact, few people will seek counsel from "perfect" individuals. Real-life situations need real-life people to appreciate and understand them.

I find that the vast majority of people can handle the situations they face if they understand them, know the limits they can expect, and trust the Lord for His lovingkindness.

Are you trusting the Lord to help you face some situation in your life? Without a doubt, He will provide.

"Bless the Lord, O my soul, and forget none of His benefits; . . . who satisfies your years with good things, so that your youth is renewed like the eagle. . . . For He Himself knows our frame; He is mindful that we are but dust" (Psalm 103:2, 5, 14).

DAILY SCRIPTURE READING: Psalms 5, 6, 7, 10, 11, 13, 17

GODLY INHERITANCE

"Train up a child in the way he should go,
even when he is old he will not depart from it"
(Proverbs 22:6).

THE most important inheritance we can offer our children is a Christian influence that leads to salvation. We think of an inheritance coming after someone's death, but godly inheritance—training in Christian living—cannot be left until then.

Neither should we neglect training our spouses and our children in the use of handling the inheritance. I challenge every Christian to develop a godly approach to inheritance, beginning right now. Establish a few fundamental absolutes about your inheritance.

Knowing how to manage money is basic in preparing for the future. Teaching your children to give to God's work out of their earnings is the most essential step in molding them into good money managers and is the best inheritance you can give them.

God promises wisdom to those who trust Him.

"The beginning of wisdom is: Acquire wisdom; and with all your acquiring, get understanding. Prize her [wisdom], *and she will exalt you; she will honor you if you embrace her"* (Proverbs 4:7–8).

DAILY SCRIPTURE READING: Psalms 23, 26, 28, 31, 35

DISHONESTY

"Do all things. . .that you may prove
yourselves to be blameless and innocent,
children of God above reproach in the midst of
a crooked and perverse generation"
(Philippians 2:14–15).

IN his book, *When Nations Die,* Jim Nelson Black pointed to a 1993 report that revealed 33 percent of high school students and 16 percent of college students admitted they had stolen from a store in the past year. The same report showed that one-third of high school and college students said they would lie on a résumé or job application to get a job.

Not surprisingly, people's respect for other people's honesty seems to be decreasing.

In his book *Virtual Reality,* George Barna revealed that when people were asked to rate honesty and integrity, compared to 10 years ago, only 9 percent believed things had gotten better in the last decade. Thirty-five percent believed things had stayed the same, and 53 percent believed things had gotten worse.

Considering these statistics, we may think that being honest is no longer possible. But no matter how dishonest anyone else becomes, we still answer to a higher authority and should live above reproach.

We are lights in this world and were placed here by God so He can reveal Himself through us. For this to happen, we must avoid the devices of Satan and hold to the standards of the Lord.

Lord, help me to have clean hands and a pure heart.

DAILY SCRIPTURE READING: Psalms 41, 43, 46, 55, 61, 62, 64

MAY 9

WHY THE DISHONEST PROSPER

"Get behind me, Satan! You are a stumbling block to Me;
for you are not setting your mind on God's interests, but man's"
(Matthew 16:23).

"MY people did not listen to My voice. . . . So I gave them over to the
stubbornness of their heart, to walk in their own devices" (Psalm
81:11–12).

There is no doubt that many dishonest people prosper and
gain material things. Why? Because Satan, in his limited authority over us, can provide riches.

However, the problem with Satan's supply is that it's accompanied by fear, anxiety, anger, greed, resentment, and eventual judgment.

Christians, on the other hand, must accept God's Word as
the only standard for honesty and integrity. Only the Lord's provision is accompanied by peace and contentment.

Many Christians conform to this world and, as a result, they
fail to experience God's blessings.

God has the power and the desire to grant material blessings
to those who faithfully follow His directions.

"I would feed you with the finest of the wheat; and with honey
from the rock I would satisfy you" (Psalm 81:16).

God-Ordained Marriage

"Consequently they are no longer two, but one flesh.
What therefore God has joined together, let no man separate"
(Matthew 19:6).

FROM the beginning, God designed marriage to be the ideal setting for perpetuating the human race. He developed the union to consist of a man and a woman, committed to each other for life and to raising their offspring.

God knew that a mother and a father were needed to create the best environment for children. Couples are warned in their marriage vows not to take this union lightly.

There are times in every marriage when it seems barely tolerable. I know that was true of my marriage for the first several years. Judy and I came out of non-Christian backgrounds, with little or no training for a good marriage relationship. Consequently we argued about nearly everything, and this caused hurt feelings on both sides.

We live in a generation that has not been taught the importance of keeping vows. The words "until death do us part" don't really have any significance to many couples. Marriage is entered into with the idea, "If it doesn't work out, I can always get out."

It is only when two people make an absolute commitment to each other that a marriage can function as God intended. It is unrealistic to think that conflicts won't occur. They will, but if spouses know that both of them are irrevocably committed to the marriage, the problems can be resolved.

There are steps to take to help keep a marriage strong: Keep the lines of communication open and spend time together in Bible reading and prayer. *"Hear my prayer, O God; give ear to the words of my mouth"* (Psalm 54:2).

DAILY SCRIPTURE READING: Psalms 83, 86, 88, 91, 95

JUDGING OTHERS

"Do not judge lest you be judged.
For in the way you judge,
you will be judged"
(Matthew 7:1–2).

I THINK this is one of the most misunderstood areas of God's Word—not to judge others.

This doesn't mean that we are not to exercise any judgment or discipline. To do so means that the whole structure of society and Christianity would fall apart.

When God's Word says to not judge others, lest we be judged, it means don't hold a standard up against somebody that is different from what God would establish.

However, we are told that when we see people living in sin we're to go to them, correct them, and win them over; so there's got to be a fine balance.

We are to execute judgment based on God's Word in a loving and kind way, to restore someone, not to condemn that person.

Luke wrote, *"Jesus is ordained of God to be the Judge of all—living and dead"* (Acts 10:42 TLB).

DAILY SCRIPTURE READING:
Psalms 108, 109, 120, 121, 140, 143, 144

POSITIVE ATTITUDES

"Choose for yourselves today whom you will serve...
but as for me and my house, we will serve the Lord"
(Joshua 24:15).

ACCORDING to God's Word, having a positive attitude simply means that we trust God, we are thankful for whatever He provides, and we seek His help in knowing how to use what we have.

Not only should we be positive about what is going on in our lives, but we should be able to praise God when He benefits someone else.

If we can praise God when someone else is prospering, we will have positive attitudes about whatever we are experiencing. Then, in God's timing, our lives will be blessed according to His riches in glory.

Lord, help me to be renewed in the spirit of Your mind. (Read Ephesians 4:23.)

May 13

Taking Responsibility

*"No soldier in active service entangles himself
in the affairs of everyday life,
so that he may please the one
who enlisted him as a soldier"*
(2 Timothy 2:4).

I FEAR that we are seeing an anemic generation of Americans, Christians included, who've had everything done for them and handed to them.

We grow strong physically, mentally, and spiritually through struggles, but this is impossible when parents shelter their children and never make them accountable for their decisions.

Government and society add to the problem by promoting the "victim" mentality and labeling overindulgence as "illness" or "addiction."

With these excuses to fall back on, people refuse to take responsibility for their actions and their own destinies. Instead of persevering, they wimp out. What an effective tool for Satan to stifle the work of the church!

We're in God's Army, and He requires commitment from His recruits. To fulfill that commitment, we must surrender our all to Him and separate ourselves from the world's system.

When we are tempted to see ourselves as victims, we should instead take full advantage of the golden opportunities we have to work for Christ and become victors.

DAILY SCRIPTURE READING: Psalms 40, 49, 50, 73

DON'T QUIT

"He who prepared us for this very purpose is God, who gave to us the Spirit as a pledge. Therefore, being always of good courage, and knowing that. . .we walk by faith, not by sight"
(2 Corinthians 5:5–7).

THOMAS Edison was born into a world that had changed little in 200 years. The horse was the primary means of transportation, gaslights were the latest rage since coal lamps, and electricity was a novelty in college labs.

By his early 20s, Edison's driving motivation was to create a light source powered by electricity. After three years and over 250 failures, he discovered that a string impregnated with carbon and enclosed in an airless jar would glow twice as brightly as the best gas lamp.

Many years later, a reporter asked him how he found the motivation to keep going after so many failures. Edison replied, "I guess I never considered them failures. I just found a lot of things that didn't work."

Like Edison, other men and women throughout history persevered in the face of overwhelming odds, and many of these were Christians.

William Tyndale was determined to enlighten the people of England by translating the New Testament from Greek into English. He knew his activities were unpopular among leaders of the established church in that day, but he persevered, even in the face of death. He was burned at the stake as a heretic in 1536.

No matter what your mission is, facing opposition, becoming discouraged, or getting sidetracked are not valid reasons for quitting.

DAILY SCRIPTURE READING:
Psalms 76, 82, 84, 90, 92, 112, 115

MAY 15

PERSISTENCE

"The steps of a man are established by the Lord;
and He delights in his way.
When he falls, he shall not be hurled headlong;
because the Lord is the One who holds his hand"
(Psalm 37:23–24).

THE apostle Paul persevered even to the point of giving his life for the cause of Christ. His persistence will benefit all generations until the Lord returns.

If you did a study of the men and women that God has used, I believe you'd find that this attribute is a common thread among them. They have been doggedly persistent in what they were called to do.

Consider Joseph. He could have hanged himself in prison after he was sold into slavery in Egypt and then falsely accused of attempted adultery, but he persevered and became second in command to Pharoah.

Likewise, David was determined not to give up in the face of adversity. God chose him to subdue Israel's enemies and clean up the camp, which he did until the end of his life.

Remember the widow in Luke 18 who kept coming to an unrighteous judge asking for protection? She pestered him so much that he eventually did what she asked. Jesus used that parable to demonstrate that we should pray and not give up.

Persistence is an attitude that Christ desires in His followers. If you quit because things get difficult in your Christian walk, you might as well not start, because if you serve the Lord it probably will get tough.

DAILY SCRIPTURE READING: Psalms 8, 9, 16, 19, 21, 24, 29

INSTILLING BASIC VALUES

"The righteous man leads a blameless life;
blessed are his children after him"
(Proverbs 20:7 NIV).

GOD'S instructions are neither complicated nor harsh. In fact, they are designed to free us, not bind us to a set of rigid rules. However, God's principles in the area of finances have been largely ignored for the last 40 years, and now we are reaping what has been sown.

I read a magazine article that vividly brought this into focus. A large mail-order seed company was forced to go out of business, despite the fact that sales were higher than ever. For nearly 50 years the company had been supplying seeds to children who would sell them door to door to raise money.

The nonpayment rate to the company began to rise steadily until it reached 70 percent. The average age of this delinquent sales force was ten. The final straw came when the company attempted to contact the parents, hoping they would help in collection, only to find that the parents actually encouraged the kids.

The symptom is nonpayment of a just debt; but the problem runs much deeper. It involves basic values that parents fail to instill in their children. It's an attitude of dishonesty. The lack of integrity in the parents is reflected and amplified in the lives of their children.

It's unfortunate that later these parents probably won't understand why the irresponsible children became irresponsible adults.

DAILY SCRIPTURE READING: Psalms 33, 65, 66, 67, 68

MAY 17

SURRENDER

"[Christl] did not come to be served, but to serve,
and to give His life a ransom for many"
(Matthew 20:28).

CHRIST'S willingness to sacrifice on behalf of others may seem far beyond our reach. We want to be more like Him, but to do so we must cross the hurdle of surrendering everything to God.

It is at this point that Satan warns us about all the things we might lose. But all that we have belongs to God anyway. The important thing is that we learn obedience.

When we study the lives of the greatest people in the Bible, we find that they did not demand and direct. They followed, just like Shadrach, Meshach, and Abed-nego did when they refused to bow before the golden image of a pagan king. (Read the story in Daniel 3.)

They understood God's power, they knew their right to petition God, they accepted God as the final authority, and they surrendered themselves to Him.

We would do well to follow the example of Shadrach, Meshach, and Abed-nego.

DAILY SCRIPTURE READING: Psalms 75, 93, 94, 97, 98, 99, 100

May 18

Cheerful Giving

"Let each one do just as he has purposed in his heart;
not grudgingly or under compulsion;
for God loves a cheerful giver"
(2 Corinthians 9:7).

TRUSTING God is one of the first steps toward overcoming Satan and becoming the cheerful giver the apostle Paul spoke about in today's Scripture verse.

Trust stems from love toward God, which produces love toward others. Love toward others produces giving.

The great American minister, Jonathan Edwards, said, "Love will dispose men to all acts of mercy toward their neighbors when they are under any affliction or calamity. . .for we are naturally disposed to pity those we love when they are afflicted. It will dispose men to give to the poor, to bear one another's burdens, and to weep with those that weep, as well as to rejoice with those that rejoice."

This giving spirit was evident in the Philippians, who faithfully supported the ministry of the apostle Paul. By their support, these people were counted as fellow laborers in Paul's work.

By the same token, everything we do for others we also do for Christ.

DAILY SCRIPTURE READING: Psalms 103, 104, 113, 114, 117

PURPOSEFUL GIVING

"It is more blessed to give than to receive"
(Acts 20:35).

IF we allow Satan's tools of fear, doubt, and selfishness to prevent us from surrendering all to God, we never can enjoy the rewards that await us when we serve, share, and give.

But if we seek God's will in giving, give only to please Him (not to impress others), and give cheerfully, we won't have to worry about our needs.

This may mean giving up having the world's "best," but that's a very small sacrifice compared to those being made by Christians in countries where professing faith in Christ means death.

God's Word says, *"Do not neglect doing good and sharing; for with such sacrifices God is pleased"* (Hebrews 13:16).

We forget that each of us has been called to suffer for Christ. For most of us, our service has not required material or physical sacrifice. However, it does require an understanding that our abundance is intended to further the kingdom of God. It is not a reward for being "nice."

How purposeful or sacrificial is your giving?

HONORING A VOW

"When you make a vow to God, do not be late in paying it,
for He takes no delight in fools.
Pay what you vow!
It is better that you should not vow
than that you should vow and not pay"
(Ecclesiastes 5:4–5).

A PRINCIPLE that has been greatly overlooked in our generation is that of making a vow. A vow is literally a promise.

When someone borrows money, he or she makes a promise to repay according to the agreed-upon conditions of the loan (no matter whether it's a bank loan, personal loan, or use of a credit card). Once an agreement is sealed, repayment is not an option. It's an absolute as far as God is concerned.

As representatives of Jesus Christ before the world, Christians are admonished to think ahead and consider the consequences of their actions.

Once a Christian borrows money, the vow must be honored and the money repaid.

If you can't keep your vows, don't make them.

A SPIRITUAL INDICATOR

*"Do not merely look out for your own personal interests,
but also for the interests of others"*
(Philippians 2:4).

GOD'S Word teaches that how we handle our money is the clearest reflection of our spiritual value system. Excessive debts, even bankruptcies, are not our problems; they are the external indicators of internal spiritual problems. Literally, they are a person's attitudes being reflected in actions.

I received a call from a pastor who was considering filing for bankruptcy because of a very heavy debt burden. He was fearful of his creditors obtaining judgments or even garnishments against him. "It's not fair that they can attach my salary," he said. "I won't be able to feed my family." I asked if they had tricked him into borrowing. They had not.

I asked him to consider what Christ would do if He were in his position. After all, isn't that what we're instructed to do as Christ's followers? We are to be imitators of Christ. *"Therefore be imitators of God, as beloved children"* (Ephesians 5:1).

This pastor stood up to his burden, asked for the forgiveness of his creditors, and cut up all his credit cards. He confessed his error before his church and found several kindred spirits in the congregation.

We are a generation of "quick-fix" attitudes, and the idea of absolutes has not been taught for a long time, even in Christian living.

DAILY SCRIPTURE READING:
Psalms 122, 124, 133, 134, 135, 136

May 22

An Easier Gospel

"The time will come when they will not endure sound doctrine;
but wanting to have their ears tickled,
they will accumulate for themselves teachers
in accordance to their own desires"
(2 Timothy 4:3).

PAUL'S letter to Timothy outlines the fact that trials are normal for the dedicated believer and, as a result, many fall away and seek an easier Gospel.

This easier Gospel teaches that Christ provides a buffer from all problems and provides unlimited prosperity and the freedom to spend profits as desired. In other words, God is so blessed to have us on His team that He is forced to intercede for fear that we will get discouraged and quit (as a great many do).

The truth is, God doesn't promise to buffer us from all difficulties for two basic reasons.

First, anyone would have to be simpleminded not to follow Christ if He buffered His followers from every problem. Instead, as Paul said, our faith must be tested by fire—in other words, faith for sustaining us through trials, not paving a path around them.

The second reason for not buffering a believer from all problems is so others will witness God's peace in the midst of turmoil. The unsaved can rely on money and position during good times, but during bad times emotional chaos usually reigns.

The Lord has promised a "crown of life" to those who persevere under trial and learn to love Him even more.

DAILY SCRIPTURE READING: Psalms 138, 139, 145, 148, 150

WE CANNOT BE DOUBLE-MINDED

"Draw near to God and He will draw near to you.
Cleanse your hands, you sinners;
and purify your hearts, you double-minded"
(James 4:8).

"I'M sorry, Mr. Burkett. Your son is listed as DOA."

This is the news I received several years ago when my son was in a serious automobile accident. I was out of town on a speaking engagement when the news came. I was shocked—stunned actually—but I can honestly say that the peace of God surpasses all understanding. I knew God was in control and I could trust Him—totally.

My wife Judy and I spent the next 73 days in the hospital with Dan, who was in a coma while his body went from crisis to crisis. The longer the crises extended, the more I was convinced of the truth in today's Scripture verse: In order to have faith we cannot be double-minded. We must be willing to follow Christ and be used as He decides.

I also realized that I had fallen into Satan's most subtle trap: fearing the loss of what really belongs to God anyway.

The doctors and nurses did their best and never quit trying to save Dan, but it was God who made the final decision.

Dan woke up. God spared my son, not because he was ours but because He wanted to show Himself strong to us and because we were trusting and relying solely on Him (read 2 Chronicles 16:9).

DAILY SCRIPTURE READING: Psalms 4, 12, 20, 25, 32, 38

ABUNDANT COMFORT

"Just as the sufferings of Christ are ours in abundance,
so also our comfort is abundant through Christ"
(2 Corinthians 1:5).

OFTEN those God has used most effectively are the ones who have suffered the greatest trials.

Perhaps no principle in God's Word is less understood than that of brokenness. Brokenness does not mean broke financially; it's a condition during which God allows circumstances to control our lives to the point that we must totally depend on Him.

It seems the greater God's plan for a person, the greater the brokenness. The life of the apostle Paul reflects both great power and great brokenness. Yet Paul never considered his personal circumstances as punishment. He consistently asserted that his sufferings were a direct result of service to Christ.

Dear Lord, I am totally dependent on You. Please help me in all the circumstances over which I have no control. I ask You in Jesus' Name. Amen.

DAILY SCRIPTURE READING:
Psalms 42, 53, 58, 81, 101, 111, 130, 131, 141, 146

THE PURPOSE OF BROKENNESS

*"Consider it all joy, my brethren, when you encounter various trials,
knowing that the testing of your faith produces endurance"*
(James 1:2–3).

*"THE Lord is near to the brokenhearted, and saves those who are
crushed in spirit"* (Psalm 34:18).

In God's wisdom, He realizes what it takes to keep us
attuned to His direction: We must read His Word, accept His
teachings, and be completely dependent on Him. Once we make
a total surrender of ourselves to God, then, and only then, can He
begin to use us.

No matter how many times we think we have surrendered
ourselves to Him, we find ourselves falling into old habits and we
have to try again.

Many times, as Christians, we pray, "God, mold me into a vessel you can use," and then when God's work begins and things don't
happen just like we had planned we are ready to call "time out."

When things are going well, we seldom complain, but when
our goals are blocked—even temporarily—we become frustrated or
irritated—a bit like spoiled children when they don't get their way.

If you set your mind on your own desires and not on God's
will or His timing, you will not attain the happiness or satisfaction
you seek.

If you want the perfecting of your faith, it comes by way of
following God's leading and being in His will.

I pray that the God of peace will *"equip you in every good
thing to do His will,"* working in you what is pleasing in His sight
(see Hebrews 13:20–21).

DAILY SCRIPTURE READING: Psalms 2, 22, 27

DIVORCE FROM THE WORLD

*"They are surprised that you do not run with them into the same
excess of dissipation, and they malign you;
but they shall give account to Him who
is ready to judge the living and the dead"*
(1 Peter 4:4–5).

THIS principle is easier to talk about than to live. The teaching is very clear in the lives of those whom God has chosen to use throughout the Bible.

The more success you have in your service for God, the greater the potential for ego and self-centeredness. Thus, the greater the necessity for you to maintain a "God-first" spirit. The process of being molded into Christ's image must be continual.

Clearly, the purpose of being totally dependent on God is so you will be divorced from a marriage to this world and all it has to offer.

The world has its way of doing things; but, as a Christian, you should have an entirely different agenda.

Paul wrote to the Christians in Rome, *"Do not be conformed to this world, but be transformed. . .that you may prove what the will of God is, that which is good and acceptable and perfect"* (Romans 12:2).

John wrote that the world is passing away, *"but the one who does the will of God abides forever"* (1 John 2:17).

May 27

Run or Relax?

*"I ask you not to lose heart at
my tribulations on your behalf,
for they are your glory"*
(Ephesians 3:13).

OUR first reaction to the pressures of life is to run. It's simply easier to withdraw and feel sorry for ourselves than it is to stand against the enemy.

No one can question Elijah's courage or commitment to God. He regularly risked his life to deliver God's messages. And yet, right after he had called down God's fire from heaven and had destroyed the prophets of Baal, he ran when Jezebel threatened him.

In 1 Kings 19:4 he is found under a juniper tree, asking God to let him die. Instead, God comforted him, fed him, and told him to relax and rest. Later when Elijah was refreshed, God sent him back into the battle.

Then there's the apostle Paul: He must have had some real doubts about the difficulties he faced while serving the Lord. But the overwhelming characteristic we see in Paul's letters is the ability to relax and enjoy life—to be content—regardless of external circumstances.

When you are in the midst of difficult circumstances, can you say that you—like Paul—are relaxed? Or do you—like Elijah—run?

To honor God, we must be more like Paul: relaxed and content with our circumstances.

"I call upon the Lord, who is worthy to be praised, and I am saved from my enemies" (Psalm 18:3).

DAILY SCRIPTURE READING: 2 Samuel 23:1-7; 1 Kings 1:1-2:12

CARING ABOUT EACH OTHER

*"Whoever has the world's goods, and beholds his brother
in need and closes his heart against him,
how does the love of God abide in him? . . .
Let us not love with word or with tongue,
but in deed and truth"*
(1 John 3:17–18).

GOD is in control. If we are serving Him, nothing can befall us unless He allows it. It will rarely seem beneficial at the time, but if we believe God's Word we must believe He will ultimately receive the glory.

One important aspect of living for the Lord is to love and care about each other. When Christians are suffering from a financial disaster, the last thing they need is an accusation: "Well, she wasn't very careful with her money." or "He could have gotten a better job if he had really tried." or "Have you seen the car they drive?"

In fact, when people need help, they need your help. You must show compassion during their time of testing, and God's Word admonishes us to show our love with deeds.

Whatever you have is not intended solely for your personal enjoyment. God intends for you to give to others the way He has given to you—in love. What if God withheld blessings from you because you have made unwise decisions? or have been careless?

People usually make their decisions based on whatever information or motivation they have at the time. It's not for us to judge their behavior. Rather, we are to care enough to help, knowing that some day we might be on the receiving end.

DAILY SCRIPTURE READING:
1 Kings 2:13–3:28; 2 Chronicles 1:15–17

SOCIAL GOALS

*" [Their] seed was sown among the thorns; these are the ones who
have heard the word, and the worries of the world,
and the deceitfulness of riches, and the desires for other things enter in
and choke the word, and it becomes unfruitful"*
(Mark 4:18–19).

CHRISTIANS get trapped into a discontented life by adopting world goals. These goals always boil down to more, bigger, best. Scripture defines them as indulgence, greed, and pride.

Often successful Christians come to the Lord out of desperation when they realize that their lives are characterized by fear and anxiety, and the accumulation of assets has neither alleviated the fear nor provided happiness.

For a while after accepting Christ as Savior, there is peace and a real desire to commit everything to God. Unfortunately, many Christians continue to live in the natural, and the tendency is for them to fall back into the same old routine. They only go through the motions of serving the Lord.

The evidence to the contrary is a lack of peace, a lack of spiritual growth, and a growing doubt about God.

Satan's ploy is to use the riches of the world to keep you away from God's salvation and His blessings. If that fails, he will simply use riches to steer you away from God's path.

Don't let Satan get the upper hand in your life by adopting worldly goals.

God's Word says it best: *" 'Come out from their midst and be separate,' says the Lord. 'And do not touch what is unclean; and I will welcome you' "* (2 Corinthians 6:17).

DAILY SCRIPTURE READING: 1 Kings 5, 6; 2 Chronicles 2, 3

May 30

Memorial Day

"Righteousness exalts a nation, but sin is a disgrace to any people"
(Proverbs 14:34).

WE should honor those who died to ensure our freedoms. It seems to me that we take these freedoms for granted, but I can guarantee you that our forefathers didn't.

Ben Franklin, Alexander Hamilton, Thomas Jefferson, George Washington, and other men met in 1774 to pledge their fortunes, their lives, and their good names to secure our right to decide our own destinies.

We owe these men, but we have an even greater debt to our fallen soldiers. Every one of the original "generals," whom Christ chose and called apostles, gave his life to ensure that we would have a right to decide our eternal destinies and a right to tell others about it.

George Washington had been a wealthy man, but he was willing to pledge everything he had—fortune, fame, good name, family, even his life—for a cause he really believed in.

When people in the armed forces go to war, they must lay aside their families, businesses, and their own selfish desires and surrender themselves to the ones who have enlisted them.

The apostle Paul said that, as believers, we must do the same thing. He wrote, *"No soldier in active service entangles himself in the affairs of everyday life, so that he may please the one who enlisted him as a soldier"* (2 Timothy 2:4).

That's an important principle to remember. I encourage you to give thanks for all the fallen Americans who have preserved our freedom and our right to hear, teach, and spread the Gospel of our Lord Jesus Christ.

DAILY SCRIPTURE READING: 1 Kings 7; 2 Chronicles 4

MAY 31

THE DANGER OF ABUNDANCE

*"Beware, and be on your guard against every form of greed;
for not even when one has an abundance
does his life consist of his possessions"*
(Luke 12:15).

THE majority of warnings in Christ's messages were to the wealthy, not the poor. In poverty, the issue is usually black or white—honesty or dishonesty.

In affluence, it is much more subtle. I believe that in America nearly everyone would be graded as wealthy by any biblical standard.

Our anxieties and worries are not related to the lack of things but, rather, to the loss of things. Many, if not most, Christians inwardly fear they might lose what they have acquired materially.

Therefore, they compromise God's best in their lives to hang on to the very way of life that brought so much worry and turmoil before they met the Lord.

This does not necessarily mean surrendering the assets. It means being willing to surrender them. It boils down to what your priorities are, doesn't it?

Remember the story in Acts: *"All those who had believed were together, and had all things in common; and they began selling their possessions and were sharing them with all, as anyone might have need"* (Acts 2:44-45).

Could you do that? How important are your possessions to you?

Pray about it.

JUNE 1

FATHERS

*"It is vain for you to rise up early, to retire late, to eat the bread of
painful labors; for He gives to His beloved even in his sleep"*
(Psalm 127:2).

THE following definition of a father was in a letter I received. "My
father is the one who slips me an extra $10 for a really big date, the
one who never misses my ball game even though we are 0 and 12 for
the season, and the one who punishes me but always defends me
against everyone else, because he's my dad, and he's my best friend."

It is customary to honor fathers at this time of year, but I want
to *address* fathers. I encourage you not to invest in the urgent things
of today, while letting the important things slip by.

There are three important investments we have to make in our
families. The first is *time*. God used the Scripture verse for today in
my life many years ago when I was working 12 to 16 hours a day.
Spend time with your children.

Second, give them your *attention*. Sometimes, even when we
are at home, our minds are elsewhere. Nothing is worth the consequences later.

Third, give them *discipline*. The proverbs say that poverty and
shame will come to them who lack discipline. I don't mean punishment; I mean setting an example for them to follow so you can mold
them into God's image.

If your father is still living, tell him how much you love and
appreciate him.

If you are a father, be the very best one you can be—with
God's help.

DAILY SCRIPTURE READING: 1 Kings 9:1-10:13;
2 Chronicles 7:11-9:12

ATTITUDE EXTREMES

"Godliness actually is a means of great gain,
when accompanied by contentment"
(1 Timothy 6:6).

THERE are many people who seemingly have little or no regard for material possessions. They accept poverty as a normal living condition, and their major concern is where they will sleep each night.

Are they living lives of contentment? Hardly so, because that description aptly fits the homeless people found in the cities of our nation. That is one extreme.

In contrast are the affluent who have the best our society has to offer at their disposal. Their homes are the community showplaces, their summer cottages are actually small hotels, and their automobiles cost more than most families' houses. But does their abundance guarantee contentment?

Considering the amount of alcohol many of them consume, the therapists they see, and the tranquilizers a lot of them take, it's hard to imagine this group is any more content than the one I first described.

If poverty doesn't provide it and money can't buy it, how can you be content?

"Give me neither poverty nor riches; feed me with the food that is my portion, lest I be full and deny Thee and say, 'Who is the Lord?' Or lest I be in want and steal, and profane the name of my God" (Proverbs 30:8–9).

To be content is to know God's plan for your life, have the conviction to live it, and believe that God's peace is greater than any problem.

DAILY SCRIPTURE READING: 1 Kings 4, 10:14-29;
2 Chronicles 1:14-17, 9:13-28; Psalm 72

LIFE'S STRUGGLES

"It is time for judgment to begin with the household of God;
and if it begins with us first, what will be the outcome for
those who do not obey the gospel of God?"
(1 Peter 4:17).

ALL of us struggle with one thing or another in our lives. I remember the struggles I had when I was growing up in a poor family. Our family was philosophically poor—they thought "poor."

My mother and father came through the Great Depression, and my father didn't work regularly for about eight years, and it left a great impression on him. So, from that time we always lived poorly and never spent money—even on a decent house.

Every discussion I can remember about money was, "We can't afford it." So, that has haunted me all of my life. But even negative circumstances can bring positive results, because I determined I would never be poor.

Over the years, I've had the opportunity to make a lot of money—in business and from writing. The Lord has convicted me to give my surplus away, because if I didn't I would never trust Him. If we have more than we need, there isn't much need to trust in Him, is there?

We will be judged for the way we have used our resources: Have we hoarded them for ourselves or have we given to those with needs?

The first generation church set an example for us, so the question is whether we will be doers of the Word instead of hearers only.

"I delivered the poor who cried for help, and the orphan who had no helper" (Job 29:12).

DAILY SCRIPTURE READING: Proverbs 1, 2, 3

A LACK OF SELF-DISCIPLINE

*"Cease listening, my son, to discipline,
and you will stray from the words of knowledge"*
(Proverbs 19:27).

A PERSON lacking discipline will develop a poor self-image, live in a state of confusion, and suffer from indefinable anxieties. Why? Because of the inner conviction that life is out of control.

Lack of discipline can be seen everywhere but especially in the area of money. People are duped by the "buy now, pay later" advertising, and they end up buying things on credit they can't afford. A glance at any bank's bad check ledger also indicates the prevalence of this lack of self-discipline.

There are several symptoms associated with a lack of self-discipline: confusion, indulgence, sloppiness, and a lack of prayer and Bible study.

The symptoms can be glossed over by pretending to be spiritual, but the residual effects (debt, depression, divorce) can be solved only by correcting the lack of discipline.

The best way to correct a bad habit is to replace it with a good habit.

CHOOSING GODLY COUNSEL

"Blessed is the man who does not walk in the counsel of the wicked"
(Psalm 1:1).

PEOPLE have often asked me, "Should a Christian ever use non-Christian counselors, such as lawyers, doctors, accountants?" I believe the answer to that question is in today's verse.

God's Word teaches that we should seek our counsel from other Christians—godly men and women who understand and try to obey God's Word.

For example, if you are going to choose a doctor, you want to know that the person who is going to take care of you has God's wisdom, as well as being skilled in the medical profession.

If you have a non-Christian counselor (doctor, dentist, attorney), God's Word teaches that you should not get rid of that person. That can be a bad witness to an unsaved person. Perhaps God put you with that person for the purpose of leading him or her to the Lord. If these counselors have been wise, ethical, and honest, then stick with them.

I counseled a Christian businessman who had a non-Christian accountant and attorney. For about 10 years this businessman had been doing unethical, dishonest practices, at the encouragement of his accountant, in order to save taxes. His attorney kept him from being caught.

As this man's relationship with God grew, it became evident that he couldn't continue these business practices. He had to stop the dishonest practices and make restitution. The accountant and attorney quit; he has since made restitution and now has godly counselors.

Do you need to make any changes in your own life?

DAILY SCRIPTURE READING: Proverbs 7, 8, 9

POWER OVER SATAN

"Our struggle is not against flesh and blood,
but against the rulers, against the powers,
against the world forces of this darkness,
against the spiritual forces of wickedness
in the heavenly places"
(Ephesians 6:12).

WE are told that Satan is a defeated foe. He was defeated from the beginning of eternity; he just didn't realize it. Satan thought he had won when Christ was crucified, but when Christ arose from the grave, Satan realized what a mistake he had made.

The only threat Satan has over God's creation is the threat of death. Once the threat of death was removed by the resurrection of Jesus, Satan's hold over us was lost.

Those who have accepted Jesus as Lord know that death has no meaning because we pass from life in this world to an eternity with God.

Satan may try to influence our minds, but God's Word says for us to *"take up the full armor of God, that you may be able to resist in the evil day, and have done everything, to stand firm"* (Ephesians 6:13).

CHRISTIAN LOGOS AND SIGNS

"Let not your adornment be merely external"
(1 Peter 3:3).

I RECEIVED a letter that said, "I'm a Christian businessman and I love the Lord, but I am really turned off by these people who display Christianity on their cards and have signs on their trucks. Either they are trying to sell Christianity or they are trying to use God to increase their business. What do you think?"

I know a lot of people who use Christian logos on their business cards and on their vehicles, and unfortunately some are phony. Some people use this means to proselytize customers. But I believe that for everyone who is phony there are a hundred more who are sincere, born-again believers, trying to serve God in a real way.

I caution everyone I come in contact with to be sure they know what that means. It doesn't just mean being a better businessperson. It means being a different businessperson because of the principles he or she is committed to live by.

Read today's verse again. In other words, don't just show your Christianity on the side of a truck or a logo on a business card. Let your behavior show that you are committed to Christ.

How can you do that? By being honest, treating your customers fairly, and by always giving them the better deal than you do yourself. You also do that by paying your employees a fair wage and treating them with honor. Then your adornment is not only external, it is internal.

If you display Christ by using symbols, live by what you are displaying. Hold up the standards of the Lord before others.

DAILY SCRIPTURE READING: Proverbs 13, 14, 15

JUNE 8

HE DRIVES A WHAT?

*"You will do well to send them on their way
in a manner worthy of God"*
(3 John 1:6).

MANY in our society pray the following prayer for pastors: "Lord, You keep him humble; we'll keep him poor." I think sometimes that's the mentality toward full-time Christian workers.

I got a letter from a man who was disturbed because his pastor was given a $50,000 Mercedes by a member of the church. The man who wrote thought it was a bad witness for the pastor to drive such an expensive automobile because it would give the church a bad image.

The first question I would ask is, "Are you just jealous? Or does it hurt your pride for the pastor to have a better car than you have?"

Why does a pastor have to look underprivileged? Why is any full-time Christian worker required to look poor? They have to live on the donations or gifts of other people. Remember that we all live on the gifts of God.

If the pastor had gone deeply in debt to get the car or had demanded a salary that would allow him to buy a $50,000 auto, then that man might have had some concern. It was a gift, given by someone who obviously could afford it.

Therefore, if the Lord gives a spirit of peace to the pastor and his wife, the car was truly a gift from God, and it is no one else's business.

Pray for those you know who are in full-time service for the Lord and ask that He will provide all their needs and allow them to walk in His favor daily.

DAILY SCRIPTURE READING: Proverbs 16, 17, 18

HOW TO CHEAT

"Whether, then, you eat or you drink,
or whatever you do, do all to the glory of God"
(1 Corinthians 10:31).

I HEARD of a Christian couple who, in order to qualify for a low income, subsidized government loan, had the wife's employer reduce her working hours. Because she made too much money to qualify for the loan, she reduced her working hours from 40 to 20, which also dropped her salary enough to help them qualify for the loan.

Then, after getting the loan, she went back to working her original hours. They believed there was nothing wrong with doing this since they actually didn't have too much income when they qualified for the loan.

This couple lost the concept of being able to be honest and also failed to trust the Lord for their needs. In order to get the loan they thought they needed, they relied on human devices, trickery, and deceitfulness.

If I could have talked to this couple I would have asked them to consider what God thought of what they had done. He knew all about it, of course.

Our purpose in life is to serve God. The government may never find out what this couple did; but, let me assure you, we all have to answer to a higher power than the government.

We are told in God's Word that if we regard iniquity in our hearts, God will not hear us (Psalm 66:18).

No matter what other people are doing, do not conform to the image of this world.

JUNE 10

YOU MUST BELIEVE

"Without faith it is impossible to please Him. . .
He is a rewarder of those who seek Him"
(Hebrews 11:6).

WE must believe God in order to receive His best. As our Scripture verse for today says, it is impossible to please Him unless we have faith—unless we really believe what He says in His Word and act accordingly.

Most Christians say they believe God, but their lives don't show it. They can exercise discipline in their lives, but they don't exercise faith. They don't step out beyond their own boundaries.

The Pharisees were very spiritual men from outward appearances: They tithed, fasted, and prayed, but it was always with a self-motivated attitude. They tithed but expected to get money back. They fasted but wanted everyone to know it, so they made a show of looking very pitiful. That is exercising discipline—not faith.

Luke 18:1 says to pray and not to lose heart. You have to believe that God hears you. A lack of faith keeps the majority of Christians from ever receiving what God promised them.

Envision God sitting on the throne in Heaven and Jesus sitting at His right hand. They are looking down on you. God says, "I want to bless that person but she doesn't act like she believes My Word. She never gives more than she thinks she can afford. She never helps unless she thinks she can get something in return. Doesn't she know that I can bless her abundantly if she will only trust in Me?"

God does want to bless us. We are His children and He loves us. He can't bless us unless we are able to come to Him unreservedly and believe His Word and His promises.

DAILY SCRIPTURE READING: Proverbs 22, 23, 24

KNOW GOD'S WORD

*"Faith comes from hearing,
and hearing by the word of Christ"*
(Romans 10:17).

HOW can you claim God's promises? You must know what God's Word says and believe it. If you don't know what God's Word promises, you can't claim His best for you. You can't claim what you don't know.

Spend time with God to get to know about Him. Study and meditate on His Word. You must believe so thoroughly that God loves you and cares about your needs that, when you ask, you expect to receive.

Make a commitment today to spend time every day, without fail, learning what's in God's Word. Study it. Pray about it. Claim it for yourself.

Spending time in God's Word is evidence of a commitment to God's way and will open new avenues of blessings in your life.

DAILY SCRIPTURE READING: Proverbs 25, 26, 27

JUNE 12

PUT FAITH TO WORK

*"Are you willing to recognize. . .
that faith without works is useless?"*
(James 2:20).

MANY Christians don't like to hear that they must put faith to work. I've even heard the comment, "I thought faith was a free gift from God." No, grace—unmerited favor—is a free gift of God. Faith requires action.

Hebrews also says that faith is the assurance of things hoped for. If you already have it, you don't need faith to receive it. It's putting something to work that says, "I believe God's plan, and I'm going to exercise God's plan."

Our responsibility is to put faith to work. Unless you live by the principles in God's Word, He can't bless you. He is bound by the same principles we are.

If we really trust God's Word, we will step out in faith. Once we add action to our faith, then things will begin to change, but we do have to be "doers" as well as "hearers."

Think of something you have been praying about but you have never applied the corresponding actions. Take that first step. Add actions to your faith.

JUNE 13

STEPS TO FREEDOM

"The steadfast of mind Thou wilt keep in perfect peace,
because he trusts in Thee"
(Isaiah 26:3).

JUST as the plans we make for ourselves sometimes cause frustration and worry, God's plans always provide peace and freedom.

Peace and freedom show themselves in every aspect of our lives: release from tension and worry, a clear conscience, and the sure knowledge that God is in control.

We are human and, as such, subject to making mistakes, but once God is in charge of our lives His divine correction will bring every area under His control.

There are steps to achieving God's plan. For every promise He makes, He has a condition. In each case, some action is required to bring His power into focus in our lives. That might be prayer, fasting, or simply believing, but it will always require a free act of our wills.

If we are seeking God's best in this life, we must be willing to submit to His will and His direction.

Pray that you will be able to keep your wishes and desires in line with God's will for your life so that you will experience peace and freedom and will receive His best for you.

JUNE 14

WHAT IS WEALTH?

"As for every man to whom God has given riches and wealth, He has also empowered him. . .to receive his reward and rejoice in his labor" (Ecclesiastes 5:19).

HOW well do you understand God's attitude about wealth? There is so much religious folklore in the financial realm that few Christians understand what is from God's Word and what is not.

There are approximately 700 direct references to money in the Bible and hundreds more indirect references. Nearly two-thirds of all the parables Christ left us deal with the use of money. After studying these verses we have to conclude that God equates our use of wealth with our commitment to Him.

God gives us financial principles in His Word, and that's exactly what they are: principles, not laws. He will not punish anyone for violations. Those who fail simply will not receive His blessings in the area of finances and will suffer along with the unbeliever.

Historically, wealth has been related to ownership, but wealth is also related to our creative ability and our credit or borrowing ability: the trust others have in us. Thus wealth becomes an extension of our personalities. It can be used creatively—to spread the Gospel and build hospitals and churches—or it can be wasted on frivolous activities. It can even be corruptive—to purchase influence—or destructive —to buy guns and bombs.

Wealth is neither moral nor immoral. There is no inherent virtue in poverty or in wealth. Rather, God condemns our preoccupation with wealth.

We must learn to trust God in every circumstance, believing that He loves us and gives us only what we can handle without being tempted beyond what we can withstand.

DAILY SCRIPTURE READING: Song of Songs

Opposites Attract

*"Enjoy life with the woman whom you love all the days
of your fleeting life which He has given to you under the sun;
for this is your reward in life"*
(Ecclesiastes 9:9).

I RECEIVED a letter from a young lady saying, "I'm engaged to a nice man, but we are so opposite it seems we never agree on anything. Do you think we are so incompatible that we will not get along in a marriage?"

Possibly they are incompatible, but I know for a fact that if two people in a marriage are just alike one of them is unnecessary. In great part, God puts opposites together because opposites really do attract. In most marriages, one gets up early; the other prefers to stay in bed. One splashes in the sink; the other cleans up.

All of this is so that one will offset the extremes of the other one. If we look at differences as a problem rather than as a balance, we will end up arguing a lot. By recognizing the differences as an asset, a couple can become one working unit. That is what God desires.

Unless you have an absolute commitment to make the marriage work, it won't, because when the going gets tough you'll want out.

Whether you are already married or you are about to get married, think about what you are willing to do to fulfill your commitment to a happy marriage.

If you are already married, think about what you believe has helped you to make a success of your marriage.

If you are unmarried, with no plans for such, think about a couple you know and then pray for them.

DAILY SCRIPTURE READING: 1 Kings 11:1-40; Ecclesiastes 1, 2

June 16

Reject a Fearful Spirit

*"The peace of God, which surpasses all comprehension,
shall guard your hearts and your minds in Christ Jesus"*
(Philippians 4:7).

ONE of Satan's favorite tools is to get you to question "What if?"
Dedicated Christians get trapped into hoarding because they fear
the "what if" of retirement, disability, unemployment, or economic collapse.

Obviously, God wants us to consider these things and even
plan for them, within reason. But when fear dictates to the point
that giving to God's work is hindered, foolish risks are assumed
and worry becomes the norm, rather than the exception. Then
contentment is impossible.

Christians must consciously reject this attitude of fear.

To claim God's victory, it may be necessary for you to face
your fear. If your fear is a lack of surplus, it may be necessary to live
without it in order to conquer that fear.

But remember above all else, *"My God shall supply all your
needs according to His riches in glory in Christ Jesus"* (Philippians
4:19).

DAILY SCRIPTURE READING: Ecclesiastes 3, 4, 5, 6, 7

A REASONABLE LIVING STANDARD

"The man who lays up treasure for himself. . .
is not rich toward God"
(Luke 12:21).

ALTHOUGH many Scriptures teach about the dangers of material riches, God's Word does not teach that poverty is the alternative. God wants us to understand that money is a tool to use in accomplishing His plan through us.

Just having surplus does not mean that it's all right to use it as we want. It is important to develop a lifestyle based on conviction —not circumstance.

Since there is no universal plan suitable for everyone, this must be a standard established among husband, wife, and God. Obviously, God will assign Christians at every economic level.

If God's plan puts you in the upper level of income, there will be a purpose for the abundance and a ministry through it. But just having an abundance is not a sign of God's blessings. Satan can easily duplicate any worldly riches.

God's riches are without sorrow and for bringing others to salvation.

Living a disciplined lifestyle with an abundance is a much stronger witness than having the abundance ever could be.

DAILY SCRIPTURE READING: 1 Kings 11:41-43;
2 Chronicles 9:29-31; Ecclesiastes 8, 9, 10, 11, 12

June 18

Respond or React?

"I say to you, love your enemies,
and pray for those who persecute you"
(Matthew 5:44).

WHEN we are hurt or betrayed by friends or business associates, our initial impressions are purely emotional ones, and unless we are controlled primarily by God's Word the first impressions are rarely correct.

In fact, I have discovered that many initial impressions run opposite to God's direction. Therefore, we must turn to His Word.

The Scriptures present an interesting perspective of strength and compassion when dealing with those who cause us harm or hurt.

Read the account of David's confrontation with Nabal in 1 Samuel 25:2–39. In spite of David's noble gesture to protect Nabal's property, when David needed help Nabal refused even to acknowledge him. This obvious affront infuriated David.

In anger (sometimes our first reaction), David decided to take matters into his own hands and destroy Nabal. God used Nabal's wife to stop David from taking vengeance, and in the face of godly counsel David cooled off and withdrew.

His withdrawal could have been interpreted as weakness by others; however, the result was that God executed judgment in His own time. Thus, the use of restraint was more effective than the use of strength.

It is always better to respond to situations (with patience, prayer, understanding) than to react (with anger and retaliation).

DAILY SCRIPTURE READING: 1 Kings 12;
2 Chronicles 10:1-11:17

JUNE 19

WHAT IS STRENGTH?

"The God of all grace, who called you to
His eternal glory in Christ,
will Himself perfect, confirm,
strengthen and establish you"
(1 Peter 5:10).

EVEN a cursory review of Scripture reveals that strength does not always mean the exercise of power. More often, it means the relinquishing of personal rights to God.

The opposite of strength is cowardice. Those who flee from any confrontation display cowardice. What's the difference? It's whether God receives honor from the action.

If you allow others to cheat and abuse you because you are fearful of any conflict, you are displaying cowardice. Cowardice is generally motivated by self-preservation—not compassion.

A classic example is found in Numbers 13 and 14. God's people refused to occupy their promised land because of the giants living there. Were they demonstrating compassion for their enemies? Hardly! They were self-motivated.

Strength is demonstrated when you exercise the proper use of power to accomplish God's assigned tasks.

God works through your life if you are surrendered to Him. Will you display cowardice or strength? It's your choice.

DAILY SCRIPTURE READING: 1 Kings 13, 14;
2 Chronicles 11:18-12:16

JUNE 20

AID THE ENEMY?

*"Jesus said to them,
'Watch out and beware of the leaven
of the Pharisees and Sadducees' "*
(Matthew 16:6).

LOVING your enemies (anyone who does you harm) is different from aiding them. Christ loved the Pharisees (He loved everyone), but He certainly did not help them.

To the contrary, as we see in today's Scripture verse, He opposed them and warned His disciples to stay away from them. They represented a counterforce that was anti-Christian.

This is not meant to imply that all our enemies fall into the same classification as the Pharisees. But when others purposely set themselves against your interests and God's, they certainly cannot be classified as friends.

God wants us to love others both prayerfully and spiritually, but that does not mean to aid what they are doing. On occasion God may direct you to aid someone who is doing you wrong, but it is so you can provide a strong and effective witness for Him.

Helping someone who has wronged you is the only type of "revenge" God would sanction.

"Vengeance is Mine, and retribution. . . . For the Lord will vindicate His people, and will have compassion on His servants" (Deuteronomy 32:35–36).

DAILY SCRIPTURE READING: 1 Kings 15:1-24;
2 Chronicles 13, 14, 15, 16

JUNE 21

SELFISHNESS

"I said to myself, 'Come now,
I will test you with pleasure.
So enjoy yourself.'
And behold, it too was futility"
(Ecclesiastes 2:1).

THE theology of selfishness is an easy one to promote because most of us were raised with it, and today it virtually dominates our society. It's the philosophy called "get all you can out of life today; live with gusto." This certainly is not a new philosophy. As you can see in today's Scripture, Solomon wrote about it in the book of Ecclesiastes.

Selfishness, ego, and pride are about as opposite from biblical concepts as light is from darkness.

It is important to discern the difference between the pride of wealth and the wealth itself. Christ never condemned wealth; He condemned the wealthy-minded of this world.

God has blessed many people with both spiritual and material wealth. Those who are selected by God to manage a large surplus —to feed His sheep—should manifest humility, not pride.

DAILY SCRIPTURE READING: 1 Kings 15:25-16:34, 17;
2 Chronicles 17

JUNE 22

COMPROMISE

*"Do not love the world, nor the things in the world.
If anyone loves the world, the love of the Father is not in him. . . .
The one who does the will of God abides forever"*
(1 John 2:15, 17).

FEW Christians willfully violate the Ten Commandments. Most appear to be basically moral. But what about inward doubts, temptations, and failures? Are these sins?

Compared to overt sins (like lying or stealing), compromises don't seem so bad. If God were merely an accountant, weighing good against bad and one person against another, there would be no problem.

However, God deals in absolutes, not comparisons. His Word is straightforward and any compromises of what it says are usually just symptoms of spiritual problems.

J. R. Lowell said, "Compromise makes a good umbrella, but a poor roof; it is a temporary expedient."

As an individual, you are responsible and accountable for your own actions, regardless of what others do.

Dear Lord, forgive me if I'm guilty of compromising anything in Your Word and help me make the changes in my life that are needed.

GOD'S ABSOLUTES

"If our hearts do not condemn us,
we have confidence before God and
receive from him anything we ask,
because we obey his commands
and do what pleases him"
(1 John 3:21–22 NIV).

THE actual violations of God's commandments involve attitudes that develop over a period of time and are difficult to guard against. Most of us simply find ourselves doing them without realizing how or when the attitudes started.

It's apparent from God's Word that He also recognizes this and has provided an objective question we can ask ourselves to measure our internal attitudes: How do we respond to temptations?

God's minimum acceptable attitudes are developed by accepting the two conditions mentioned in the verse following today's Scripture verse: *"This is his command: to believe in the name of his Son, Jesus Christ, and to love one another as he commanded us"* (1 John 3:23 NIV).

Christ said that loving God more than anything else is a prerequisite to receiving God's best, and I believe that's what most of us want, isn't it?

Use the words of a hymn by Frances Havergal and Henry Malan as your prayer: *Take my life and let it be consecrated, Lord, to Thee. Take my moments and my days and let them flow in ceaseless praise.*

DAILY SCRIPTURE READING: 1 Kings 20, 21

JUNE 24

IS GREED ACCEPTABLE?

*"People who want to get rich fall into temptation and a trap
and into many foolish and harmful desires that
plunge men into ruin and destruction"*
(1 Timothy 6:9 NIV).

GREED has become such an accepted attitude that most major advertisements for luxury products are built around it. Many committed believers are convinced (often by other believers) that it is God's absolute responsibility to make them wealthy and successful.

Just to help Him out (in case God neglects His responsibility), they are willing to borrow large amounts of money to invest in get-rich-quick schemes, abandon their families to provide the good life for them, and rob God of His tithes and offerings. Then they rationalize their behavior under the guise of doing what they have to do to succeed.

God does have a plan for success, and, although it is unique for each individual, it is common in three ways.

God never provides success at the expense of serving Him first.

God never provides success at the expense of our peace.

God never provides success at the expense of the family.

Albert Einstein said, "It is high time that the ideal of success should be replaced by the ideal of service."

DAILY SCRIPTURE READING: 1 Kings 22:1-40; 2 Chronicles 18

JUNE 25

GOD'S WAY:
OPTIONAL OR MANDATORY?

"Become blameless and pure,
children of God without fault in a crooked
and depraved generation,
in which you shine like stars in the universe
as you hold out the word of life"
(Philippians 2:15–16 NIV).

IT seems abundantly clear from God's Word that when we accept Christ as our Lord we are to live by a much higher standard than the rest of the world—not because as Christians we are supposed to be pious or super spiritual but simply because we are to be normal.

It is God's way that is normal and the world's way that is abnormal—not the other way around, as some would think.

We are to be lights in a dark world, for the express purpose of leading others to a saving knowledge of Jesus.

What we say is not enough. God requires that we "show and tell." When others observe our attitudes and our behavior, they will either see Christ in us or they won't. It is as clear as that.

True believers possess a serenity and joy that comes from knowing Christ and living for Him. And true believers set standards for their lives that are in tune with the Word of God.

"As for me, I shall walk in my integrity; redeem me, and be gracious to me. My foot stands on a level place" (Psalm 26:11–12).

DAILY SCRIPTURE READING: 1 Kings 22:41-53;
2 Kings 1; 2 Chronicles 19:1-21:3

JUNE 26

PRECONDITIONED RESPONSE

"Should a man like me run away?
Or should one like me go into the temple to save his life?
I will not go!"
(Nehemiah 6:11 NIV).

As Christians, we learn a great deal about discipline and dedication from the secular world. It is interesting that those in the secular business world are sometimes more punctual and reliable in their work than Christians are in serving God.

Sadly, some Christians apply a degree of excellence and dedication to their business careers that are woefully lacking in their walk with the Lord.

The secular business world practices what is called "preconditioned response." For instance, the airlines have found that it is not feasible to wait until in-flight emergencies occur to acquaint pilots with emergency procedures. Therefore, they attempt to precondition their responses.

Even a cursory scan of Scripture will reveal that the truly successful servants of the Lord made decisions on the preconditioned belief that God's way wasn't the best way; it was the only way.

Just as Nehemiah did when he refused to compromise God's way even to save his own life, a Christian must precondition all responses to temptations and problems on the basis of what God says, not what is normal and acceptable to the world.

God promises that He will protect us so that He may receive the glory. *"Call upon me in the day of trouble; I will deliver you, and you will honor me"* (Psalm 50:15 NIV).

DAILY SCRIPTURE READING: 2 Kings 2, 3, 4

IS WELFARE SCRIPTURAL?

*"There will always be poor people in the land.
Therefore I command you to be openhanded toward your brothers and
toward the poor and needy in your land"*
(Deuteronomy 15:11 NIV).

THE issue of welfare is very clear biblically: We are to help those in need. There may be disagreements about how much help is necessary and who should receive it, but there should be no disagreement about the necessity to feed, clothe, and shelter the poor.

Welfare for the poor is biblical and necessary. The fact that the government has assumed that function of caring for the poor does not negate our responsibility.

No one can realistically deny that the church is no longer the prime source for meeting the needs of the poor; the government is.

Nor can there be any doubt that from this base of government welfare the "great society" has grown. From this society developed many families in permanent poverty. Because of this, many Christians have developed resentment and indifference to those who really are poor.

God's Word says there will always be needs in the world around us. The purpose is twofold: to test our commitment to obedience and to create an attitude of interdependence.

We are given clear and absolute direction about welfare in God's Word. Fortunately, the standards for welfare also are given.

Indiscriminate welfare traps the recipients by making them dependent. Biblical welfare meets needs and always looks toward restoring individuals to positions of productivity.

How do you feel about the poor? What are you doing about it?

DAILY SCRIPTURE READING: 2 Kings 5, 6, 7

JUNE 28

CHRISTIAN RESPONSIBILITY

*"He who gives to the poor will lack nothing,
but he who closes his eyes to them receives many curses"*
(Proverbs 28:27 NIV).

CHRISTIANS are doing a miserable job of caring for the physical needs of the poor. If we can't meet the needs of those around us, we won't meet the needs of those in other countries.

Few churches today have any organized program for helping the poor of their own fellowship or community. Some have a benevolence fund to help meet some emergencies but nothing to meet continuing needs.

Obviously vision and leadership come down from the top. If the churches don't practice the body concept of Christianity, it is a certainty that they will never reach the unsaved community.

At present, the governments of the world account for nearly 95 percent of all the care to the aged, ill, and impoverished, and the evidence shows they are using it as a tool to spread atheism.

Is it any wonder that the unsaved are rejecting Christianity? In the matter of caring, it has become just another religion, rather than a way of living. It is not a question of ability or direction. Christians in America have the resources to do at least ten times what we are presently doing for the poor, with little or no alteration of lifestyles.

Many of us are going to be very ashamed to face the Lord and explain how we hoarded money for indulgences while others were in need.

DAILY SCRIPTURE READING: 2 Kings 8, 9; 2 Chronicles 21:4–22:9

WHAT IS A CHRISTIAN BUSINESS?

"Blessed is the man who finds wisdom,
the man who gains understanding,
for she [wisdom] *is more profitable*
than silver and yields better returns than gold"
(Proverbs 3:13–14 NIV).

OBVIOUSLY, as any thinking person knows, there is no such thing as a Christian business. A business is a legal entity, such as a corporation, partnership, or proprietorship; and, as such, it has no spirit or soul.

The business may, however, reflect the values of the principal owners or managers. It is the reflection of these values that determines whether a business is labeled Christian or non-Christian.

A business is a tool to be used by God in demonstrating the truth of the Gospel. A business is the perfect environment for obeying Christ's truths.

When we are truly committed to Jesus and to serving God's purposes, our businesses (or our work) will be conducted according to scriptural principles.

So, whether you are a business owner, an employee, or you just patronize businesses to provide your needs, the main objective in life is to live in such a way that you demonstrate the truth of the Gospel.

DAILY SCRIPTURE READING: 2 Kings 10, 11;
2 Chronicles 22:10-23:21

June 30

Balance in Business

"Do not merely listen to the word,
and so deceive yourselves. Do what it says"
(James 1:22 NIV).

THE purpose of a Christian's business is to glorify God. The day-to-day functions are the things we do to accomplish that purpose. No one function is more or less important, and each must be done with excellence.

For instance, if the business aspects are neglected to do evangelism, quite often the business will fail. If the ministry functions are neglected to generate profits, the business loses its witness in the world.

This certainly can be observed in our society today. Often the term Christian, in conjunction with a business, brings to mind an image of people who don't pay their bills and tell the creditors they are just "trusting the Lord" for their money.

The truth is, there are many Christian-run businesses that are extremely profitable and are operated honestly and ethically, but few people even know the owner is a Christian, because that person is keeping his or her beliefs a secret.

Obviously these extremes do not constitute every Christian-run business. But of the more than 250,000 Christian-run businesses in America, few present a balanced image of good business practices based on biblical principles.

"A false balance is an abomination to the Lord" (Proverbs 11:1).

If you don't own or operate a Christian business, pray today for someone who does. Ask God to give that person wisdom and discernment of His will.

DAILY SCRIPTURE READING: Joel

NEWNESS OF LIFE

"We have been buried with Him through baptism into death. . .
so we too might walk in newness of life"
(Romans 6:4).

IN many ways, I think I have a great advantage by not being saved until age 32, because I clearly recognize what newness of life is. It's being snatched out of the clutches of Satan and thrust into the Spirit of God.

The apostle Paul addressed this issue in today's Scripture verse and the surrounding verses. When you and I accept Jesus Christ and the Holy Spirit comes to dwell within us, we literally have a new life—a new spirit living within us.

God's Word tells us to be transformed by the renewing of our minds. The word transformed is a translation of the Greek *metamorphosis*, the process by which a caterpillar becomes a butterfly. Isn't that a beautiful picture?

Of course, this doesn't mean that we are immune to temptation or that we won't sin anymore. Quite the contrary. When we are trying to live for the Lord, Satan will try even harder to distract us or send us down the wrong road.

I can assure you that on any given day I am capable of letting my anger overwhelm me, bad attitudes override my actions, or my weaknesses influence my decisions. But I have found that the more I yield to the power of the Holy Spirit, the more God helps me overcome those things.

If you haven't experienced that newness of life, it is never too late.

DAILY SCRIPTURE READING: 2 Kings 12, 13; 2 Chronicles 24

July 2

Christian Athletes

*Everyone who competes in the games exercises
self-control in all things"*
(1 Corinthians 9:25).

Since about 1975, I have worked with Christian professional athletes on their personal finances. I've met some really neat guys and many of their wives.

One of the finest athletes was a middle linebacker with the Atlanta Falcons. He was saved shortly before I met him and was in the process of living like a professional athlete: buying the biggest house and best cars. However, after hearing the financial principles, he began to put them into action.

For a period of time I mentored him and we spent lots of time together. I can remember going into fast-food restaurants with him. He would go place his order and then twist the microphone around and share Christ with everybody in the place. Not exactly the way I would have chosen, but it worked for him (he was a large man and most of the people in Atlanta knew him).

One time a young kid came up to him and said, "Man, who do you think you are, sharing that Christian stuff?"

The athlete, still a relatively new Christian at the time and a bit rough around the edges, reached over and grabbed the kid by his jacket, lifted him about an inch off the ground, and said, "You want to hear about Jesus?" You should have seen the kid shaking his head and saying, "Yeah, sure! I do!"

I'm not advocating his methods, but I do suggest that you pray for Christian athletes everywhere—that they will be godly witnesses to their unsaved families, teammates, coaches, and fans.

DAILY SCRIPTURE READING: 2 Kings 14; 2 Chronicles 25; Jonah

WHAT IS WEALTH?

*"Instruct those who are rich in this present world not to be conceited
or to fix their hope on the uncertainty of riches, but on God,
who richly supplies us with all things to enjoy"*
(1 Timothy 6:17).

A MISSIONARY had been invited by a church pastor to bring a message one Sunday morning. The missionary had one married son and five married daughters, all of whom were in Christian work and present at that service. His five daughters had just finished singing a special song before the congregation.

As he rose to speak, a friend whispered, "Emil, you are a very wealthy man." The missionary didn't have much money, yet his friend considered him wealthy. Emil's friend was correct. He was truly wealthy. His trust was in God.

There are some Christians who are wealthy in the riches of this world, but their conceit and trust in money have robbed them of their spiritual wealth.

Your spiritual wealth is more than just possessions and money. It is all of God's blessings: family, friends, health, home, spiritual gifts, job—and much more.

How wealthy are you?

Jesus said, *"Not even when one has an abundance does his life consist of his possessions"* (Luke 12:15).

Give thanks to the Lord now for your "wealth."

DAILY SCRIPTURE READING: Hosea 1, 2, 3, 4, 5, 6, 7

JULY 4

INDEPENDENCE DAY

*"All who are being led by the Spirit of God,
these are sons of God"*
(Romans 8:14).

WHAT does Independence Day mean to most of us? Firecrackers? Picnics? Parades? I'm afraid that's about all our children understand about it.

It's easy to look back and just assume that the Declaration of Independence from our forefathers was just one of the steps down the road to liberty. In fact, it was the break point—the final step—before war.

These men were saying, "We declare ourselves to be a free nation." They were coming against the strongest military power in that day. There was no Constitution, no Bill of Rights, no country in existence. It was a small group of men who, as the leaders of our country, said they believed it was their right to choose their own destiny. We can all praise God for their commitment.

One of the things I encourage all Christian parents to do is to check out a copy of the diary of General George Washington. He kept a fairly complete diary all during the Revolutionary War and I believe it should be required reading for all American children.

Not only was Washington a great patriot and the father of our nation, he was a born-again Christian who believed that what he was doing was God's will for this nation.

Let's give thanks for our forefathers, who were willing to confront the establishment of their day to secure the freedoms we have in this most influential nation in the world—a nation that stands as a bastion of freedom.

DAILY SCRIPTURE READING: Hosea 8, 9, 10, 11, 12, 13, 14

JULY 5

NOT FOR SALE

"Even Simon himself believed; and after being baptized,
he continued on with Philip;
and as he observed signs and great miracles taking place,
he was constantly amazed"
(Acts 8:13).

SIMON, a magician during the time of the apostle Peter, believed on the Lord Jesus and, after being baptized, went with Philip. He noticed that the Spirit was being bestowed by the laying on of hands by the apostles.

When Simon offered money to receive this authority, Peter responded by saying, *"May your silver perish with you, because you thought you could obtain the gift of God with money! You have no part or portion in this matter, for your heart is not right before God"* (Acts 8:20–21).

It was a terrible thing for Simon to try to buy the power of God with money. We need to realize one thing about Simon, however: He did recognize the value of God's power and was willing to spend his money to get it. Too often Christians do not value God's power at all but spend money on the power of the world.

God's power is not for sale; it is given freely by Him. He will not refuse us His power when we give ourselves completely to Him.

The apostle Paul wrote about his desire: *"That I may know Him, and **the power of His resurrection** and the fellowship of His sufferings, being conformed to His death"* (Philippians 3:10, emphasis added).

DAILY SCRIPTURE READING: 2 Kings 15:1-7;
2 Chronicles 26; Amos 1, 2, 3, 4

WHAT HAS GOD PREPARED?

*"No mere man has ever seen, heard or even imagined
what wonderful things God has ready for those who love the Lord"*
(1 Corinthians 2:9).

IT was 9:00 A.M. and the doctors had just finished working frantically to save the life of an elderly woman. Several times during the operation the doctors thought they had lost her. The last time there was no breathing, her pulse had stopped, and there were no vital signs whatsoever. But death had lost and the doctors' efforts had prevailed.

The operating room was silent for a few moments; then everyone began to smile as life began to flow back into the body of the patient. In a few moments she regained a brief state of consciousness, looked at the doctor with tears in her eyes, and asked, "Why did you bring me back? I wanted to stay with Jesus!"

Too often we look at death as an end when it is only a beginning. It is not a time of sadness; it is one of gladness. We get our eyes on the things of this world—money, possessions, and good times—and the world blinds us to the things He has for us. If we walk in the Spirit, the things of this world will not have a hold on us.

And, as we walk in the Spirit, the apostle Paul's testimony—*"for me to die is gain"*—will become our testimony.

You will know you are walking in the Spirit when the things of this world are overshadowed by the eternal things of heaven.

DAILY SCRIPTURE READING: 2 Kings 15:8-18; Amos 5, 6, 7, 8, 9

DUPED BY ADVERTISING

*"For all that is in the world, the lust of the flesh
and the lust of the eyes and the boastful pride of life,
is not from the Father, but is from the world"*
(1 John 2:16).

WHEN we get caught up in the desire to satisfy our senses, we become vulnerable to a lifestyle that has as its goal the accumulation of money, because, if we are to have the things we see advertised, we will need to have money to purchase them. God equates this commitment to riches with sin.

It's not that God wants us to live in poverty; neither does He mean for us to be drawn into the allure of advertising. Our lives should not be characterized by the extravagance and foolish sensualism promoted by the mass media.

Solomon explains the result of indulgence in Ecclesiastes 2:10-11: *"And all that my eyes desired I did not refuse them. . . .and behold all was vanity and striving after wind and there was no profit under the sun."*

We deeply desire something, work for it, finally get it, and shortly thereafter we experience boredom or emptiness. This is why God wants to fulfill the desires of our spirits—because these other desires never can be totally gratified. They always bring with them the quest for more.

But, when our spirits are satisfied, we have peace. If you haven't committed your desires to the Lord, do it now.

"Thou, O Lord, hast made me glad by what Thou hast done, I will sing for joy at the works of Thy hands" (Psalm 92:4).

DAILY SCRIPTURE READING: Isaiah 1, 2, 3, 4

FREEDOM THROUGH RESTRICTION

"Having been freed from sin, you became slaves of righteousness. . . .
Now having been freed from sin and enslaved to God,
you derive your benefit. . .the outcome, eternal life"
(Romans 6:18, 22).

As the directors of a child care center watched the children playing outside, they noticed them staying quite close to the building, even though the yard itself was quite large. It was evident that the busy intersection and passing cars had frightened the children into huddling together in one spot.

One of the directors suggested putting up a fence, and the day after it was erected the children were seen playing happily all over the yard. The fence represented security and, consequently, freedom. Knowing their limits expanded the children's sense of freedom and their capacity to enjoy it.

If God's love did not provide fences in our lives, the result would be chaos, disorder, and unhappiness. God's restraints produce freedom, which brings satisfaction and fulfillment.

What fences do you think God has provided for you in order to avoid unhappiness?

During his predicament Job said, *"He has walled up my way so that I cannot pass; and He has put darkness on my paths"* (Job 19:8). But we read later in Job: *"And the Lord restored the fortunes of Job when he prayed for his friends"* (Job 42:10).

So, no matter what your situation is now, no matter how many "fences" you think there are in your way, trust the Lord to remove them at the right time.

DAILY SCRIPTURE READING: 2 Kings 15:19-38;
2 Chronicles 27; Isaiah 5, 6

WATCHING IN VAIN

"Unless the Lord builds the house, they labor in vain who build it;
unless the Lord guards the city,
the watchman keeps awake in vain"
(Psalm 127:1).

MANY years ago I was given the responsibility for the security and safekeeping of the facilities of a Christian college. It was then I learned an extremely valuable lesson about the practical application of God's Word.

The cost of providing security for the college facilities was approximately $50,000, plus another $50,000 for insurance cost. The college president asked me what could be done to cut costs without jeopardizing safety and security.

I began praying, seeking God's wisdom and direction in the use of His money. That's when I found today's Scripture verse and was reminded that all efforts to watch and insure, apart from God's help, would be in vain.

A proposed reduction in insurance coverage saved approximately $38,000 in premiums; a reduction in our security expenses lowered it to $28,000. Both proposals were based on studies and then adopted. The college did afford reasonable protection, but the practical application of Scripture saved $66,000 annually.

On the other hand, we cannot fail to take precautions and just sit back and expect God's protection. We must take sensible, practical steps to insure safety and then trust God to be in control.

Be sure to seek God's guidance as you endeavor to become informed in all the details of your own particular life situation.

Lord, *"With Thy counsel Thou wilt guide me, and afterward receive me to glory"* (Psalm 73:24).

DAILY SCRIPTURE READING: Micah

DEDICATE YOUR HOME

"Who is the man that has built a new house and has not dedicated it?"
(Deuteronomy 20:5).

MANY years ago, we arrived home to find that one of the apartments in our building had been vandalized, and the thieves had broken three locks to get in our neighbor's back door. Then we noticed that our back door was open.

We ran upstairs, looked throughout our apartment, but found nothing missing. Judy then remembered that she had unintentionally failed to close the back door that morning. Even though it was open and easily observed from the bottom of the stairs, nothing was missing from our apartment.

Our neighbors were robbed of their TV, stereo tape deck, radio, CB, and other valuable possessions. When they found out we had lost nothing, they couldn't understand why the thieves had broken through three locks to get in their apartment but had not touched ours.

However, we understood. Our apartment had been dedicated to God. Just as the Israelites did, we dedicated our home to God. We shared this with our neighbors, but it wasn't clear whether they believed that it was really God protecting our things. That wasn't important; what was important was that we believed it.

Of course, we learned a lesson from this experience. Although we trust God, we must not disregard safety measures. We must do all we can; He will do the rest.

"He will give His angels charge concerning you, to guard you in all your ways" (Psalm 91:11).

DAILY SCRIPTURE READING: 2 Kings 16;
2 Chronicles 28; Isaiah 7, 8

Firstfruits

"Cain brought an offering to the Lord of the fruit of the ground. And Abel, on his part also brought of the firstlings of his flock. . . and the Lord had regard for Abel and for his offering"
(Genesis 4:3–4).

CAIN brought an offering to God at the end of the harvest. Abel, on the other hand, brought of the first of his flocks, demonstrating faith, because he trusted God.

Just like Abel, Uncle Frank was a man who gave God the first of what he produced. He believed that God was his sustenance and that giving God the firstfruit (tithe) was a top priority.

On one occasion, there was absolutely nothing to eat in their home—not even a slice of bread. He did, however, have $5 in a drawer, but that was God's tithe and he refused to use it to buy groceries for the family.

"God doesn't expect you to starve your family!" his wife said. But he remained firm in his conviction: the tithe is the Lord's. Uncle Frank would not use God's money.

Shortly before supper time, there was a knock at the front door. There stood a woman with $20 in her hand—payment for some sewing Aunt Dot had done nearly two years earlier. The money had come in the time of need.

Uncle Frank went on to become a very successful and prosperous businessman, and the needs were always met.

Tithing from the first of our produce shows how we honor God and opens the doors for His provision. Read in Deuteronomy 28:1–11 about all the blessings that will be yours if you will diligently obey the Lord. Then in verse 12: *"The Lord will open for you His good storehouse."* Obedience is the underlying factor.

DAILY SCRIPTURE READING: Isaiah 9, 10, 11, 12

JULY 12

TRANSCENDING LINES

"It is not an enemy who reproaches me, then I could bear it. . .
but it is you, a man my equal"
(Psalm 55:12–13).

REGARDLESS of what we might say, we seldom treat all people equally. In fact, it may not even be possible, since we all have preconditioned biases and prejudices of one kind or another.

As Christians, we must transcend lines of culture, race, denomination, or age. If we can't it's because we think more highly of ourselves than we should.

The apostle Peter said, *"I should never think of anyone as inferior"* (Acts 10:28 TLB). Everyone is of value to society and of value to the Lord Jesus Christ.

Of course, there are people we may not like to spend time with—because of their attitudes or because we enjoy doing different things. But if we avoid anyone because of a preestablished mindset, then we are bigoted.

We live in a country in which we have the freedom to worship as we please with those who believe the same as we do. But to ignore someone or mistreat someone because that person is from a different background or skin tone is displeasing to God.

God does not see what shade our skin is or what nationality or denomination we are. He looks into our hearts, and it's what's in there that matters.

When Jesus gave the commandment to "love one another," He didn't add, "if everything about them pleases you." It was an unqualified commandment.

"A new commandment I give to you, that you love one another, even as I have loved you, that you also love one another" (John 13:34).

DAILY SCRIPTURE READING: Isaiah 13, 14, 15, 16

July 13

Authority over Satan

*"Submit therefore to God. Resist the devil
and he will flee from you"*
(James 4:7).

WHEN Satan was cast out of Heaven, the only authority granted to him was the authority given by God: authority over this world.

We read in the book of John that Jesus said, *"The thief* [Satan] *comes only to steal, and kill, and destroy"* (John 10:10).

As Christians we have authority over Satan. James said in today's verse that we are to *"resist the devil and he will flee."*

The apostle Paul wrote, *"Our struggle is not against flesh and blood, but against the rulers, against the powers, against the world forces of this darkness, against the spiritual forces of wickedness* [Satan] *in the heavenly places. Therefore, take up the full armor of God, that you may be able to resist in the evil day, and having done everything, to stand firm"* (Ephesians 6:12–13).

When the devil tempted Jesus, He fought him off with the phrase, "It is written." We can do the same thing. We can use God's Word to raise hedges around us.

Jesus told the disciples, *"He who believes in Me, the works that I do shall he do also. . . . And whatever you ask in My name, that will I do"* (John 14:12–13).

It seems pretty clear to me that we have authority over Satan as long as we are living in the power of the Holy Spirit, following God's Word, doing God's will, and resisting him in Jesus' name.

DAILY SCRIPTURE READING: Isaiah 17, 18, 19, 20, 21, 22

July 14

Citizenship and Christianity

"Let your light shine for all the nations to see!
For the glory of the Lord is streaming from you"
(Isaiah 60:1 TLB).

HAVE you ever considered the relationship between citizenship and Christianity? Which takes priority?

As Americans, we have all the rights and privileges granted to us by the Constitution and the Bill of Rights. And, I believe we are bound according to God's Word to obey the legal authority over us, including the IRS.

"Let every person be in subjection to the governing authorities. . . . Because of this you also pay taxes, for rulers are servants of God" (Romans 13:1, 6).

Although I don't like paying taxes, and I think the amount we have to pay is unfair, I am bound by God's Word.

But, is there any point at which I am no longer bound by government authority? In my opinion, there is when that authority violates the superior authority of the Word of God.

For example, although abortion is legal according to the law of our land, it is totally immoral and is abhorrent to the Word of God. Therefore, I must take a stand against abortion.

We haven't started euthanizing elderly people, but it's not impossible that we might find that legal in the future.

As God's people, we are also citizens and therefore we have the right to appeal any laws of this land to protect our constitutional rights.

When the laws of this land try to supersede the law of God, that's when we must take a stand, even to the point of imprisonment, if necessary.

DAILY SCRIPTURE READING: Isaiah 23, 24, 25, 26, 27

July 15

Shades of Gray

"Wash yourselves, make yourselves clean; . . . learn to do good"
(Isaiah 1:16–17).

SOMETIMES the lessons we learn in life are hard ones. Let me tell you about one that comes to mind.

When I was a new Christian, living in Florida, some friends came to visit and wanted to go to Disney World. At that time, if you were a Florida resident you could get free passes. A friend of mine had passes so, instead of writing to Disney for my own passes, I decided to borrow his.

When we returned from Disney World, I went to this man's house to return his passes. His wife confronted me and accused me of lying. She said, "Those were not your passes, but you presented them to the people at Disney World as if they were; therefore, you lied. I will never believe anything else you say."

That really irritated me and I stormed out of her house. But, after I left I began to feel the conviction of the Holy Spirit. I went back, asked for her forgiveness, and then I sent in the difference in what it would have cost us to go to Disney World without the passes.

I have no idea what the Disney Company did with the money. They might not have even wanted it. It probably amused them that someone would do that, but I felt it was my obligation to do the right thing.

So, we can learn lessons—sometimes hard ones—and God taught me one in that regard. Honesty is a black-and-white issue. It does not come in shades of gray.

"Put on the Lord Jesus Christ, and make no provision for the flesh" (Romans 13:14).

DAILY SCRIPTURE READING: Isaiah 28, 29, 30

July 16

Faith and Works

"Faith, if it has no works, is dead, being by itself"
(James 2:17).

I HEARD a Christian teacher one time say that he wished the book of James had never been written. He felt the book emphasized works and not faith. I don't agree with his conclusion at all.

If you'll read James, you'll see that the point he was making is that if you are saved you have made Jesus the Lord of your life; therefore, you will have works in your life.

After saying that faith without works is useless, James uses the example of Abraham, who was *"justified by works, when he offered up Isaac his son on the altar"* (James 2:21). Abraham's faith *"was working with his works, and as a result of the works, faith was perfected"* (verse 22).

We are not saved by our works. The apostle Paul tells us in Ephesians 2:8–9 that we are saved by grace, through faith, and it is not a results of works.

Then in 2 Timothy 1:9 Paul says that the power of God has saved us and called us, *"not according to our works, but according to His own purpose and grace which was granted us in Christ Jesus."*

I believe that James was saying that if we are saved, our lives will show it by our works. The works are evidence that the Holy Spirit is residing within us.

DAILY SCRIPTURE READING: Isaiah 31, 32, 33, 34, 35

One God

*"One Lord, one faith, one baptism,
one God and Father of all who is over all
and through all and in all"*
(Ephesians 4:5–6).

GOD is sovereign. He is the omnipotent (all powerful), omniscient (all wise), omnipresent (present everywhere at once) creator of all things and the absolute authority.

Sometimes we live our lives as if God were a genie in a bottle. We go about doing what we please until we need help. Then we uncork the bottle and ask the "genie" to come out and solve our problems. Then when things are running smoothly, we just put Him back into the bottle and put the cork back in.

Unfortunately, that's not the way it works. Our responsibility as followers of the sovereign God is to obey His instructions on a day-by-day basis, knowing that He will guide us.

"You will call, and the Lord will answer; . . . 'Here I am.' . . . The Lord will continually guide you" (Isaiah 58:9, 11).

The great joy we have is that God is also a loving, caring, comforting Father. All He wants is our fellowship with Him. He likes doing good things for us.

With our finite thinking, it is hard for us to grasp the immensity of a sovereign God. When we pass from this life into the next life, we will understand the sovereignty of God and His love, because He is waiting with open arms to welcome us.

How much fellowship with the Lord do you experience? What can you do to make it better?

DAILY SCRIPTURE READING: 2 Kings 18:1-8;
2 Chronicles 29, 30, 31

JULY 18

WHEREVER YOU ARE

*"Walk in a manner worthy of the calling with which
you have been called, with all humility and gentleness,
with patience, showing forbearance to one another in love"*
(Ephesians 4:1–2).

AN evangelist, speaking at a church on the subject of loving people and being a witness for Christ, went to buy a pair of shoes the next day. Little did he know that the shoe clerk, an antagonistic unbeliever, had been in his meeting the night before.

She recognized the evangelist and did everything she could to be rude to him, to see how he would react. She even insulted him, but he responded politely. He thought to himself, *She must be having a rough day.*

He bought a pair of shoes and that evening, when he started to put them on, he discovered that one was two sizes smaller than the other. He knew the ones he tried on were the same size, so he was sure she had switched the shoe deliberately.

When he returned to the store, the woman argued with him and was insulting, but again he was polite.

That evening when the evangelist gave the invitation, the first person down the aisle to accept Jesus was the shoe clerk. You see, his witness to her was not what he had said from the pulpit; it was said by his actions at the store. That was the message she needed to win her to Christ.

I think that, as Christians, we need to treat with love and kindness our next-door neighbors, the people who work on our cars, the store clerks—everyone with whom we come in contact.

This is what separates us from unbelievers.

DAILY SCRIPTURE READING: 2 Kings 17, 18:9-37;
2 Chronicles 32:1-19; Isaiah 36

Servant/Leader

*"You have been given freedom: not freedom to do wrong,
but freedom to love and serve each other"*
(Galatians 5:13 TLB).

A CHINESE communist official, under Mao Tse-tung, was assigned to lead an execution squad in China. The purpose was to eliminate all opposition to the party.

In one village a man came down the road pushing a wheelbarrow full of manure. The Chinese official asked who was the leader of the village, and the man answered, "I am."

"You can't be. Leaders don't do what you are doing," the communist replied.

The man with the wheelbarrow said, "Well, I am. This is a community of Christians, and in the community of Christ the leader is the servant of everyone."

Ultimately this revelation lead to the communist accepting Christ. What kind of witness would Christians be if we truly lived as if we were servants to other people!

I try to have a servant's attitude on a regular basis, but I find it difficult, don't you? I try to serve my spouse; I try to be a servant to the employees of our organization and consider each of them as more important than myself. But all too often the old "self" takes over.

To the extent we are able to put others first is how effective our lives will be for Christ. It is through this kind of witness that we can lead people to salvation.

DAILY SCRIPTURE READING: 2 Kings 19;
2 Chronicles 32:20-23; Isaiah 37

July 20

Carnal Minds

"The mind set on the flesh is hostile toward God"
(Romans 8:7).

WE'VE all heard the expression, "people with carnal minds." In Romans I believe the apostle Paul was talking about people with what we call "lower natures" and people who live only to please themselves.

He went on to say that following after the *old nature leads to death, because the old sinful nature within us is against God"* (Romans 8:7 TLB).

Christians who continue to live in their old sinful ways cannot please God.

If we're following the Spirit of God and living by the principles of God's Word, the Holy Spirit will convict us when we are out of the will of God.

Those who set their minds on worldly things and are motivated by them, have carnal minds, and need to repent. *"Repent of this wickedness of yours, and pray the Lord that if possible, the intention of your heart may be forgiven you"* (Acts 8:22).

If you have a particular weakness, the smart thing to do is to avoid any contact with it.

A man who travels in business and finds a pornographic channel on the television in his hotel room must make a decision. Will he allow the Holy Spirit to take control of his life or give in to his carnal nature?

Airline pilots spend many hours training in a simulator for every potential problem they might face when flying an airplane. They train themselves for every contingency so they cannot be caught unaware. We must do the same in our spiritual lives.

DAILY SCRIPTURE READING: 2 Kings 20;
2 Chronicles 32:24–33; Isaiah 38, 39

July 21

Academic Achievement

*I have chosen him, in order that he may command
his children and his household after him to keep
the way of the Lord by doing righteousness and justice"*
(Genesis 18:19).

SAMUEL Johnson said, "Knowledge always desires increase; it is
like fire, which must first be kindled by some external agent, but
which will afterward propagate itself."

The homeschooling movement has literally exploded because
of the steady deterioration of our public schools and the soaring
costs of private schools. Parents are desperate to insulate their children from the permissive attitudes taught in public schools, declining achievement scores, and the total denial of basic religious values
at any level in public education.

In order for our children to have good futures, we must give
them the best training possible, both academically and spiritually.

In his article for *Home School Researcher,* Richard Medlin
noted that homeschooled children are "not educationally disad-
vantaged" and that their achievement scores are, in fact, "above
average."

The success or failure of homeschooling depends on parents'
willingness to do their jobs, and only parents who are seriously
committed to teaching their children at home should try it.

Ask God to bless the parents who are homeschooling their children, and pray for the children as they learn in a home environment.

July 22

Law or Grace

"Sin shall not be master over you,
for you are not under law,
but under grace"
(Romans 6:14).

It's interesting as we look back into the time of the apostles and see how many of the Jews who had accepted Christ tried to apply both law and grace at the same time.

They required the Jewish converts to Christianity to adhere to all the ritualistic laws of the Old Testament and, to a large degree, subjugated grace to a secondary role.

The apostle Paul writes about this issue in Romans. Following the Scripture verse for today, he said, *"Shall we sin because we are not under law but under grace? May it never be!"* (Romans 6:15).

What Paul was saying to his generation is, "We are not controlled by the law; it is not the governing force over your life. God's grace is."

However, because we are saved by grace (see Ephesians 2:8–9) and live under grace, we don't have a license to do whatever we want when we want to do it. We are bound by God's Word, and it teaches that we should abstain from anything that would bring dishonor or disservice to God's name.

Therefore, under grace we have a greater responsibility to live in a purer way than anyone ever did under the Law.

"The higher a man is in grace, the lower he will be in his own esteem." —Charles Spurgeon

DAILY SCRIPTURE READING: Isaiah 41, 42, 43

KINGDOM ADDRESS

"My kingdom is not of this world"
(John 18:36).

WHEN Christ was on Earth, He said, "My kingdom is not of this world." If it had been, He could have called a legion of angels to His defense and nobody could have hanged Him on Calvary's cross.

We know that Satan has power in this realm—at least for the time being. Perhaps it's to see whether we will be faithful to the Lord.

Peter wrote, *"Be all the more diligent to make certain about His calling and choosing you. . . for in this way the entrance into the eternal kingdom of our Lord and Savior Jesus Christ will be abundantly supplied to you"* (2 Peter 1:10–11).

So, Christ's kingdom is coming, and when it does it will be an absolute monarchy—a spiritual theocracy of the highest order.

I don't know about you, but I'm looking forward to spending eternity with a loving, kind, and gracious Ruler.

Maranatha!

DAILY SCRIPTURE READING: Isaiah 44, 45, 46, 47

MORAL LAW/GOD'S LAW

"The Law is holy, and the commandment is holy and
righteous and good. . . . The Law is spiritual; . . .
I agree with the Law, confessing that it is good"
(Romans 7:12, 14, 16).

THERE is no way to separate moral law from God's Law, unless it's through the situational ethics that we see in our generation.

God established the moral laws. The Ten Commandments are simple, straightforward, and absolute. If you follow those, you will follow moral law.

C. S. Lewis wrote, "Morality is indispensable: but the Divine life, which gives itself to us and which calls us to be gods, intends for us something in which morality will be swallowed up. We are to be remade."

In our society we have adopted situational ethics. Basically that means that the times and the situations dictate morality. Therefore, if everyone believes that abortion is okay, then it is. Or if everyone says that homosexuality is acceptable, it is.

When it comes to morality, God's Word is piercingly clear. Right is right, and wrong is wrong.

Clearly, our "enlightened" society could use a good dose of God's biblical absolutes. I grieve that the youth of this generation have been deceived by "situational ethics."

DAILY SCRIPTURE READING: Isaiah 48, 49, 50, 51

MORTIFY THE FLESH

"If you are living according to the flesh, you must die;
but if by the Spirit you are putting to death
the deeds of the body, you will live"
(Romans 8:13).

INSTEAD of saying *"putting to death the deeds of the body,"* the King James version of the Bible uses the term *"mortify the deeds of the body."*

I think what the apostle Paul was saying is that if you're living according to your fleshly desires, just doing whatever you happen to think is right, you're going to die—physically and spiritually.

Then he goes further and says, *"All who are being led by the Spirit of God, these are sons of God"* (Romans 8:14).

Paul was giving his generation (and now ours) a spiritual attitude check. If you are living in the flesh and doing all the things the world around you is doing, you'd better check your spiritual condition.

Personally, I don't want to be a part of the group identified in verse 13. I prefer the group he wrote about in verse 14.

Think about this: *"Those who are in the flesh cannot please God. However, you are not in the flesh but in the Spirit, if indeed the Spirit of God dwells in you. But if anyone does not have the Spirit of Christ, he does not belong to Him"* (Romans 8:8–9). *"It is the Spirit who gives life; the flesh profits nothing"* (John 6:63).

Father, I ask in Jesus' name that You will help me to put to death the fleshly desires in my life.

DAILY SCRIPTURE READING: Isaiah 52, 53, 54, 55, 56, 57

JULY 26

UNRIGHTEOUSNESS

*"Do not go on presenting the members of your body
to sin as instruments of unrighteousness"*
(Romans 6:13).

THERE were very few moral absolutes during the dark days of the Roman empire. It appears to me that our generation is as caught up in the same relativism as the first century people were.

The apostle Paul addressed the basic sins and abominations of his society when he wrote, *"Consider yourselves to be dead to sin, but alive to God in Christ Jesus. Therefore do not let sin reign in your mortal body that you should obey its lusts"* (Romans 6:11–12).

When you look around today, there is very little that is considered immoral, unethical, or illegal. We have moralized homosexuality, sexual promiscuity, filthy movies, and pornographic magazines. The government even hands out condoms in the public schools. We accept, and even reelect immoral, degenerate politicians. And the list goes on. . . .

Christians are to be examples of righteousness in a sinful world—lights in the darkness.

A fallen, dying generation does not need more tolerant Christians; they need more lights in their dark world.

Read the eighth chapter of Romans. Then ask the Holy Spirit to reveal to you how you can help make a difference.

DAILY SCRIPTURE READING: Isaiah 58, 59, 60, 61, 62

INTERNATIONAL VIEW

"How blessed will you be, you who sow beside all waters"
(Isaiah 32:20).

I BELIEVE every American should travel, especially to Third World countries, to see what it really means to live in the blessed society in which they were born.

I traveled to the island of Haiti, spent a little time there, and got to know some of the people. I went through a couple of orphanages and witnessed the hopelessness of the children who were abandoned by their families. The poorest person in America would be wealthy compared to the people of Haiti.

Judy and I traveled through Eastern Europe shortly after communism fell. What a stark contrast it was, going from Western Europe, where things were modern and well-kept with plenty of food and everybody working.

We went ten miles across the border—to the East—and saw people who were still plowing their fields with oxen, with barely enough food to survive, wearing ragged clothing, and living in run-down buildings.

Another observation in Europe was to see how far those Christian nations have fallen. There is virtually no vestige of Christianity left in most of Europe. In the huge cathedrals, which could hold thousands of people, there might be a handful of old people there.

Their society has been dragged down with immorality, open homosexuality, promiscuousness, and lewdness. I don't mean to condemn the European people. I love them. My daughter-in-law is European and I love her and her family dearly.

It just grieves me to see what has happened to the countries and to the people spiritually. It should be a warning to our society.

DAILY SCRIPTURE READING: Isaiah 63, 64, 65, 66

The Powerful Word

*"So shall My word be which goes forth from
My mouth; it shall not return to Me empty,
without accomplishing what I desire"*
(Isaiah 55:11).

WE know that God is all powerful (omnipotent), and His Word is as powerful as He is.

The Bible says that Christ spoke the world into existence, so we know how powerful the voice of God (His Word) is. The apostle Paul tells us, *"He [Jesus] is the image of the invisible God, the first-born of all creation, for by Him all things were created. . . all things have been created by Him and for Him"* (Colossians 1:15–16).

God says that His Word will not return to Him without accomplishing what it says it will.

If you are just beginning to read the Bible, you have a great treat ahead. If you've read it for years, you can testify to how rich it is and what a comfort. If you don't read it every day, you are cheating yourself (that's my opinion, of course).

When David wrote about God's Word he said, *"The precepts of the Lord are right, rejoicing the heart; the commandment of the Lord is pure, enlightening the eyes. . . . The judgments of the Lord are true. . . . They are more desirable than gold. . .sweeter also than honey. . . . In keeping them is great reward"* (Psalm 19:8–11).

Martin Luther said, "The Bible is alive, it speaks to me; it has feet, it runs after me; it has hands, it lays hold on me."

How much does your Bible mean to you?

DAILY SCRIPTURE READING: 2 Kings 21:19-26;
2 Chronicles 33:21-34:7; Zephaniah

FOREORDAINED

"[God] paid for you with the precious lifeblood of Christ. . . .
God chose him for this purpose long before the world began"
(1 Peter 1:19–20 TLB).

PREDESTINATION is a concept that has been argued for a long time. It came into focus during the ministry of John Calvin and has many followers. Are the events in the lives of human beings foreordained by God: predetermined and can't be changed under any circumstances?

If Christ had asked His Father to save Him from death on the cross, God could have sent a legion of angels. But Jesus chose to do the Father's will.

The omnipotent Creator of the universe could have done anything He wanted. But when Jesus was arrested He told the soldiers to put away their swords and said, *"Don't you realize that I could ask my Father for thousands of angels to protect us, and he would send them instantly? But if I did, how would the Scriptures be fulfilled that describe what is happening now?"* (Matthew 26:53 54 TLB).

God has always been here and always will be. Time is irrelevant to Him. He exists in the past, the present, and the future. Did God know that Christ was going to the cross? Read today's Scripture verse again for the answer to that.

When Adam sinned He could have destroyed the whole creation and started again. But He is a loving, caring, kind, and gracious Creator. He was willing to do whatever it took to redeem us—even allowing His Son to become the sinless sacrifice for all sin.

Jesus paid the price for you and for me. There's a hymn that says "Jesus paid it all; all to Him I owe. Sin had left a crimson stain; He washed it white as snow" (by Elvina M. Hall and John T. Grape).

DAILY SCRIPTURE READING: Jeremiah 1, 2, 3

HOLINESS

*"Walk in a manner worthy of the calling
with which you have been called"*
(Ephesians 4:1).

D. L. MOODY said, "Next to the might of God, the serene beauty of a holy life is the most powerful influence for good."

The scribes and Pharisees of Jesus' day were hypocrites who concentrated on appearing holy, even though they were neglecting real holiness: of their hearts.

There's a saying that sometimes people are so busy being religious they fail to be spiritual. Outward acts of goodness can never make up for hearts that are cold or empty.

"Whoever believes in Him should not perish, but have eternal life" (John 3:16). After we accept Jesus as Lord and Savior of our lives, how can we have clean hearts? *"If we confess our sins, He is faithful and righteous to forgive us our sins and to cleanse us from all unrighteousness"* (1 John 1:9).

To be holy, we must have pure hearts. James says, *"Purify your hearts. . . . Humble yourselves in the presence of the Lord"* (James 4:8, 10).

Oswald Chambers said, "Holiness is not only what God gives me, but what I manifest that God has given."

Have you had your heart checked lately? Imagine you are strapped into a machine that can see into your heart and measure the holiness there. What would the diagnosis be?

Holiness just means being separated to God. It's what you do with your life every day; it's ordering your conduct according to the Word of God and being of one mind with God. No one ever said it would be easy. But it is possible.

DAILY SCRIPTURE READING: Jeremiah 4, 5, 6

JULY 31

RUNNING AHEAD

"Hagar bore Abram a son;
and Abram called the name of his son, whom Hagar bore, Ishmael"
(Genesis 16:15).

HAVE you ever run ahead of God because you became impatient with His timing? You probably know how much pain that can bring and you quickly learned why it is so important to do things in God's timing.

God's covenant with Abraham included the fact that he would be the father of nations. God took him outside, showed him the heavens, and told him to see how many stars there were. Then He said, *"So shall your descendants be"* (Genesis 15:5).

But perhaps childless Sarah got impatient, or maybe she didn't have Abraham's faith. She suggested that Abraham go in to her handmaiden; he did and Hagar bore him a son. As a result, Hagar's son grew up to be in competition with Isaac, Sarah's son and rightful heir of the covenant.

God did bless Abraham and Sarah, but they always remembered that they had attempted to go around His plan.

If or when you have that kind of experience—of running ahead of God—you should realize that you've made a mistake and ask God's forgiveness. Since you can't undo what has been done, forgiveness is the most important thing—not guilt.

Ask God to help you know His timing in everything you do. *"The Lord is not slow about His promise, as some count slowness, but is patient toward you"* (2 Peter 3:9).

DAILY SCRIPTURE READING: Jeremiah 7, 8, 9

CHRISTIAN DISCOUNTS

"A righteous man hates falsehood,
but a wicked man acts disgustingly and shamefully"
(Proverbs 13:5).

HAVE you ever been guilty of using your Christianity in order to get a good deal? I read an article in a Christian magazine about how many Christians expect discounts from other Christians for virtually everything they buy.

If you are offered a discount because you are in full-time Christian ministry, that's a different matter.

I have been in the ministry of Christian Financial Concepts for over 20 years and I find consistently that when I do business with people they think they have to give us a discount because we are a ministry. I always say that we are capable of paying what we are buying, and we don't need a discount unless the Lord has led them to give it. God doesn't want us to be beggars.

I believe that God wants us to give more to Christians in business—not less. If I find a Christian who owns a business and that person has a good service or good product, I believe I should pay more, particularly if I know that a portion of the money I pay will be going back into the kingdom of God.

Instead of looking for a "good deal," we should be looking for opportunities to witness through our attitudes and actions.

Before you buy something, pray about it. Ask God to show you where to shop and what you should pay. Be generous with Christians in business or in a ministry.

"Do not withhold good from those to whom it is due, when it is in your power to do it" (Proverbs 3:27).

DAILY SCRIPTURE READING: Jeremiah 10, 11, 12, 13

NO ONE IS PERFECT

"In Him we have redemption through His blood,
the forgiveness of our trespasses,
according to the riches of His grace"
(Ephesians 1:7).

COMMITTING sin has its consequences. One of the best examples of that is the story of David and Bathsheba. They committed adultery and a child was born. However, the child didn't live, even after David pleaded with God to spare the life of his baby.

David knew he had sinned and he was consumed with guilt and remorse. He didn't try to deny his sin or makes excuses for it by claiming the temptation was too great. Instead David owned up to his sin and sought God's forgiveness.

Because you are human, you are going to sin, but you don't have to live with your guilt. If you truly repent of your sin, God will readily forgive you and restore you to His favor. That's what grace is all about.

Just open your heart to His forgiveness and allow Him to deal with you right where you are. What we have done isn't as important as what we are going to do about it.

God knows you aren't perfect and He doesn't love you any less when you sin. When Jesus shed His blood on the cross and died in our place, He opened the door to full redemption. The only criteria for forgiveness is true repentance.

"Our Redeemer, the Lord of hosts is His name" (Isaiah 47:4).

DAILY SCRIPTURE READING: Jeremiah 14, 15, 16

COMMUNING WITH GOD

*"The God of peace, who brought up
from the dead the great Shepherd. . .
even Jesus our Lord, equip you in
every good thing to do His will,
working in us that which is pleasing in His sight"*
(Hebrews 13:20–21).

OSWALD Chambers says that when you stay in contact with God so much that you never need to ask Him to show you His will, you have gotten close to the final stages of being disciplined in the life of faith.

When you stay in constant communion with God, you develop a delightful friendship with Him. You read His Word, pray without ceasing; then go ahead and make the everyday, commonsense decisions, assured that He will let you know if what you plan to do isn't what is best for you.

Have you ever decided to do something but felt a sort of scratchy feeling in your spirit? That's a sure sign you may not have made the right decision. Listen to that inner voice. It can save you a lot of heartache.

God never gets tired of hearing you call out to Him. He promises good things for those who seek Him. Your fellowship with Him through your faith in Jesus Christ opens the door to communication.

Father, thank You for being so accessible to me at all times.

DAILY SCRIPTURE READING: Jeremiah 17, 18, 19, 20

ONLY YOU WILL DO

*"I have known you by name,
and you have also found favor in My sight"*
(Exodus 33:12).

DID you ever audition for a play or for a chorus? Usually you have to do a bit of acting or singing—whatever is required—and then leave, hoping to get chosen and called back. You have to be absolutely perfect for the role you tried out for.

You have a role in life that only you can fill. You don't have to audition for it, because you are the only one who can do exactly what it calls for. God has chosen you to do a specific thing. And, the best part is, you aren't in competition with anyone else for the "part." No one could be as good a YOU as you can be.

You could follow Billy Graham around for weeks or months, study his preaching, mannerisms, talents, and learn to sound just like he does. But you could never be a better Billy Graham than he is. That's because God called him to be just who he is.

The same is true of you. You don't need to be jealous of anyone else, because when God calls for you there is nobody else who can answer your call. You have no contenders. You are the "star." You won the "audition."

You are a unique individual. God's Word says, *"The very hairs of your head are all numbered"* (Matthew 10:30).

If God calls you to the task that is specifically yours and you don't accept His call, your blessings will go to someone else. Pay close attention to the prompting of the Holy Spirit so you won't miss your blessings.

DAILY SCRIPTURE READING: 2 Kings 22:1-23:28;
2 Chronicles 34:8-35:19

GOD'S CREATION

"In the beginning God created the heavens and the earth. . . .
Thus the heavens and the earth were completed,
and all their hosts"
(Genesis 1:1, 2:1).

DON'T you wonder why the world is living so far away from God and spiritual values, when technology has brought us access to so much information?

You would think that the advanced technology would draw people closer to God. However, learning more about God's creation and how complex it is has done the opposite: It has pushed people away from God; some even believe that science refutes God.

When we split the atom and created the atomic bomb, basically, we didn't create anything that hadn't been there since the beginning of time. The ability of that atom to be separated and to release energy has been there since the world began.

What we've realized now is that since the beginning of the world God's creation has been doing exactly what we "discovered" in 1944. We haven't invented anything. All we've done is discover another one of God's marvelous creations.

In great part, technology in our generation has been the single greatest tool used by Satan to deceive people into believing there is no God.

Science is not incompatible with creation. In fact it confirms it. It is our refusal to accept God's authority that causes us to rebel.

However, His Word says, *"In the beginning was the Word. . . and the Word was God. He was in the beginning"* (John 1:1–2). That's what is vital to our lives.

DAILY SCRIPTURE READING: 2 Kings 23:29-37;
2 Chronicles 35:20-36:5; Jeremiah 22:10-17; Nahum

PROVING GOD

*"Know that the Lord Himself is God; it is He who has made us,
and not we ourselves; we are His people and the sheep of His pasture"*
(Psalm 100:3).

Do you know someone who doesn't believe there is a God? You may never convince an atheist there is a God.

I was an agnostic in my earlier life, so I understand. As an unbeliever no one could convince me that God existed.

People either believe there's a God or they don't. If there were absolute proof, faith would be meaningless. If God allowed absolute truth to be discovered that He exists, there no longer would be a need for faith. So, I think the mystery surrounding His existence is purely by God's own design.

The more technology tries to disprove God's existence, the more it is proved. We're now discovering things that nobody thought was even possible just a decade ago. The more we learn about our universe, the more it becomes evident that things don't "just happen."

You'd think, when we look out into space, it would show us how little, how finite, we really are compared to God. He has been spinning out galaxies since the beginning of time, and we haven't made our first one; so we're not as great as we think we are.

As Christians, we should not avoid technology or science; we should use them to demonstrate God.

The creation scientists at Creation Science Research Institute make absolute perfect sense. What they're doing is using nature and science to prove, or at least to demonstrate, that God is real.

How real is He to you? Think about who you believe He is and what He means to you in your life.

DAILY SCRIPTURE READING: Jeremiah 26; Habakkuk

AUGUST 7

MIRACLES

"Believe Me that I am in the Father, and the Father in Me;
otherwise believe on account of the works themselves. . . .
He who believes in Me, the works that I do shall he do also;
and greater works than these shall he do"
(John 14:11–12).

SOME people question whether miracles are still happening today —like they were in the early church—or if we are we just blind to the workings of God. Are people really healed but attribute the healing to medicine or to coincidence?

I believe that miracles are happening in other countries. I haven't been there to witness them but I have heard from credible people who have been there.

A good friend of mine recently told me about someone working in Mexico who had witnessed incredible miracles among the Native Indians. When asked why he thought similar miracles weren't being witnessed in America, he said that skepticism and complacency were impeding the Holy Spirit's work.

He went on to say that many of the people in underdeveloped countries are like little birds with their mouths open, ready to receive. But when he has to come to America to raise his ministry funds, he senses that people are cold toward God, compared to where he works in Mexico.

But I do believe that miracles are being performed here in America; they are just being attributed to something else. I'm speaking from experience. I know at least three people who are alive today only because of God's miraculous intervention. One of them is me.

Jesus said, *"All things are possible to him who believes"* (Mark 9:23).

DAILY SCRIPTURE READING: 2 Kings 24:1-4;
2 Chronicles 36:6-7; Jeremiah 25, 35, 46, 47

AUGUST 8

FAMILIES

*"The lovingkindness of the Lord is from everlasting to everlasting
on those who fear Him, and His righteousness to children's children,
to those who keep His covenant,
and who remember His precepts to do them"*
(Psalm 103:17–18).

IN the past, many generations have lived and died under the same roof, but the family unit has pretty much been dissipated in America. What has that done to us spiritually and what can we do in our own homes to build families?

There are several contributing factors that made the family more of a unit in past generations: distance, transportation, and economics.

We are much more mobile these days, and it is common for children to grow up and relocate several hundred miles away. And with modern technology, that allows us to keep in touch daily if we wish. There's no reason not to relocate.

However, relocation is only one factor. I think what affects the family unit more than anything else today is television. When everyone is glued to the television, there is little or no personal interaction or communication—things that are necessary if we are going to operate as families.

Furthermore, we are all going in different directions, either to fulfill obligations or to be entertained. That means we only see each other occasionally to exchange hurried greetings.

We must make this a matter of prayer and ask God to show us what we can do to salvage the family unit. One suggestion would be to have a TV-free day per week.

Reread today's Scripture verse in Psalm 103.

DAILY SCRIPTURE READING: Jeremiah 36, 45, 48

AUGUST 9

A SERVANT'S ATTITUDE

"The greatest among you shall be your servant.
And whoever exalts himself shall be humbled;
and whoever humbles himself shall be exalted"
(Matthew 23:11–12).

ONE of the finest examples I can think of when I read in God's Word about humility or having a servant's spirit is my friend and brother in the Lord, Dr. Larry Hyde. He has gone to be with the Lord now, but he was one of the kindest people I have ever known. This book is dedicated to his memory.

Of course, he had some faults, but mostly they were the result of being too personable. At least five times (that I know of) he took people into his home who were terminally ill. Usually they were people whose families wouldn't take care of them.

He actually set up a hospital room in his home, with oxygen and a hospital bed—at great inconvenience to his own family. He and his wife cared lovingly for them, changing their beds (and their diapers if that's what was needed).

Wouldn't it be wonderful if all Christians had that kind of a servant's heart? It's all too easy to say, "Oh, that's the gift of mercy, and I don't have that gift." But, we are all supposed to have that kind of mercy. Jesus did, and He set the example for us.

We need to redefine our lives in terms of what the church (the body of Christ) is supposed to be.

Jesus said, *"If I then, the Lord and the Teacher, washed your feet, you also ought to wash one another's feet"* (John 13:14).

DAILY SCRIPTURE READING: Jeremiah 49:1–33; Daniel 1, 2

TIME TRAVEL

"May the Lord cause you to increase and abound in love for one another, and for all men. . . so that He may establish your hearts unblamable in holiness before our God and Father"
(1 Thessalonians 3:12–13).

HAVE you ever thought about what it would have been like to have lived in another time period? If you could be at any event in history, which one would you choose?

Perhaps most Christians would choose to have lived during the time Christ was on the earth. I don't think I would, and I'll tell you why. I'm not absolutely sure which side I would have been on. Would I have believed what Jesus was teaching, or would I have been one of those who opposed Him? Would I have been a zealot, screaming unbelief at Him, like everyone else? I'm not sure. I'd like to think I would have accepted His teaching, but I'm not sure.

I know that if I had lived during Christ's life and had accepted His teaching, the crowds would have done to me what they did to Paul, because I would have refused to compromise.

If the Lord would just allow me to do it, I'd go back to 1775, when the first of the real Freedom Movement began to take hold in America. The value systems and attitudes were being shaped by the Founding Fathers.

To me, outside of the birth, death, and resurrection of Christ, that is the most exciting time in all history. There are others, to be sure.

However, we were created for this particular time and environment, and it is great, because we can be a driving force for Christianity to the entire world.

"God is with the righteous generation" (Psalm 14:5).

DAILY SCRIPTURE READING: 2 Kings 24:5-20;
2 Chronicles 36:8-12; Jeremiah 22:18-30, 24, 29, 37:1-2; 52:1-3

GOING BACK

"After those days, says the Lord:
I will put My laws into their minds, and I will write them upon
their hearts. And I will be their God and they shall be My people"
(Hebrews 8:10).

TO continue the subject from yesterday, about going back in time, I'd love to be able to sit down and talk to Benjamin Franklin and just pick his brain. Madison and Monroe were my kind of guys. I would really enjoy the opportunity to sit and talk with them.

What a marvelous time in history that was! When we think about what they did and how sound their value system was, it should inspire us to sit down and read the Declaration of Independence, the Constitution, and the Bill of Rights. That would remind us of their values. They were unshakably sound.

They did compromise a little bit along the way in things like slavery and other things they didn't really believe in. Though, again, you can't fault them for that, because even their foundation, which was the Bible, doesn't prohibit slavery. It didn't encourage it, but it was not prohibited.

When you realize that what they did has lasted this long, until we allowed the federal court to pervert it, it's the soundest biblical foundation of framework ever.

I would have enjoyed living during that time. But as I said before, we are designed and destined for this time and must do all we can to preserve the value system established by our Founding Fathers.

Our allegiance is to the time in which we are living and to our Lord. The important thing isn't what year or century we were born. We were made in God's image and we are made to glorify Him in all that we do.

DAILY SCRIPTURE READING: Jeremiah 23, 27, 28

QUESTIONING GOD

"My God, My God, why hast Thou forsaken Me?"
(Matthew 27:46).

THE question in today's Scripture verse is one of the most poignant questions ever asked in history. It makes me wonder what I would say if I could ask God one question.

If we are made in God's image, as the Bible says we are, that means that we think, to some degree, like Him. Now, if I were God and saw all the ungodliness and sin, I would have destroyed all of creation. I would have just wiped it out and started all over again. At some point, why didn't He just start over?

Yes, I know that at one point He did wipe out all but Noah and his family. But I would have taken the "modeling clay," rolled it into a ball, and said, "Okay, we'll try this thing again. And, remember that angel that was such a bother to me? I'll just do away with him too."

All the angels in Heaven would have been a witness to that and would have left God's creation alone.

Think of all the grief that has been caused and is being caused as a result of God allowing Satan to infect the earth.

It seems that the mess we are making of things just keeps getting worse. Of course He has a reason for it, because He's God. He can do whatever He wants.

He gave us the ability to think on our own (another thing I'm not sure about). He gave us the ability to make decisions. He gave us the ability to love; and He longs for us to love Him and fellowship with Him. What we do is left up to us.

"The Lord is the portion of my inheritance and my cup. . . . I have set the Lord continually before me" (Psalm 16:5, 8).

DAILY SCRIPTURE READING: Jeremiah 50, 51

WHY?

"Not one of us lives for himself, and not one dies for himself; for if we live, we live for the Lord, or if we die, we die for the Lord; therefore whether we live or die, we are the Lord's"
(Romans 14:7–8).

NEARLY everyone has experienced the sorrow of losing a loved one or close friend. Perhaps it was a son or daughter who seemingly had everything to live for or the wife or husband of a happily married couple.

Usually the first question we ask is "Why, Lord?" At those times it is pretty hard (or impossible) to say with the apostle Paul that to live is Christ and to die is gain.

One of my friends lost his father at age 40—a man who had founded 22 churches and had an orphans' home where he placed over 5,000 kids into Christian homes. The same friend lost his wife to cancer and he couldn't help but ask why. If husbands and wives truly become one (as the Bible says), why is a couple separated by death?

Another friend was in a military squad with 22 men, who were all killed. He was placed in another squad and was the only one to survive that group. He wondered, "Why was I spared?"

We look at death as something bad—a punishment. I can only say, if you look at it from God's eyes, death is a reward. That's the only way it will ever make sense to us in our grief.

When you look at eternity and how long it is, even if we suffered every day for 80 years, it is so insignificant in comparison to what's ahead. Of one thing we are sure: God never makes mistakes.

Sir Walter Scott was quoted as saying, "Is death the last sleep? No, it is the final awakening."

DAILY SCRIPTURE READING:
Jeremiah 49:34-39; 34:1-22; Ezekiel 1, 2, 3

I SHALL RETURN

"If I go and prepare a place for you,
I will come again,
and receive you to Myself;
that where I am, there you may be also"
(John 14:3).

"I SHALL return" was made famous during the years of World War II. Gen. Douglas MacArthur visited the people of the Philippine Islands while they were under enemy occupation, and when he left he promised them he would return.

We have that same promise from Jesus, and that should counteract any gloom, confusion, disappointment, sadness, or lack of hope we might have in this life.

We get so Earth-bound that we forget that this earth is not our home; we are just visitors here. Our real home is with Jesus Christ in Heaven, if we have accepted Him as Lord and Savior of our lives.

We should be looking forward to that day when His promise is fulfilled and He comes back to receive us unto Himself.

"The Lord Himself will descend from heaven with a shout, with the voice of the archangel, and with the trumpet of God; and the dead in Christ shall rise first. Then we who are alive and re-main shall be caught up together with them in the clouds to meet the Lord in the air, and thus we shall always be with the Lord" (1 Thessalonians 4:16–17).

We should do what verse 18 says, *"Comfort one another with these words."*

DAILY SCRIPTURE READING: Ezekiel 4, 5, 6, 7

AUGUST 15

BE THE BEST

"Concerning spiritual gifts, brethren, . . . There are varieties of gifts,
but the same Spirit. . . . and there are varieties of effects,
but the same God who works all things in all persons"
(1 Corinthians 12:1, 4, 6).

NOAH was told to build a ship; Abraham was instructed to leave his home for a strange land; David came to be known as Israel's finest king; Daniel was appointed to interpret dreams; Saul (later called Paul) was called to become the church's first missionary/evangelist/pastor.

When I was very young, I decided that, no matter what, I was going to be better at one thing than anybody else. That made many decisions much easier, because when I got in a job I knew I wasn't good at I would leave.

I tried a lot of things: I was an electrician; in electronics in the Air Force; and an electrical engineer at the Space Center, involved with an experiments ground station; but, every day I was there I knew I was working around people who were better at what we were doing than I was.

At one point in my life—after I got into what I do now—I felt that in the area of biblical finances I knew more about it than anyone else. Perhaps other people have passed me now, and that's okay, but at that point I was functioning at my best and I knew I was where God wanted me to be. There's nothing better than that!

If I could emphasize one thing for my grandchildren—outside of a love for the Lord and a personal relationship with Him—I'd tell them to find out what they are good at, what they enjoy, and be the best they can be, with the Lord's help.

"I will instruct you and teach you in the way which you should go" (Psalm 32:8).

DAILY SCRIPTURE READING: Ezekiel 8, 9,10, 11

August 16

End Times

"Behold, the day of the Lord is coming, cruel,
with fury and burning anger, to make the land a desolation;
and He will exterminate its sinners from it"
(Isaiah 13:9).

THERE are many views on end–time prophecy. My philosophy is twofold. I got part of it from my former pastor, who said, "Live like you're going through the tribulation, and pray that you don't have to."

Will we or won't we go through the tribulation? I can't honestly say. I've heard some intelligent people argue, very convincingly, in any number of positions—at least three: premillennial, amillennial, and postmillennial. All of them were convincing.

My other philosophy was set by John Wesley. Someone asked him what he would do if he knew the Lord was coming back tomorrow. He said, "If I were a gardener, I'd go out and plant another tree today." I agree with that.

The apostle Paul, in his early ministry, wrote like he expected the Lord's return any day and stressed the urgency of being ready. After he had lived many years and knew that he was going to die, you can see the shift in his writing, placing the emphasis on maintaining the church (the body of Christ).

My closing thought would be that we should live as if Christ were coming back tomorrow.

"The nations of the world will see me arrive in the clouds of heaven, with power and great glory" (Matthew 24:30 TLB).

GOD'S WORD

*"Be diligent to present yourself approved to God as
a workman who does not need to be ashamed,
handling accurately the word of truth"*
(2 Timothy 2:15).

I READ the Bible in my private devotion time. I don't actually study during those times. Rather, I'm looking to see if God might reveal something to me out of a passage of Scripture that I might have already read many times but had missed. Often you'll do that, because at different stages of your life you're more open to specific things.

Sometimes when I study the Bible I am looking for something —a particular word—and I'll look up all the verses that deal with that word or subject.

I use different translations: the New International Version in my private devotions or when I'm just reading the Bible. If I'm studying, I use the New American Standard version, and that's primarily because I grew up using it. Once you've used one translation that long, it's hard to change.

If I ever find what I think is a discrepancy in one translation, I'll look that up in several translations or I'll get out a lexicon and see if that determines for me the root meaning of a word.

If that doesn't work, I'll go to someone who knows the root languages of Greek and Hebrew. Whatever they say pretty well settles it for me.

Unless we read God's Word, we cannot know what God is saying to us. When we pray we talk to Him. When we read the Bible, He is talking to us. His Word is full of rich history, exciting events, instruction for daily living, encouragement, and strength.

DAILY SCRIPTURE READING: Ezekiel 15, 16, 17

EATING HABITS

"Food is for the stomach, and the stomach is for food;
but God will do away with both of them"
(1 Corinthians 6:13).

THE majority of Americans have poor eating habits. I think the problem we're having with food is the same problem we have with almost every other thing we do: We tend to overindulge and not be very discerning.

When I think back to when I had my heart attack (eight years before I was diagnosed with cancer), I remember what changes had to be made. I changed my diet—drastically! I got busy and lowered my cholesterol from about 245 down to 90, and I kept it there or below for eight years.

Looking back, and having read a lot more about it, I believe that I might have overreacted. That drastic measure could possibly have contributed to my having cancer.

After both illnesses, I knew that to do what God wanted me to do, which is to teach and to write, I had to make some fundamental decisions, either in treatment or in diet.

After researching many diets, some of which were so rigid I knew I would never stick to them, I decided I would have to establish my own regimen—one that would not prohibit my work for the Lord.

We are responsible for the way we take care of our bodies. Being a good steward is not limited to how we manage our money. It also includes taking care of the "temple."

The apostle Paul wrote, *"Do you not know that you are a temple of God, and that the Spirit of God dwells in you?"* (1 Corinthians 3:16).

DAILY SCRIPTURE READING: Ezekiel 18, 19, 20

JOYFUL NOISE?

"Shout joyfully to the Lord, all the earth;
break forth and sing for joy and sing praises"
(Psalm 98:4).

EVERYONE has his or her own opinion about what music is approved by God. Is some music bad?

Well, from a humanistic perspective, we know that children who have been raised hearing quality music—that's music with good rhythm, harmony, and balance—will have more intelligence and be more well-rounded. It has been proved that music somehow affects brain development.

From a personal perspective, I love all music. I can listen to anything from the classics to country to 50s music, which is what I grew up on. I do not like hard rock or heavy metal; the music's consistent beat agitates my spirit somehow.

As Christians, we can pray about what kind of music is honoring to God and what is displeasing to Him. As in all other areas of life, we must follow our convictions. What is all right for someone else may not be right for you. Pray about it.

"Praise Him with trumpet sound; praise Him with harp and lyre. Praise Him with timbrel and dancing; praise Him with stringed instruments and pipe. Praise Him with loud cymbals" (Psalm 150:3–5).

Reread today's Scripture verse in Psalm 98.

DAILY SCRIPTURE READING: Ezekiel 21, 22, 23

In Space

"All that is in the world. . . .is not from the Father,
but is from the world. . . . And the world is passing away. . .
but the one who does the will of God abides forever"
(1 John 2:16–17).

WHEN I worked in the space program at Cape Canaveral, I was in charge of an experiments test facility that served the Mercury, Gemini, and Apollo manned space programs.

We experimented with transistorized computers, developed specifically and primarily for the space program. We tried to figure out how to launch the biggest bomb we could on the Russians.

Most of our major technological breakthroughs have come through war, and this was a major breakthrough period when we didn't have to go to war to do it.

Many of the products we use now evolved from the space program. For instance, the first microwave: a radar dish aimed at our lunches to warm them, and it worked great! What a great device for the housewife! Also, the Teflon in the bottom of your cookware came out of the space program, developed as a high-grade insulation on electrical wires that were used in rockets. I saw many innovative things that later came out on the commercial market.

It's remarkable to see how many ways we have benefited from the space program. I don't think God has any objection to our exploring space. In fact, I think that the moment we die we'll realize just how archaic our space program really was.

There are benefits for us in every kind of technology if the right people are in control.

DAILY SCRIPTURE READING: 2 Kings 25:1; 2 Chronicles 36:13-16; Jeremiah 21:1-22:9, 32:1-44, 52:4; Ezekiel 24

REACHING THE GOAL

*"I do all things for the sake of the gospel,
that I may become a fellow partaker of it"*
(1 Corinthians 9:23).

IT is important to set goals in life. It's just as important to be sure we aren't distracted from those goals.

I have found myself being pulled away from my original goals for Christian Financial Concepts. Fortunately, before I get too far off the field, God usually kind of jerks me back to the center line. My board of directors will ask, "Why are we doing this?"

We had that discussion when we started Life Pathways—the career division. I had to convince them that careers and money go together. If you don't steer people into the right career field, they waste enormous amounts of money in college; they waste numbers of years—some of them their entire lifetime—doing things they'll never be equipped to do well.

I have gotten distracted, though, many times. One thing in particular was the training center we had for a while. I finally was convinced that God didn't want us to manage our own training center and all that property, so we put it up for sale.

I do listen to the Lord and when He says "You're off the path," I get back on. You can do things that are good and right for other people to do but still be in the wrong. So, when I sense that, I step back and say, "Okay, God, I understand. I'll straighten that out."

Just as Paul wrote about in his letter to the Corinthians, *"Do you not know that those who run in a race all run, but only one receives the prize? Run in such a way that you may win"* (1 Corinthians 9:24).

DAILY SCRIPTURE READING: Jeremiah 30, 31, 33

A TWO-EDGED SWORD

"The word of God is living and active and sharper than any two-edged sword. . .able to judge the thoughts and intentions of the heart"
(Hebrews 4:12).

TATE was driving me to the airport when he told me about a difficult dispute in his company, which had been handled through the reading of God's Word.

He was addressing a meeting of salespeople when they began to argue about sales territories. Just before the conversation became heated and name-calling began, Tate reached for his Bible and read the following. *"You were called to freedom, brethren; only do not turn your freedom into an opportunity for the flesh, but through love serve one another"* (Galatians 5:13).

Tate closed his Bible and, without comment, continued the meeting. The Word of God had gone out, and it did not return void. Even though several of the sales force were not Christians, the Word of God, sharper than a two-edged sword, had cut and convicted them.

A short time after the meeting, a man came admitted that their dispute could only have resulted in their devouring each other; but, after hearing God's Word, the argument was settled.

Thank God for Christian businesspeople who are not afraid to be a witness with God's Word. If we don't take this stand and are ashamed of our Savior, we are guilty of hiding our lights—to our own detriment.

Martin Luther said it best: "The Bible is alive, it speaks to me; it has feet, it runs after me; it has hands, it lays old on me."

Do your coworkers know where you stand concerning God and His Word?

DAILY SCRIPTURE READING: Ezekiel 25, 29:1-16, 30, 31

PRIDE OR CONFIDENCE

"Let another praise you, and not your own mouth;
a stranger, and not your own lips"
(Proverbs 27:2).

OUR society has taught us that if we don't show self-confidence others won't have confidence in us either. We live in a time when a great deal of emphasis is placed on personal credentials.

Qualifications are based on personal achievements, education, and experience. And, when viewed in the right perspective, these things are good; but, when they produce pride, they lose their value from a godly perspective.

There is no doubt that we should work with all our might in whatever we do; but, the presence of pride indicates confidence in self rather than in Christ, who enables us.

Pride is an enemy of God, the cause of the fall of both Lucifer and of man. The attitude God wants us to have is demonstrated by the story of a convicted prisoner.

With Napoleon's permission, a Russian prince was allowed to pardon one convict in a French prison. As he talked with the prisoners, they all professed innocence and said they had been unjustly punished. Finally, he found a man who sorrowfully confessed his guilt and acknowledged that he was deserving of the punishment. To this man the prince said, "I have brought you pardon in the name of the emperor."

Isn't this the way we receive our salvation? And isn't it the way we live our Christian lives? The next time you are tempted to "watch out for number one," remember that Number One (Jesus) died nearly 2,000 years ago and now lives in the hearts of the humble.

DAILY SCRIPTURE READING: Ezekiel 26, 27, 28

PROUD OR PLEASED?

*"Who regards you as superior? And what do you have
that you did not receive? But if you did receive it,
why do you boast as if you had not received it?"*
(1 Corinthians 4:7).

THERE was a time when I found it difficult to accept that everything I possessed was not a direct result of my hard work and superiority. I often observed those who had less than I did, and I concluded that their lack was because they didn't work as hard as I did.

On the other hand, I looked at others who had more and calculated that I needed to work harder and become wiser in order to have what they did. After reading today's Scripture verse I had to change my thinking.

Consider the farmer. He prepares the ground and plants and waters the seed, but God gives the increase. To say that the farmer grew the crops would be incorrect. He only harvested the crops that God grew. There's no question that the farmer had to be faithful in doing his part; however, the farmer can't boast in the crop that is harvested. He can only be thankful that God blessed the work of his hands.

Don't discount your efforts completely, though. Faithfulness is required. God doesn't honor slothfulness; He honors faithfulness. And the most significant thing about faithfulness is that even the most untalented or unskilled person can be faithful.

Pride says, "Look what I did." Humility says, "Look what God did through me."

Father, thank You that everything good and perfect comes to us from You, the Creator of all things.

DAILY SCRIPTURE READING: 2 Kings 25:2-21;
2 Chronicles 36:17-20; Jeremiah 37:3-39:10, 52:5-30

JUMPING THE GUN

"He who is spiritual appraises all things,
yet he himself is appraised by no man"
(1 Corinthians 2:15).

SEVERAL contestants entered a race, which was to start with the firing of a gun. But, in anticipation, one of the contestants started before the gun fired. He "jumped the gun."

Christians can be guilty of spiritually jumping the gun. The apostle Peter was guilty of this more than once but the Lord just said, "Get thee behind Me, Satan."

Jumping the gun can be a conditioned response from Satan. The Scriptures clearly demonstrate that God is patient, and everything He does is thought out in advance.

God does not anticipate. He prepares. The Christian also should prepare, through appraisal or investigation. The spiritual person investigates first—then acts. The natural man simply reacts, almost always resulting in disaster.

How many times have you jumped into a conversation impulsively, only to regret it later? Remember, *"He who gives an answer before he hears, it is folly and shame to him"* (Proverbs 18:13).

It is vitally important in everything to allow the Lord to prepare your heart. An immediate response or quick reaction is rarely ever from the Lord.

Pray before you act, or speak, or react. Jumping the gun can result in all manner of problems.

Lord, in Your Word, James said that if I could control my tongue it would prove that I have perfect control over myself in other ways. Help me, Lord!

DAILY SCRIPTURE READING: 2 Kings 25:22;
Jeremiah 39:11-40:6; Lamentations 1, 2, 3

THE KING'S BUSINESS

"We are ambassadors for Christ,
as though God were entreating through us"
(2 Corinthians 5:20).

A BUSINESSMAN was summoned before England's queen. When he appeared, she requested that he represent England as one of the country's ambassadors.

He expressed his delight and appreciation for the honor, but he told of his reluctance to leave his own business, which demanded most of his time and attention. If he were to leave for two years of service to England and the queen, his business surely would fail.

The queen said, "You take care of England's business, and England will take care of yours."

After his tenure of service, the man returned to find his business had doubled in size.

What if you were given the same offer? Well, you have been! Today's Scripture verse says that we are ambassadors and God has given us the privilege of attending to His business. He, in turn, will take care of us.

However, God has no obligation to anyone who neglects His business in pursuit of his or her own.

As long as we have our priorities right, we have an unfailing guarantee of success from God's Word: *"Commit your work to the Lord, then it will succeed"* (Proverbs 16:3 TLB).

Father, help me find balance between "taking care of business" and being Your ambassador.

DAILY SCRIPTURE READING: Lamentations 4, 5; Obadiah

FAITH AND CONSCIENCE

"Keeping faith and a good conscience,
which some have rejected and suffered
shipwreck in regard to their faith"
(1 Timothy 1:19).

OUR Scripture verse likens faith to a ship. The conscience can be likened to the hull of that ship. When the conscience (hull) gets a hole in it, faith (the vessel) can become shipwrecked and sink.

Picture a ship sailing down a channel. The ship is faith and the channel is love. If the ship (faith) gets outside of the channel (love) it will run aground, puncture the hull (conscience), and sink.

When we operate our lives outside of love, we will cause our consciences to become defiled and suffer shipwreck with regard to our faith. And we know from God's Word that without faith it is impossible to please God.

Augustine said, "The words of God come like fire, so that when your heart is cleared, Christ can be built in you."

How can we clean up an evil conscience and restore faith in a shipwrecked condition? Through confession of sin.

A very practical and easy way to do this is to ask God to reveal the things in our lives that aren't pleasing to Him. Write them down, repent of them, receive His forgiveness, and then destroy the list. After you've been forgiven, the list no longer exists, because God's Word promises, *"Their sins and their lawless deeds I will remember no more"* (Hebrews 10:17).

Pray a prayer of thanksgiving for this very special blessing as God's child.

DAILY SCRIPTURE READING: 2 Kings 25:23–26;
Jeremiah 40:7-44:30

Eliminate Failure

*"Commit your works to the Lord,
and your plans will be established"*
(Proverbs 16:3).

JIM operated a business with another man who was both his friend and partner. When the business began to generate losses, rather than profits, Jim called and shared his concern with me, stating that they were losing up to $1,000 a day.

As I reviewed the nature of the business, I learned that it was a liquor store. Jim hadn't wanted to go into this particular business, but he did so because of his friendship with his partner.

I asked Jim if he had dedicated his business to God, and he said that he hadn't. I explained that before God can establish our plans our works must first be committed to Him. But could the sale of beer and wine be dedicated to God? Jim and I agreed—probably not.

The verse for today is a guide to help us to begin eliminating some of our failures. If we are going to commit our works to God, there are prerequisites that must be met.

First, is the nature of our work honoring to God? Second, what is the purpose of our efforts? In 1 Peter 4:11 we read that the purpose is that *"in all things God may be glorified through Jesus Christ."*

Jim's liquor business was really a "planned failure" from God's viewpoint. In all good conscience, he could not ask God to bless the business, because the works couldn't be committed to the Lord.

Remember, works committed to God will be supported by God.

DAILY SCRIPTURE READING: Ezekiel 33:21-36:38

GETTING EVEN

"See that no one repays another with evil for evil, but always seek
after that which is good for one another and for all men"
(1 Thessalonians 5:15).

IT had always been Charlie's dream to be involved full time in the Lord's work. He left a successful business and went to work for a Christian ministry. But the dream was turned into a nightmare when he was fired. He was told never to set foot on the ministry's property again.

Charlie thought, *I'll get even. Just wait.* Vindictiveness is the word to describe Charlie's attitude: getting back at someone for what has been done. It's almost a national pastime. At one time or another most of us have made the same statement Charlie made, "I'll get even."

We are instructed not to get even but to leave the matter of justice to God.

Newton's third law, a law of nature, says that for every action there is always an equal and opposite reaction. For example, if we fire a shotgun, the charge goes forward and the barrel goes backward. When we render evil for evil, we violate a spiritual law that is the counterpart of the natural law, and we suffer the outcome.

There must always be an equal and opposite reaction for every action. Rendering evil for evil is not opposite; it is the same. When Jesus was being reviled, He didn't revile in return. In fact He uttered no threats. He entrusted Himself to the One who judges righteously (paraphrase of 1 Peter 2:23).

Rendering good for evil is God's way of justice.

Think of a time when you returned evil for good. How did it make you feel? Talk to the Lord about it.

DAILY SCRIPTURE READING: Ezekiel 37, 38, 39

HASTE MAKES WASTE

*"The plans of the diligent lead surely to advantage,
but everyone who is hasty comes surely to poverty"*
(Proverbs 21:5).

BILL and Jayne were seminar sponsors for their city. Bill, as usual, took little interest and left the preparation to Jayne. However, in addition to coordinating the seminar, Jayne also had her family obligations, which often caused her to make last-minute plans. They were habitually late and Bill continually remarked about Jayne's poor planning.

Some people seem to constantly have emergencies or are always in a frantic rush to get things done. This is the result of failing to plan, which indicates something important: Usually there's a failure to pray.

If Bill and Jayne had recognized the principle of stewardship, they would have realized that Jesus is Lord and that we are His stewards. And, as His stewards, we should seek His direction through prayer.

When we think of being good stewards, often we think only of how we use our money. But being good stewards involves far more than money; we are to be good stewards of our time.

Prayer is the instrument for planning. If we will start the day with prayer and then spend more time in prayer throughout the day, there will be better planning, and proper planning will eliminate most emergencies and haste.

Ask the Lord to reveal to you how you can be a better steward of your time. If you already have that under control, pray for someone else you know who has more than he or she can handle.

DAILY SCRIPTURE READING: Ezekiel 32:1-33:20; Daniel 3

AUGUST 31

LESS SPURS, MORE REINS

*"The Lord is good, a stronghold in the day of trouble,
and He knows those who take refuge in Him"*
(Nahum 1:7).

LAST century in the Wild West mail was dispatched through a relay system known as the Pony Express. Occasionally an Express rider was attacked by hostile Indians. However, because the rider's mount was stronger than the Indian ponies, he could spur his horse to a gallop and outrun his attackers before his horse would tire.

The scenario wasn't repeated many times before the Indians changed their plan of attack. Realizing they couldn't outrun the Express rider, they stationed some of their number every few miles along the route. Then, just when the rider had outrun the first group of attackers, the second band would appear, causing him to spur his horse on without rest. This tactic was repeated until the rider's horse would drop from exhaustion.

I believe our economy faces the same peril as that Pony Express rider. We have spurred our mount to a gallop, thinking we can outdistance our problems.

However, at least eight "bands of attackers" are poised along the way: our aging population, declining youth population (as a result of abortions), increasing government regulations, declining savings, rising health care costs, declining industry, lawsuits, and growing government debt.

I'm convinced that these factors, combined with our lack of resolve to "rein in" spending, will lead to a major crisis. We'll kick this economy along until it finally drops dead in its tracks.

Our hope is in the Lord and the ultimate victory is His. God is able. I invite you to join with me in prayer that the Gospel will be preached unhindered throughout the world.

DAILY SCRIPTURE READING: Ezekiel 40, 41, 42

LENDING TO OTHERS

*"Give to him who asks of you, and do not turn away
from him who wants to borrow from you"*
(Matthew 5:42).

DOES it bother you when someone wants to borrow something that belongs to you? I suppose we all have had bad experiences and don't want to be "taken" again. But there is an attitude problem in the hearts of Christians who have difficulty lending, and God will deal with that attitude.

Personal attachment to the things of this life is contrary to Scripture. Anyone who loves the world and what it offers doesn't have the love of God abiding in him or her.

God may allow us to lose an item just to show us how much we love the things of this world. Lending grudgingly or refusing to lend should be seen as a red light of warning by a Christian. Also, demanding replacement of a lost item should be an indicator of attachment to things.

Our Scripture verse for today may be difficult to live by, but it is not impossible or Jesus wouldn't have expected it of us.

God can help us overcome the attitude of greed (an attitude that makes us think our possessions actually belong to us).

Even though we may have worked hard for what we have, the truth is that God has provided our material blessings. They are all from Him, and it is not a matter of ownership; it is a matter of stewardship. Being a good steward is miles apart from being a concerned owner.

Recognize the true ownership of your possessions and transfer ownership to Christ. Think of what all you "own." Then acknowledge God's ownership by turning it all over to Him.

DAILY SCRIPTURE READING: Ezekiel 43, 44, 45

September 2

Deceitfulness of Riches

"Some rich people are poor, and some poor people have great wealth!"
(Proverbs 13:7 TLB).

OLD man Cates was a very rich man—one of the richest in the islands. He had a sizable plantation and prospered financially from its produce; but he had few friends. He was very tight with his money, and the wages he paid his hired labor were low. Over the years he spent little and amassed quite a savings. And through those years he didn't have time for God; he was too busy building "bigger barns."

After many years, old man Cates became extremely ill. Because he suffered from pain that hindered his sleep, he often rocked during the evenings. His condition grew worse until it was evident that he wouldn't live.

One evening, hearing his screams, his wife ran to him and heard him cry out, "Oh, my God! Jesus of Nazareth has passed me by!" With that on his lips, he died.

Time ran out for the man who had no time for God. The expression of terrible fright remained on his face and the sounds of his agonizing cries about the intense heat of the fire into which he was passing haunted his wife.

Just like the rich man of Luke 16, old man Cates would have traded his wealth for Lazarus' poverty, if he had only realized the deceitfulness of his riches.

We need to remind ourselves that we cannot trust in riches. Only our trust in Christ will secure our future—now and in the hereafter.

DAILY SCRIPTURE READING: Ezekiel 46, 47, 48

THE LAW OF FAITH

*"Whatever is born of God overcomes the world;
and this is the victory that has overcome the world—our faith"*
(1 John 5:4).

PRAYER is probably one of the most talked about and least understood topics in the Bible. How does prayer really work? Many Christians say that they pray, but they seldom get an answer. Have you ever felt that way?

The reason prayer goes unanswered is because God answers prayer based on faith. Romans 3:27 tells us that faith is a law—just like gravity. You can't jump off the top of a building and ignore the law of gravity without suffering a grave consequence.

However, many of us ignore the law of faith, expecting God to violate His own principle.

Since faith works by love (see 1 Corinthians 13:1–3), all prayers must be based on love.

Anytime we pray, we should search our hearts for the true motives behind our requests. Are our prayers motivated by greed or by love? Without love, prayer will not be answered, because it is not according to faith. Faith works through love, which pleases God. He then rewards that faith.

How can you be sure your prayers are according to faith and will please God and evoke His response? Weigh your motives. Is the prayer for selfish benefit, or will it benefit someone else?

Look up James 4:3 and write it down. Continue to read it over until you know you have come to terms with what it says. What about your motives? God wants to give you His best, but you must follow the teaching in His Word.

DAILY SCRIPTURE READING: 2 Kings 25:27-30; Psalm 44;
Jeremiah 52:31-34; Ezekiel 29:17-21; Daniel 4

THE "KEEPING UP WITH" DISEASE

*"Rest in the Lord, and wait patiently for Him:
do not fret because of him who prospers in his way"*
(Psalm 37:7).

DO you worry or become overworked because someone else is prospering and you aren't? This is caused by a malady called "keeping up with the Joneses," and there are many Christians who have this disease in its final stages.

There is a cure; it's called patience. The prescription is faith, and it can be obtained from your Great Physician.

In trying to keep up with the Joneses, we suffer an "attack" of money shortages. But for too many Christians with this disease the "infection" of impatience is severe. Many cannot wait for God to act; they must put a "bandage" on the shortage now. This might be done by taking a second mortgage, a second job, a get-rich-quick scheme.

The Great Physician doesn't administer human salve. The answer to money problems isn't more money. We wouldn't give more sugar to a diabetic. Instead, He prescribes a "double dose" of patience, the very deficiency that brought about the "Jones" disease.

More work to meet higher financial demands may keep us from the Lord's rest and bring on fatigue. If we refuse His "treatment," we will take our own medicine.

How can you avoid catching this dread disease? Avoid contact with others who have the disease, and read Psalm 37:1–7. Confess your envy and ask for the Lord's "treatment."

DAILY SCRIPTURE READING: Psalms 74, 79, 80, 89

MINE OR GOD'S?

"The earth is the Lord's, and all it contains,
the world, and those who dwell in it"
(Psalm 24:1).

WHEN my children were young I shared with them the importance of recognizing that everything we have is from God and that we should transfer ownership back to His care and protection.

Years ago two friends and I purchased a chain saw for a project on which we were working. After using the saw, it was placed in what we thought was a safe place. But, a day or two later, we discovered it was missing.

My oldest son asked if I had given the saw to God. I had forgotten to do this. I immediately asked my two friends if they had committed the saw to God and they hadn't either.

This made me sure of two things: My son had learned the scriptural lesson I had wanted to teach him, and I needed to practice what I had preached to my family.

Keep in mind that God isn't responsible for what we do not give to Him.

How do we protect what we have? Make a list of your possessions and give them all to God. He will protect what has been committed to Him.

DAILY SCRIPTURE READING: Psalms 85, 102, 106, 123, 137

PUT GOD FIRST

*"Seek first His kingdom and His righteousness,
and all these things shall be added to you"*
(Matthew 6:33).

IT'S a simple thing to say, "I do put God first." But, is He the first thing on your mind in the morning and the last thing on your mind at night?

What if God looked at the use of our time during any given day? How much time do we really put into the study of His Word or talking with Him? If He is first, we should be studying the handbook of life, the Bible, and spending time in prayer.

The man who invented most of our road-grading equipment in America was R.G. LeTourneau, an uneducated man with a sixth-grade education. He was told by his own college-graduate engineers that the equipment he designed wouldn't work.

What they didn't know was that every evening before he went to bed he would study God's Word thoroughly and spend the last thirty minutes of his evenings in prayer before going to sleep. When he awoke in the morning, he had a fully formed design for a new piece of equipment, given to him by God, with an absolute assurance from God that the piece of equipment would work.

LeTourneau designed some truly remarkable equipment. In fact, long after his death, that equipment is still operating and, in great part, no one has ever improved on the initial design. Why? Because he put God first in his life.

Not only did he give God a portion of his money (90 percent!), but he gave God a portion of his time. He made it clear that God was first in his life.

Where does God rank in your schedule for the day?

DAILY SCRIPTURE READING: Daniel 5, 7, 8

BE A GOOD FOLLOWER

"If anyone serves Me, let him follow Me;
and where I am,
there shall My servant also be;
if anyone serves Me,
the Father will honor him"
(John 12:26).

WOULD you rather be a follower or a leader? Leaders earn more money, get more recognition, and are more popular. Who wouldn't rather be a leader?

God didn't call us to be leaders. He called us to be followers, and as followers we honor others and build them up.

I truly believe with all my heart that one of these days we are going to show up in Heaven at the judgment seat of Christ, and when He calls all the nations of the world together we will be working for some little old lady we never heard of during our life-time. She never received any recognition, never received any great rewards in this life, but she was doing what God called her to do.

As a result, God blessed her and gave her a number one position in the kingdom of God, along with other deserving followers.

Are you a leader or a follower?

September 8

Serving Others

"Many who are first now will be last then;
and some who are last now will be first then"
(Matthew 19:30).

At the Last Supper, when Jesus went into the upper room, He took off His clothing, except for a loincloth, put a towel over His shoulders and, then, as His apostles came into the room, He began washing their feet.

When He came to Peter, who was more impetuous than the others, *"Peter said to Him, 'Never shall You wash my feet!' "* (John 13:8). Why do you think he said that? What would you have said?

There was a hierarchy in Jerusalem at the time, and at the bottom of the system were the people Jesus called His disciples: workmen, fishermen, carpenters, and laborers. Below them were slaves, and at the lowest level of slavery was a foot servant—someone who washed other people's feet.

When Peter refused to let Jesus wash his feet, the Savior said, *"If I do not wash you, you have no part with Me"* (John 13:8). Then he went on to say (in verses 14–15), *"If I then, the Lord and the Teacher, washed your feet, you also ought to wash one another's feet. For I gave you an example that you also should do as I did to you."*

Jesus was on His way to being the most exalted person in the kingdom of God; therefore, He had to show them that He was willing to take the very least position in the kingdom. He wanted to be the least glorified before He became the most exalted.

Jesus set an example of how to put others before self. Could you humble yourself to wash someone else's feet like He did?

Daily Scripture Reading:
2 Chronicles 36:22-23; Ezra 1:1-4:5

SUING CHRISTIANS?

"Does any one of you, when he has a case against his neighbor,
dare to go to law before the unrighteous?"
(1 Corinthians 6:1).

A LAWSUIT is nothing more than a legal recourse for an assumed loss. Suing is not a new concept. The apostle Paul wrote about it almost 2,000 years ago. He said it is better to be defrauded and lose everything you have than to take a fellow Christian to court and present a poor witness to an unsaved world. There are alternatives to suing available to us.

God cannot bless our attitudes until we forgive the ones we feel like we have the right to sue. No matter what wrong they have done, we must forgive them, because the principles of God's Word are for restoring people—not punishing them.

The next step is to go to the guilty party and confront that person face-to-face. If this doesn't do any good, then you are to take the person before the church.

God's Word teaches restoration—not vengeance.

Is there someone you need to forgive? A relationship that needs to be restored?

DAILY SCRIPTURE READING: Daniel 10, 11, 12

September 10

Suing Non-Christians

*"Give to everyone who asks of you,
and whoever takes away what is yours, do not demand it back"*
(Luke 6:30).

WE know from reading Paul's writings to the Corinthians that we are not to sue Christians, but what about non-Christians? The Bible is not quite as specific, but just because God didn't make it a "thou shalt not," that doesn't mean you should sue non-Christians.

The Scripture verse for today is a strong statement about how we are to treat other people.

I'm not saying that you have to let people take things away from you that belong to God or that you should loan them things and never try to recover them. But there are ways to recapture things without taking someone to court.

God is quite competent to protect His own business and His own people.

I know of instances in which a person was saved because of the actions of a Christian not being willing to sue a non-Christian.

However, this means giving up our "rights" rather than pursuing vengeance.

Only God can tell you what is right for you to do in any given situation. Pray fervently.

DAILY SCRIPTURE READING: Ezra 4:6-6:13; Haggai

A NEW APPRECIATION

*"In the early morning, while it was still dark, He arose and went out
and departed to a lonely place, and was praying there"*
(Mark 1:35).

I'VE always been a late-night person, but following my cancer surgeries sleep was particularly hard to come by. As I lay awake because the pain prohibited sleep, one of the great blessings for me personally was to turn on my local Christian radio station and listen to the comforting music.

With so much time on my hands, I really began to focus in on the music—probably more than at any other time in my life. I was amazed at how much Christian music truly centers on the theme of the death and resurrection of Jesus Christ.

Not only did His resurrection take place, but our resurrection —the future for those who trust Jesus as Lord and Savior—to eternal life. What a comfort that message was, reasserting that death is not a curse but a reward—for God's people.

We have an enormous number of Christian radio stations throughout America. They are the best resource available to God's people to communicate quickly with one another and as a means of ministering to one another.

I pray you will help me protect the medium of Christian radio as a sacred trust from the Lord. That means, if you listen to Christian radio, you should support it. If we ever lose access to Christian radio, there will be a great gap in spreading the Gospel across the world.

Jesus told the disciples: *"You shall receive power. . . and you shall be My witnesses both in Jerusalem, and in all Judea and Samaria, and even to the remotest part of the earth"* (Acts 1:8).

DAILY SCRIPTURE READING: Zechariah 1, 2, 3, 4, 5, 6

DIFFERENT METHODS

"Since his days are determined, the number of his months
is with Thee, and his limits Thou hast set"
(Job 14:5).

LIKE many people, I have thought through the message of eternal life in Jesus many times. Thoughts of facing death can cause one to examine his or her faith.

I think of a story you've probably heard about the man who was trapped on his roof during a flood. While clinging to the chimney, he was praying that God would rescue him. A fellow came by in a boat and asked if he could help. The man said, "No, that's okay. God's going to rescue me."

The water continued to rise and another fellow came by, paddling a skimpy little raft. He offered help to the man on the roof but was told, "No, thank you. God is going to rescue me."

The water rose higher and higher and then a helicopter hovered over him. The pilot offered to lower a rope, but the man said, "No, God has this under control. He's going to rescue me." As the water continued to rise, the man was swept to his death.

When the man reached heaven he asked St. Peter why God didn't rescue him. Peter smiled as he said, "Well, my friend, He sent three people by to pick you up and you turned them all away. What did you expect?"

Though it is a fictitious story, the principle cannot be lost. Often God uses natural things to rescue His people. They are not always instantaneous, miraculous answers.

We should always be open to what God is trying to do for us.

DAILY SCRIPTURE READING:
Ezra 6:14-22; Psalm 78; Zechariah 7, 8

SAY WHAT?

"Pleasant words are a honeycomb,
sweet to the soul and healing to the bones"
(Proverbs 16:24).

CHRISTIANS can mean well and yet say some of the most inappropriate things at the wrong time. Before you make remarks to someone recovering from cancer or any other serious illness, think about how your words will impact the other person.

When I was recovering from my first cancer surgery, a young man slipped into my room. He approached my bed, introduced himself, and then said, "Larry, I'm a renal cell carcinoma patient also, and you might as well face it: You're going to die. I'm going to die and you are too, because there just isn't any cure for this type of cancer."

He may have had the best of intentions, but he offered only words of discouragement.

Later, I had a visit from another well-meaning friend whose wife had died from renal cancer and had been buried that day. He told me about the excruciating pain his wife had suffered during the last three years of her life and described all the trauma they had endured. I didn't need to hear that!

Be careful what you say when you visit friends or family in the hospital. Ask God to help you understand what the patient may be experiencing, as well as how you can be an encouragement. Sometimes the most appropriate thing may just be to pray and leave.

Be positive in what you say to anyone who is ill. Ask the Holy Spirit to guide you.

DAILY SCRIPTURE READING: Psalms 107, 116, 118

IGNORANCE

*"The naive believes everything,
but the prudent man considers his steps"*
(Proverbs 14:15).

THE word ignorance doesn't imply stupidity. It simply means not knowledgeable. Many mistakes are made because we don't know any better.

But, when it comes to stewardship—our accountability before God for what He has entrusted to us—ignorance is no excuse. God's Word is full of wisdom and advice on financial matters, and good Christian counsel is readily available. Find someone who can help you.

Learn to budget. Discipline yourself to balance your checkbook. Investigate investment options before making any decisions.

Being able to identify and subdue ignorance is crucial if we are to walk in spiritual and financial freedom.

Ask God to give you wisdom in all your financial plans and actions.

DAILY SCRIPTURE READING:
Psalms 125, 126, 128, 129, 132, 147, 149

SEPTEMBER 15

IT'S A HEART THING

"For as he thinks within himself, so he is"
(Proverbs 23:7).

THE Bible makes it clear that the battle to live godly lives is won or lost first in our hearts—long before we actually make a decision or follow a certain course.

In every area of our lives, we must determine to follow God's way, whatever the cost. Then when our old sinful nature tries to surface and take control, we have the grace to resist our natural impulses and are given strength through Christ to live lives pleasing to Him.

Open your heart to Him and allow Him to deal with you right where you are in your life. Remember, our lives are not who we are—they are who we are becoming.

Elisabeth Elliot, widow of slain missionary Jim Elliot, wrote, "[Lord] remind us that it is in losing ourselves that we find You."

If there is an attitude hidden in your heart that is contrary to God's plan for you and it is hindering your spiritual growth, get rid of it by planting God's Word there instead. Confess it to the Lord now.

DAILY SCRIPTURE READING: Zechariah 9, 10, 11, 12, 13, 14

EMOTIONAL SUFFERING

*"The righteous cry and the Lord hears, and delivers
them out of all their troubles. The Lord is near to the brokenhearted,
and saves those who are crushed in spirit"*
(Psalm 34:17–18).

MENTAL suffering revolves around our attitudes and thought patterns; emotional suffering reflects the pain we experience in our feelings. In our culture, many equate emotional struggles with spiritual weakness or even mental disturbances.

The vast majority of human beings struggle from time to time with depression. We call it "feeling blue," or "being down." Some of the great saints of the Bible struggled with these same kinds of feelings. Read about Elijah in 1 Kings 19 or about Moses in Numbers 11. Or read through the Psalms and hear the pain and despair in King David's heart from time to time.

The difference between those times and now is the way the church, in general, condemns or makes the battle against depression a moral issue. The general comments might be "You just need to pray more" or "You must have some unconfessed sin somewhere in your life." Such comments usually evoke more guilt, shame, or inadequacy, which only makes the problem worse.

God expects more out of His church than those kinds of responses. Emotional pain and suffering are very real. Unfortunately, rather than helping people see God as their merciful Father, eternally filled with compassion and care, often our responses drive people further away from Him by heaping on guilt or shame.

The Scriptures indicate that God desires for us to draw near to Him in our time of need. It also says that we are to help those in need—whatever the need.

DAILY SCRIPTURE READING: Esther 1, 2, 3, 4

GOD IS FAITHFUL

*"God is faithful, through whom you were called
into fellowship with His Son,
Jesus Christ our Lord"*
(1 Corinthians 1:9).

THROUGH my suffering I have learned one thing for sure: God is a faithful God. He also is a forgiving God who will forgive anything and everything on the basis of the sacrifice of His Son, the Lord Jesus.

In contrast, He forgives nothing, no matter how small the offense, on the basis of how good we are or how acceptable we are or whether we have more positives than negatives in our lives.

God is merciful. He cares about your suffering, whether it is mental, physical, emotional, or spiritual.

My favorite Bible character, in regard to suffering, is King David, who suffered a lot in his life. He suffered at the hands of a maniacal King Saul and ran for his life with Saul in hot pursuit. Yet God protected David because He still had plans for his life.

Yes, David did die—as all flesh must. Bear in mind, though, that no one can remove us one second before God decides it's our time.

God has plans that are at work in your life. He hasn't completed His work in you, so be sure you are putting Him first in your life and seeking His will for you.

Father, I read in Lamentations 3:22–23 that Your lovingkindness never ceases and Your compassion never fails but is new every morning. Thank You, Father.

DAILY SCRIPTURE READING: Esther 5, 6, 7, 8, 9, 10

CHURCH ASSISTANCE

"Bear one another's burdens, and thus fulfill the law of Christ"
(Galatians 6:2).

THERE will be times when Christians in need should approach their church families for financial assistance. That's totally biblical, and the precedent is seen clearly in Scripture.

Although most churches can help a family in need with daily living expenses, few are prepared to help with major, catastrophic medical bills. They just don't have the resources. Of course, we would have more available if the church would obey God's command of bringing the tithes into the storehouse.

The reason needs go unmet is because we, God's people, are mismanaging what God has provided, spending it on our own desires.

God has no shortage of funds in His economy. Rather, there is a shortage of vision among His people today. In Haggai 1:4–6 the prophet had stern words for the people of Judah because they put their own selfish needs ahead of the work within God's house. These words serve as quite a challenge to the American church today.

Ironically, by putting our own priorities first, we never have enough. Conversely, when we sacrificially obey God's commands, He will supernaturally multiply our resources, providing nothing less than an abundance.

It is the story of the five loaves and two fishes all over again. That should not take us by surprise, since God has already told us that He would respond to our faith and obedience in this manner.

Lord, show me how to help someone who is in need—either through my church or individually.

DAILY SCRIPTURE READING: Ezra 7, 8

OUR SECURITY

"It is the blessing of the Lord that makes rich, and He adds no sorrow to it"
(Proverbs 10:22).

As we fight against the rampant materialism in our society, the serious danger our world is in becomes more obvious to me daily.

The goal of our lives, according to society, is to be rich or at least to live like we are. Without a doubt, even the poor in our country would not be considered impoverished when compared to most Third World countries.

And yet, in the U.S. there are children who are going to bed hungry tonight. I believe that the materialism and monetary poverty in this country are just symptoms of a greater problem: emotional and spiritual poverty.

As a culture, because we are searching for significance and security in our lives, we put a high value on having things, on making lots of money, and on getting all we can.

As Christians, our significance comes from being the children of God—equals with Jesus, the Son of God! In John 17:21 Jesus prayed, *"That they may all be one; even as Thou, Father, art in Me, and I in Thee, that they also may be in Us; that the world may believe."*

As His children, God wants us to serve Him by loving those around us and revealing His nature to them by the way we live our lives.

Our security comes from knowing that God loves with an unlimited love—not from our income or the amount of money we have in the bank. Our significance comes from being His children.

Thank You, God, for being my Father.

Purposeful Obedience

"As obedient children, do not be conformed to the former lusts which were yours in your ignorance, but like the Holy One who called you, be holy yourselves also in all your behavior"
(1 Peter 1:14–15).

SOMETIMES it can be difficult to do the things we want to do. When we became Christians, God began to change us from the inside, as the Holy Spirit began moving in us, creating new hearts with new desires.

As a new Christian, I surprised myself with the longing to be obedient to God in ways I'd never considered before. These longings changed the way I thought, and those new thoughts began to change the way I lived.

Often, though, I found myself, like Paul, doing the things I didn't want to do and not doing the things I did want to do. My behavior frustrated and disappointed me, and I think many people are feeling the same frustration.

One area is in stewardship. The Holy Spirit has placed a longing in our hearts to become good managers of what God has given us. We truly want to control our spending, give more to help others, get out of debt, and bring a balance into our financial lives. However, we find that the path to stewardship is difficult, and it's easy to stumble.

I've learned that it's okay to stumble, because when we are aware of our shortcomings and turn to Him, He can work more powerfully through us. Being obedient means being willing to do what God's Word says—regardless.

Are there ways you have failed to be obedient to God that you want to confess? Pray about it now.

DAILY SCRIPTURE READING: Nehemiah 1, 2, 3, 4, 5

PRAYER HABITS

"Pray without ceasing"
(1 Thessalonians 1:17).

IT'S good to set aside a particular time or times each day for prayer. But, instead of being in prayer at just those times, we should be in an attitude of prayer all day—wherever we are.

Of course, I don't mean to pray aloud all day; that wouldn't be practical or reasonable. I have found, however, that it's easy to pray as you drive your car—just thanking the Lord for all you have or asking guidance for what you are about to do. If your particular job allows it, pray during your work time.

Without prayer, your life will be empty and discouraging. However, if you do pray "without ceasing," you'll find a peace that truly does pass all understanding.

If you try to make decisions without praying about them first, you'll be operating in your own strength and, in large part, just cheating yourself.

Prayer brings the blessings of God's will to your personal life and helps to keep you within God's plan. Pray when you are in trouble; pray when things are going well. Pray for forgiveness; ask for an outpouring of the Holy Spirit in your life. Pray for the salvation of others; pray for God's continued protection and grace. Pray sometimes when all you do is praise God for His goodness and faithfulness.

Make a list of some other things you can pray for, put it in your Bible, and then read Mark 11:24 as confirmation that your prayers will be answered.

Billy Graham wrote that "Heaven is full of answers to prayer for which no one ever bothered to ask."

DAILY SCRIPTURE READING: Nehemiah 6, 7

HOPE FOR THE FUTURE

"Hope does not disappoint,
because the love of God has been poured out within
our hearts through the Holy Spirit who was given to us"
(Romans 5:5).

As I read the daily newspapers and watch the local and national news on television, I am disturbed by the violence, bloodshed, chaos, strife, and international unrest.

For unbelievers the future must look pretty dark. However, we know what is ahead and can have hope. In the Bible we read about the evidences of the fulfillment of biblical prophecy.

John Baillie wrote that "the future is in the hands of One who is preparing something better than eye hath seen, or ear heard, or has entered into the heart of man to conceive."

The psalmist says that the Lord is our light and salvation and that we should have no fear (see Psalm 27:1).

And, as Christians, we know that we are promised life in a happy place where we won't have hardships and casualties. We have an assurance that life there will be happiness, joy, and peace. This blessed hope allows us to look forward to that day.

"You have need of endurance, so that when you have done the will of God, you may receive what was promised" (Hebrews 10:36).

DAILY SCRIPTURE READING: Nehemiah 8, 9, 10

EFFECTUAL PRAYER

"The effectual prayer of a righteous man can accomplish much"
(James 5:16).

ALL through the Bible we read about what was accomplished through prayer. When Elijah prayed, God sent fire from heaven. When Daniel prayed, the hungry lions were unable to hurt him. When the Assyrian army was advancing, Hezekiah prayed and his nation was spared for another generation.

In the New Testament we have example after example of the power of prayer. Peter prayed and Dorcas was brought to life. Paul prayed and many churches were established in Asia Minor and in Europe.

Seventeenth century theologian John Owen once said, "He who prays as he ought will endeavor to live as he prays."

The problems of our society could be resolved if our national leaders would go to God in prayer. Can you imagine what would happen if every session of Congress was begun with the representatives on their knees in prayer?

Our nation was founded by people who believed in prayer. Benjamin Franklin knew that there was only one power that could redeem the course of events: the power of prayer.

Abraham Lincoln said, "I have been driven many times to my knees by the overwhelming conviction that I had nowhere else to go."

How wonderful it would be if our nation's leadership lived by those values!

Have you made prayer a part of your daily schedule?

Think of several people and situations you will pray for today.

DAILY SCRIPTURE READING: Nehemiah 11, 12, 13

THE TEST OF DISCIPLESHIP

"By this all men will know that you are My disciples,
if you have love for one another"
(John 13:35).

THE message the Lord Jesus Christ gave His disciples just before going to be with the Father in Heaven is recorded in John 13 and 14. He announced His betrayal, His departure, and His return to receive His disciples unto Himself. For three years Jesus had ministered to them and taught them His way. These last words with His disciples would be vital in reinforcing all He had taught them.

There are many vital parts of the Christian's life. Caring for and witnessing to the lost is one part. Prayer, Bible study, and gathering together as a body for fellowship are all very essential to Christian growth. But caring for one another is the test of a disciple, because that, according to Jesus, is how everyone will know that we belong to Him.

We demonstrate the degree of our love for Christ by the way we give to other Christians. Giving to the needs of another demonstrates the sincerity of our love.

Remember, the household of faith is built on the foundation of brotherly love.

How do you think Christ views us if we show little concern for the needs of others? Can you pass the test of discipleship?

DAILY SCRIPTURE READING: Malachi

THE GUILT TRAP

"If you then, being evil,
know how to give good gifts to your children,
how much more shall your Father who
is in heaven give what is good to those who ask Him!"
(Matthew 7:11).

WE sometimes fail to trust God because, inwardly, we believe that God wants to deprive us and punish us. It is important to remember that God does not punish His children; He chastens us. Chastening is always directed toward correction, which is always for the benefit of the person being chastened.

Through the Holy Spirit, our Father convicts of wrong actions. On the other hand, Satan accuses. Correction of our errors is what the Lord wants; Satan's desire is that we become depressed and despondent, convinced of our unworthiness to serve God. The Lord seeks to improve our service for Him, but Satan wants our guilt to paralyze us into idleness.

We must never forget that God loves us as His children, and what He does is always for our benefit. We must never allow difficulties to keep us from our Heavenly Father.

In Hebrews we read that Jesus is sitting at the right hand of the Father, making intercession for us.

God loved us when we were sinners. He will not stop loving us now if we sin.

"Commit your way to the Lord, trust also in Him. . . . He will bring forth your righteousness as the light, and your judgment as the noonday" (Psalm 37:5–6).

DAILY SCRIPTURE READING: 1 Chronicles 1, 2

WHO ARE YOU WORKING FOR?

*"Whatever you do, do your work heartily, as for
the Lord rather than for men"*
(Colossians 3:23).

FRED was really excited about the paint job he had just finished and anxiously waited for the boss of the auto paint shop to return and see it. But when his boss returned he only remarked about the small run of paint under the left headlight that needed to be sanded out and retouched. Fred was crushed and discouraged because he had so wanted to impress his boss.

It is natural to want to be recognized and rewarded for a job. Everyone wants to be appreciated, which is important. However, if this is our ultimate motive for service, we will most likely be disappointed. That's a major reason so many Christians aren't happy in their jobs; and many are even bitter.

Consider your own situation and who you work for. Are you happy? If not, you may be employed in the right place but performing for the wrong person and for the wrong reason.

Disappointment, discouragement, and bitterness are very often symptoms of wrong motives.

If you are working to please some person rather than to please God, ask for His forgiveness and ask Him to help you develop a different motive for working.

DAILY SCRIPTURE READING: 1 Chronicles 3, 4, 5

ACCUMULATING THINGS

"All that my eyes desired I did not refuse them. I did not withhold my heart from any pleasure, for my heart was pleased because of all my labor and this was my reward for all my labor"
(Ecclesiastes 2:10).

THE tendency expressed in today's verse is what prompted Karl Marx to comment that capitalism destroys itself because it is humanistic and feeds its own greed.

Christianity in America has been the controlling influence on capitalism because we practice self-control and moderation. But now we have become caught up with everyone else in the race to see who can accumulate the most things. As a result, we have lost our witness in that area.

A Christian businessman and his wife were asked to go on a trip to Haiti with a missionary group. It was their first trip into an impoverished culture and it was a life-changing experience.

The husband said, "I had always assumed we were helping a few ignorant natives who were really too lazy to do better. But instead, we saw fellow human beings who had been born into total poverty. Twice we were offered babies by women who desired, above all else, that their children be given a chance to live."

When we recognize that these kinds of needs exist, it should become easier to curb our temptations to accumulate things.

Remember, Peter said, *"In your knowledge, self-control, and in your self-control, perseverance, and in your perseverance, godliness"* (2 Peter 1:6).

Is your focus on accumulating more things or on what you can do for someone in need?

DAILY SCRIPTURE READING: 1 Chronicles 6

WANTS OR NEEDS

*"The flesh sets its desire against the Spirit,
and the Spirit against the flesh; for these are in opposition to one
another, so that you may not do the things that you please"*
(Galatians 5:17).

BALANCE and moderation are the keys to determining what is a need, want, or desire. How can you tell when your life is indulgent?

One sign is that you or your family must always have "better" than before. This could be cars, clothes, houses, or recreation equipment.

Another sign is that you must always have better than others and find yourself trying to top their lifestyles.

Also, you find that you have a lot of things that you feel embarrassed about around other people.

Many people struggle with discerning between need and greed. The decision is not related to what we buy but, rather, to our attitude about things in general.

Without a doubt, it is easier in the short run to give in to indulgence than it is to control it. I say short run because in the long run the result is a growing sense of restlessness and distance from God.

If you have experienced this, you are the only one who can do anything about it. It is your decision to make changes. If you want to, God will supply the power.

Once we recognize the need to control indulgent spending, something else becomes obvious: The money we don't spend on ourselves is now available to help someone else's need.

"Let everyone see that you are unselfish and considerate in all you do. Remember that the Lord is coming soon" (Philippians 4:5 TLB).

DAILY SCRIPTURE READING: 1 Chronicles 7:1-8:27

INTEGRITY IN ALL THINGS

"He who walks in integrity walks securely,
but he who perverts his ways will be found out"
(Proverbs 10:9).

YEARS ago my son and I got involved with restoring a Ford Mustang, with the idea of selling it for a nice profit. Unfortunately, the deeper we got into it, the more problems the car developed. As the months passed, we both grew rather frustrated with the project and decided to put it up for sale. It looked great with the new paint job, and under the right conditions it ran reasonably well.

I found that when the first potential buyer came I had a temptation that I thought had been buried years earlier. The buyer's first question was the worst one possible: "What do you think of the car?" My first thoughts ran to the amount of money we had tied up in the car, but then I remembered today's verse.

My response to the potential buyer was, "It's the worst car I've ever owned, and I wouldn't trust it out of my driveway."

I wish I could tell you that he bought it anyway, but he didn't, and neither did anyone else until I dropped the price to half of what we had in the car. The spiritual lesson learned was worth far more than any amount of money.

Can you think of incidents in your own life when you were tempted to conceal some truth for gain? What decision did you make at the time?

Discuss these with your family or a friend and pray together that integrity will be a part of every day's experiences.

DAILY SCRIPTURE READING: 1 Chronicles 8:28-9:44

YOUR SINS WILL FIND YOU OUT

"A scoffer does not love one who reproves him, he will not go to the wise"
(Proverbs 15:12).

THERE is nothing more devastating to a believer than looking spiritual while living in defeat. The immediate consequence is the loss of esteem in the eyes of family and close friends.

One couple shared how God had used their daughter to shake them out of their complacency about deception and hypocrisy. It seems they were selling their home, which had a significant problem with flooding in a basement playroom. During the dry winter season, they replaced the carpets and put the house on the market.

They were showing it to a very interested buyer, and when they went to the playroom the potential buyer mentioned that the carpet looked new.

"Sure," the small daughter replied, "the old carpet got wet every time it rained."

This came as a shock, since the couple had skillfully avoided any mention of a water problem. The buyer left, but not without a thorough discussion of ethics and Christianity.

You see, the couple selling the home was a well-known pastor and his wife. Later he told me, "We allowed our personal needs to choke out our spiritual values. God simply used the honesty of a young child to expose us."

The truth revealed will make you truly free; concealing facts will make you a captive of your own hypocrisy.

"Do not let kindness and truth leave you; . . .write them on the tablet of your heart. So you will find favor and good repute in the sight of God and man" (Proverbs 3:3–4).

DAILY SCRIPTURE READING: Matthew 1:1-17; Mark 1:1;
Luke 1:1-4, 3:23-38; John 1:1-18

WHAT FAULTS?

"Who regards you as superior?
And what do you have that you did not receive?
But if you did receive it,
why do you boast as if you had not received it"
(1 Corinthians 4:7).

IN order to cure a disease, we must first be able to recognize its symptoms, which are visible, outside indicators. Although we may not always recognize these symptoms in ourselves, others will. So it becomes vital for us to stay open to criticism, particularly from those who are spiritually discerning.

The people most consistent in discerning our faults are usually our spouses. God has placed them in our lives as a balance, and they will help to offset our extremes if we will listen.

This works both ways, because we also are balance for them. I'll have to say that more often than not it is the husband who refuses to take counsel from his wife. Why? Pride.

Once we are trapped by pride, we can be of no service to God. We must accept criticism, humble ourselves, call on His mercy and forgiveness.

Make me aware, Father, of any pride in my life, and help me to overcome it.

DAILY SCRIPTURE READING: Luke 1:5-80

COVETOUSNESS

"You shall not covet your neighbor's wife
or his male servant or his female servant
or his ox or his donkey or anything
that belongs to your neighbor"
(Exodus 20:17).

COVETOUSNESS is desiring to have what belongs to others—the proverbial "keeping up with the Joneses." This attitude rears its head when we begin comparing ourselves with others.

We tend to measure our successes against the achievements of friends or family or even fellow church members. Often career choices are made, based on gaining the status, income, or prestige others have, rather than what is truly best.

To avoid covetousness, take the long-term view: Understand that God has a unique plan for you. Fulfillment comes by seeking His will and His way and following His plan. You'll only reap frustration when you covet the ways of someone else.

Remember, *"This you know with certainty, that no immoral or impure person or covetous man, who is an idolater, has an inheritance in the kingdom of Christ and God"* (Ephesians 5:5).

Lord, show me if there is any covetousness in me.

DAILY SCRIPTURE READING: Matthew 1:18-2:23; Luke 2

A CLEAN HEART

"Create in me a clean heart,
O God, and renew a steadfast spirit within me"
(Psalm 51:10).

WE read in Jeremiah 17:9 that our hearts are desperately wicked. Our hearts need the change that comes from receiving grace, which is a free gift from God. Grace is literally the divine influence on the heart and is reflected in the lives we live.

The heart wants its way, but there are many times when we should not follow the leading of our hearts.

Having a clean heart will come from praying for the Holy Spirit to guide you in all your attitudes and actions.

"[Jesus] *said, 'Not all of you are clean'* " (John 13:11).

DAILY SCRIPTURE READING: Matthew 3:1-4:11;
Mark 1:2-13; Luke 3:1-22, 4:1-13; John 1:19-34

GET RICH QUICK

"A man with an evil eye hastens after wealth,
and does not know that want will come upon him"
(Proverbs 28:22).

THE basic premise of all get-rich-quick schemes is to make a lot of money with very little effort—fast! A typical get-rich-quick "opportunity" involves investing in an area you know little or nothing about. It leads you to risk money you can't afford to lose and forces you to make snap decisions. Most of the time this leads to "get-poor-quicker" instead of get-rich-quick.

You can avoid falling into a get-rich-quick snare if you will set a minimum time to pray and seek God's direction, never risk money you can't afford to lose, never become involved with things you don't understand, demand enough information for a thorough evaluation, and seek counsel from knowledgeable and impartial Christians.

Be a good steward of what God has entrusted to you.

"Let no man deceive himself. If any man among you thinks that he is wise in this age, let him become foolish that he may become wise. For the wisdom of this world is foolishness before God. For it is written, 'He is the One Who catches the wise in their craftiness'" (1 Corinthians 3:18-19).

DAILY SCRIPTURE READING: John 1:35-3:36

A WILLING MIND

*"If the willingness is there, the gift is acceptable according to
what one has, not according to what he does not have"*
(2 Corinthians 8:12).

"PASTOR, if I just had a million dollars, I would really help you and
this church," remarked a church member. Have you ever said that
or something similar?

Today's Scripture verse tells us that God isn't concerned with
what we would do if we had a million dollars; rather, He's concerned with the way we are using what money we do have.

I vividly remember the first time I put $5 of my own in the
church offering. My friend quietly pointed out how much lunch
that money would have bought. If the plate had come back our way
I probably would have retrieved the $5 and dropped in a few coins.

Later, I learned that God's acceptance of our deeds is based on
a willing mind that acts obediently in spite of the feelings of a
wicked heart. My mind was obedient, and God changed my heart.

Throughout Scripture a change of heart is preceded by a change
of mind. When we, in obedience to God's Word, humble ourselves
mentally, then God is able to change our hearts by His grace.

The mind of Christ has taught me that there is always a struggle to give, not just in the giving of money but of myself in service.

Our lives can show forth Christ if we have willing and obedient minds.

King David said to his son Solomon: *"Know the God of your
father, and serve Him with a whole heart and a willing mind; for the
Lord searches all hearts, and understands every intent of the thoughts"*
(1 Chronicles 28:9).

DAILY SCRIPTURE READING: Matthew 4:12-17;
Mark 1:14-15; Luke 4:14-30; John 4

TWO WAYS TO VIEW WEALTH

"Because you. . .did not ask for riches, wealth, or honor. . .
but you have asked for yourself wisdom and knowledge. . .
wisdom and knowledge have been granted to you.
And I will give you riches and wealth and honor"
(2 Chronicles 1:11–12).

To most people being wealthy means having an abundance of money. However, this falls short of what God's Word describes as true wealth.

The worldly view of money is temporal. The biblical meaning is not restricted to money and earthly possessions. It goes far beyond the temporal values to include heavenly and eternal riches.

In Acts 5 we read about Ananias and Sapphira, shortsighted Christians who failed to realize the meaning of wealth and allowed Satan to fill their hearts with evil. As a result of their actions, they died.

On the other hand, Solomon wasn't concerned with earthly wealth and, instead, asked for wisdom to rule God's people. Because he wasn't greedy, God gave him what he didn't ask for—riches and wealth.

True wealth is never obtained by greed or selfishness; only the world's wealth is achieved that way. God's wealth is gained through ministering to others, and it lasts forever.

If you were given the choice between wisdom and wealth, which would you choose? How wealthy are you? What is the source of your wealth?

DAILY SCRIPTURE READING: Matthew 4:18-25, 8:2-4, 14-17;
Mark 1:16-45; Luke 4:31-5:16

CHRISTIAN TESTIMONY

*"My dishonor is before me,
and my humiliation has overwhelmed me,
because of the voice of him who reproaches and reviles"*
(Psalm 44:15–16).

I MET a man years ago who was using some very unethical practices in his life. In fact, I met him as a result of counseling another Christian who had just finished a real estate transaction with this man and had been cheated.

In the course of having lunch one day with the man who had cheated, I challenged him, telling him that I knew what he'd done and asking why, as a Christian, he would willfully deceive another Christian.

"Well," he said, "that's just a bad habit of mine, but I don't let anyone know I'm a Christian, because I don't want to reflect my bad image on Jesus Christ." In other words, he thought it was all right to be dishonest and deceitful as long as no one knew he was a Christian.

It is not all right for any Christian to do that. God requires us to be honest and tell the truth, with no exaggerations and without leaving out any pertinent details.

A Christian testimony is necessary, in every aspect of our lives, if God is going to be able to use us in an effective way.

"He who walks in a blameless way is the one who will minister to me" (Psalm 101:6).

Lord, help me to walk daily in a blameless way so that I can be a Christian witness for You.

DAILY SCRIPTURE READING: Matthew 9:1-17;
Mark 2:1-22; Luke 5:17-39

GIVE HONOR

"Do nothing from selfishness or empty conceit,
but with humility of mind let each of you
regard one another as more important than himself"
(Philippians 2:3).

IF you are an employer, do you give honor to those who work for you? Or does your employer give honor to you as an employee?

I'm afraid we believe that unless we elevate ourselves above others we are failures. The "Indian/Chief" principle was not established by God. There is no caste system in God's family.

If you are a supervisor or manager, are you building up or tearing down people? Are you trying to honor them? The word honor means to give a position of worth. That doesn't mean you have to pay them as much as you make. The amount is between you and the Lord.

What it does mean is that you honor them by showing the people who are making lower salaries that they are as important to the success of the business as the salespeople who are generating $1 million a year in income.

Another way to give honor is by controlling your tongue. For every fault you find in a person, you should look for two positive characteristics to build that person up. God says to give honor to those below us and above us.

God wants us to have compassion on the people around us, to care about them and to love them. There is no greater testimony a Christian can have in business than to show honor toward others.

Do you show honor to your employer (or to your employees)? Pray about what changes you can make in this area.

DAILY SCRIPTURE READING: Matthew 12:1-21;
Mark 2:23-3:12; Luke 6:1-11; John 5

THE APOSTLE PAUL

"The Lord said to [Ananias], *'Go, for he is a chosen instrument
of Mine, to bear My name before the Gentiles
and kings and the sons of Israel"*
(Acts 9:15).

MY favorite person in the New Testament, outside of the Lord, is the apostle Paul. He's my kind of guy. I think Paul probably had the same personality type I do: "D," dominant, decision maker. It could be said of us both: "often wrong, but never in doubt."

Paul was impetuous and charged ahead, and whatever God told Paul to do, he did it. On his last journey into Jerusalem, the Christians begged Paul to stay because the prophet Agabus said Paul was going to be bound and cast into prison.

Paul's response was, "Why do you break my heart so? Don't you know that God has also told me this? I must do what God has told me to do."

I admire Paul for his boldness, his ability to speak up for the Lord but, also, for his humility. He never thought more highly of himself than he should have.

I believe all of his characteristics made him useful to the Lord. I love the concise writings of Paul, which fill a large part of the New Testament.

He was a man who liked to pay his own way and was willing to suffer whatever it took to serve the Lord.

Paul said of himself, *"I can do all things through Him who strengthens me"* (Philippians 4:13). Are you claiming this for yourself?

DAILY SCRIPTURE READING: Matthew 5;
Mark 3:13-19; Luke 6:12-36

JUST A LITTLE MORE

"Do not seek what you shall eat, and what you shall drink,
and do not keep worrying"
(Luke 12:29).

WE have the greatest abundance of material things in the entire world. It's not the lack of things that concerns us; it is the worry about the lack of things.

I recall a story I heard about a fellow in India who was starving. He couldn't feed his family so he began to pray, "Oh God, I ask You to give us what we need this day. Give us just one fish, Lord, and we'll be satisfied." That day he went to a rice paddy with a bent hook, dropped it into a rice paddy, and pulled out a fish. A miracle.

After the fish was gone he began to pray that God would give him a fish every day and then he would not have a need again. Every day he pulled out a fish. A miracle.

It began to rain and his roof leaked. He asked God to provide him with materials to fix the roof. A truck came by one day and some tin fell off. It kept the rain out of his house and he was thankful.

Then he prayed, "Lord, I thank You for the fish and for the tin for my roof. Now, God, if I just had a three-bedroom, two-bath house, with two cars, a color television, and a good education for my children, then, God, I wouldn't ask You for anything else."

Of course, the story is fictitious, but does it remind you in any way of yourself? Are you ever satisfied with what you have or do you always want more? Just a little more?

"His eyes were not satisfied with riches. . . . This too is vanity and it is a grievous task" (Ecclesiastes 4:8).

DAILY SCRIPTURE READING: Matthew 6-7; Luke 6:37-49

OCTOBER 11

JUST A LITTLE EXTRA

*"The deceitfulness of riches, and the desires for other things enter in
and choke the word, and it becomes unfruitful"*
(Mark 4:19).

DR. Brown had been the pastor of one of the larger churches in
the city for only three months but had brought some fine messages
that were an encouragement to many church members.

One afternoon, Dr. Brown went through the checkout line
of one of the local grocery stores. He did not recognize the cashier
as a member of his church and the cashier didn't identify himself.

After leaving the store, Dr. Brown realized that he had
received $20 more in change than he should have. But being in a
hurry, he got in his car and went on his way. Almost immediately
the $20 began to haunt him. The next day he returned the money
to the cashier and explained what had happened. The cashier simply took the money and said, "Yes, I know. Thank you."

After the service the following Sunday morning, the pastor
was greeting the people as they left the church. One of the hands
he shook was that same grocery cashier, who said, "Pastor, I know
now that you believe what you preach."

The deceitfulness of riches did not destroy the fruitfulness of
Dr. Brown's testimony to the cashier who belonged to his church.

How sad it is when we allow ourselves to be caught in Satan's
snares—even small ones. Just a little extra change we don't return
can destroy our testimony.

Have you ever taken something that doesn't belong to you?
Kept extra change? Taken office supplies home? How did you feel
about it? Have you allowed it to *"choke the word"*?

DAILY SCRIPTURE READING:
Matthew 8:1, 5-13; 11:2-30; Luke 7

OCTOBER 12

CHRISTOPHER COLUMBUS

"Blessed is the nation whose God is the Lord,
the people whom He has chosen for His own inheritance"
(Psalm 33:12).

HISTORICALLY we have celebrated Columbus Day to honor Christopher Columbus as the explorer who is credited for having discovered America.

If you read your history books, however, you'll find that long before Columbus arrived America had been discovered by the Nordic tribes who visited America regularly—as far back as about A.D. 1000.

You probably learned the same rhyme in school that I did—"In 1492 Columbus sailed the ocean blue"—but do you remember why he faced peril to discover another continent? We are told that he was searching for a new, shorter trade route to the Dutch West Indies.

However, I've read parts of the reprint of Columbus' diary and it reveals something else. He had heard reports from some of the other navigators that there was another continent in the northern part of the hemisphere, and he believed it was his responsibility to reach that continent with the Lord's plan of salvation.

His diary, as you read it, reflects a devout Christian who daily sought the Lord both in Scripture and in prayer. Isn't it a shame that in our schools today none of that is reflected in our history books?

Was this God's way of reseeding Christianity—by sending Christopher Columbus? Was this God's method of bringing the Word to the New World? I believe it was. We are the most Christian nation in the world and God has used us as no other nation.

Join me in paying tribute to this brave Christian.

DAILY SCRIPTURE READING:
Matthew 12:22-50; Mark 3:20-35; Luke 8:1-21

WHY SOME CHRISTIANS FAIL

*"Commit your works to the Lord,
and your plans will be established"*
(Proverbs 16:3).

MANY people believe that whatever they can conceive and believe they can achieve. This kind of positive thinking and success motivation require goal setting, to which those people attribute the successes in their lives.

However, all too often these goals are centered on personal success, and the plans to accomplish them become selfish and ultimately self-defeating.

In 1 Corinthians 13, God tells us that whatever is done for self is profitless, and only that which is done out of love will benefit self. This creates a paradox: To be successful we must make someone else successful; to be leaders, we must be servants.

In order for our plans to be established, our works must be committed to God. It is evident that selfish goals cannot be committed to God—only unselfish ones.

Therefore, the prerequisite for receiving God's help in our planning is the commitment of the end result to God. The problem is that many works cannot be committed to God because of their very nature. At that point, Christians rob themselves of God's help. To paraphrase James 4:3: We ask and don't receive because we ask with wrong motives.

The answer to whether you will succeed or fail is found in today's Scripture verse in Proverbs. Read it prayerfully.

PUBLIC TELEVISION

"He who is spiritual appraises all things"
(1 Corinthians 2:15).

SHOULD we help support public television if we watch some of the programs on it and yet find some of the others offensive and anti-Christian?

I was watching an excellent program on public television when they came on asking for support and I considered sending money. Then a program came on supporting evolution—men evolving from apes—and I had to ask myself: Can I support this station?

I prayed about it and came to a decision that might help you, if this is an issue for you. I believe you either have to help support public television or stop watching it. It isn't right to be a hypocrite—watch it but not support it.

One of the reasons the humanist element of our society can take over is because they are willing to support what they believe in. Christians end up losing because we won't support something that isn't 100 percent what we believe; so, therefore, we end up not having any input.

If you are a regular supporter of a television station and you write in your objections, the station managers will take heed. You'll have their attention if money is involved.

The apostle Paul always made it a point to pay his own way (2 Corinthians 11:9), and I believe we should pay our own way. You can't have a voice unless you participate.

"The things which are seen are temporal, but the things which are not seen are eternal" (2 Corinthians 4:18).

DAILY SCRIPTURE READING: Matthew 8:18, 23-24, 9:18-34;
Mark 4:35-5:43; Luke 8:22-56

CHRISTIAN BUSINESS

"Just as you abound in everything,
in faith and utterance and knowledge
and in all earnestness and in the love. . . ,
see that you abound in this gracious work also"
(2 Corinthians 8:7).

THE goal of Christian businesspeople should be to use their organizations as vehicles to share Christ with other people.

Businesspeople should be Christ's representatives to employees, to creditors, and to customers.

Also the minimum expected from a Christian business must be a quality product or service at a fair price. Sadly, not all Christian organizations measure up to this standard. It's small wonder that so many unbelievers have a bad perspective of Christianity.

If a Christian businesses don't have excellence, they will not be able to witness to the customers.

Though there's nothing specifically mentioned in God's Word about it, I'm sure Paul made the best tents and Jesus, the carpenter's son, made excellent furniture. We can do no less.

"Do you see a man skilled in his work? He will stand before kings; he will not stand before obscure men" (Proverbs 22:29).

DAILY SCRIPTURE READING: Matthew 13:54-58, 9:35-11:1, 14:1-12; Mark 6:1-30; Luke 9:1-10

OCTOBER 16

BALANCE IN MARRIAGE

"On the day I called Thou didst answer me;
Thou didst make me bold with strength in my soul"
(Psalm 138:3).

MY greatest strength as a husband is being a Christian. I shudder to think what my life, or Judy's, might be like today if I had not accepted Jesus Christ as Lord of my life.

I believe it takes God's wisdom to be a Christian leader in your home. If I didn't know Christ, I would likely be leading my children and grandchildren down the wrong path.

Another strength God has developed in me is the willingness to serve my family. I don't mind doing the dishes; in fact, I do them pretty regularly. I also cook and iron clothes as well as anybody.

One of my weaknesses is that I tend to clam up when Judy and I get into an argument. Judy's probably the only person in the world who can really hurt my feelings, because she knows me so well. When she does, I tend to pout, hoping she'll recognize what she's done and apologize.

Achieving balance is an important goal in any marriage. If two people are similar, one of them isn't necessary. I believe God puts opposites together. That's certainly the case in our lives. The areas in which I have strengths, Judy has weaknesses, and vice versa. And I believe that's as it should be.

If a husband and wife will pray and ask for God's help, they can work through any differences and find the balance that He intended in marriage.

"Humility and reverence for the Lord will make you both wise and honored" (Proverbs 15:33 TLB).

DAILY SCRIPTURE READING: Matthew 14:13-36;
Mark 6:31-56; Luke 9:11-17; John 6:1-21

SHOULD I HAVE FEAR?

"[God] alone is my refuge, my place of safety;
he is my God, and I am trusting him"
(Psalm 91:2 TLB).

FEAR has a very useful function. If you didn't have fear, you'd be roadkill.

I have a friend who has no fear of physical peril, and it's a real detriment to him. In his lifetime, he's probably had 200 broken bones and is a terror to be around.

He goes hang gliding in the Alps, jumps off buildings, scuba dives in underwater caves, jumps motorcycles for fun—crazy things.

We are supposed to fear some things. However, there are some people who live in dread and fear, and that's wrong too. They let fear control their lives.

There should be a healthy balance for fear in your life. You should have a cautious regard for your own safety but not enough to let it control your life.

The writer of Hebrews says, *"Since we, God's children, are human beings...he became flesh and blood too.... Only in that way could he deliver those who through fear of death have been living all their lives as slaves to constant dread"* (Hebrews 2:14–15 TLB).

DAILY SCRIPTURE READING:
Matthew 15:1-20; Mark 7:1-23; John 6:22-7:1

FEAR OF THE LORD

"The fear of the Lord is the beginning of wisdom"
(Psalm 111:10).

WE know that *"perfect love casts out fear"* (1 John 4:18), so you would think that there would be no place for persistent fear. We are assured time and again in God's Word that we do not need to fear the future; He will take care of us.

But what about another kind of fear—fear of God? Do I fear God? Oh yes, but it is the kind of fear that is the beginning of wisdom. You can replace the word "fear" with "reverence" or "awe." We should be in awe of God: His power, His love, His grace, His compassion. How could we not be in awe of Him?

As believers, we should have that kind of fear, which is actually reverence for God.

Then there's the fear of God's judgment. *"Justice for man comes from the Lord"* (Proverbs 29:26). *"We shall all stand before the judgment seat of God"* (Romans 14:10).

I believe I would sum it all up by quoting yet another verse: *"The fear of the Lord prolongs life, but the years of the wicked will be shortened"* (Proverbs 10:27).

God said it. I believe it!

DAILY SCRIPTURE READING: Matthew 15:21-16:20;
Mark 7:24-8:30; Luke 9:18-21

FEAR OF SIN

"All that is in the world,
the lust of the flesh and the lust of the eyes
and the boastful pride of life,
is not from the Father, but is from the world"
(1 John 2:16).

WE all have different weaknesses or propensities toward sin. As the apostle Paul said in Timothy, if you know something is a problem for you, stay away from it.

I had a friend whose weakness was alcohol. He was a good father, husband, and provider. He had a brother who was unsaved and, in an effort to win his brother to the Lord, my friend would go where his brother was—in bars.

My friend said, "I'll just drink soft drinks while I'm there." A few weeks passed and someone offered him a beer. Months passed, and the next time I saw him he was a falling-down drunk. He should have had a fear of his weakness. If he had, he likely would never have fallen back into sin.

Good judgment is of great value when dealing with sin. If you have a weakness, fear it and avoid it.

"I urge you. . . to abstain from fleshly lusts, which wage war against the soul" (1 Peter 2:11).

DAILY SCRIPTURE READING: Matthew 16:21-17:27;
Mark 8:31-9:32; Luke 9:22-45

OCTOBER 20

LOYALTY

"A friend loves at all times,
and a brother is born for adversity"
(Proverbs 17:17).

ALTHOUGH I've taught and written a lot about integrity being important, there is another characteristic that is vital in living: loyalty. Loyalty seems to be a lost art in our society. When people are in the midst of adversity, all too often others tend to abandon them.

Webster says that to be loyal means to be "unswerving in allegiance" and to be "faithful to a person, cause, ideal, custom, institution, or product."

Christians have a reputation for being a group that "kills their wounded." When people are down, we tend to judge them instead of help them.

Even if people have brought the trouble on themselves, God's Word teaches that we are to act in love. It says that if we see someone in need and have the ability to help and don't, how can we say that the love of God abides in us?

In the Old Testament Absalom asked Hushai: *"Is this your loyalty to your friend? Why did you not go with your friend?"* (2 Samuel 16:17).

Certainly integrity should be a minimum requirement in Christians, but the second most valuable quality is loyalty.

To whom can you show your loyalty today?

Don't forget, Jesus said, *"A new commandment I give to you, that you love one another, even as I have loved you, that you also love one another"* (John 13:34).

DAILY SCRIPTURE READING: Matthew 18; 8:19-22;
Mark 9:33-50; Luke 9:46-62; John 7:2-10

FORGIVING OTHERS

"If you do not forgive,
neither will your Father who is in heaven
forgive your transgressions"
(Mark 11:26).

ONE of the most commonly taught principles in the Bible is that of forgiveness. If we expect to be forgiven of our own sins, we have to forgive others who have sinned against us.

There have been times when I had difficulty forgiving people who offended me. At the end of the day I might have mouthed words of forgiveness, and yet I knew in my heart that I really hadn't forgiven them because I hadn't forgotten the offenses.

The way to work through that problem is to continue praying until you do forget the offense.

If, as today's Scripture verse says, we fail to forgive those who hurt or offend us, then God will not forgive us our sins either. It doesn't leave much choice, does it?

In the New Testament, Luke said it clearly: *"If your brother sins, rebuke him; and if he repents, forgive him"* (Luke 17:3).

DAILY SCRIPTURE READING: John 7:11-8:59

ESTHER'S COMMITMENT

"The young lady was beautiful of form and face. . . .
And Esther found favor in the eyes of all who saw her"
(Esther 2:7, 15).

THERE are many people in the Old Testament that I admire, but a woman I greatly admire is Esther.

As you read in today's Scripture verse, she was a young, beautiful woman. But that's not all. If you'll read the book of Esther you'll find that she was willing to risk everything, including her life, to do what God wanted her to do.

It isn't often that you see that kind of commitment. Of course, there are other characters we can admire: Shadrach, Meshach, Abed-nego, Daniel, David, Moses, Abraham.

But Esther was outstanding because she wasn't an authority figure. She was a figure of submission, in total subjugation to the authority over her (her husband, the king).

I believe this is a perfect picture of what God wants us to be as Christians: bold, courageous, and totally submissive.

Take the time to read the book of Esther. You'll be blessed by her courage and faith. Would you have had her commitment?

DAILY SCRIPTURE READING: Luke 10:1-11:36

BUSINESS BONDAGE

*"Lord, my heart is not proud. . .nor do I involve myself in
great matters, or in things too difficult for me"*
(Psalm 131:1).

BUSINESS bondage is anything that disrupts your priority system
as a Christian. If you are a stay-at-home wife and your husband is
in business, you are a part of that business with him. God created
you as a working unit, so you need to understand God's principles
and then help your husband.

A Christian's priority system should begin with an active,
viable personal relationship with Jesus Christ. That means reading
and getting truth and direction from God's Word on a regular
basis. It also means communicating with and praying to God.

Any Christian who is so involved with business that he or
she has no time to study God's Word, to pray, or to get involved
with other people and their needs is in bondage.

Also, a Christian who is unable to communicate and meet
the needs of his or her spouse is in business bondage.

Third, a Christian must be able to meet the needs of his or
her children. We are responsible for the training of our children,
and if we fail in raising our children God is not pleased.

Being in balance with the world's system is risky, because the
world has never been in balance with God's system.

If you or your spouse are required to work 10, 12, or 14 hours
a day to do a good job, to make more money, or just to get ahead,
watch out. That's bondage.

If you are in bondage, because of business or for any other
reason, ask God to help you bring balance into your life today.

DAILY SCRIPTURE READING: Luke 11:37-13:21

AN HONORABLE MAN

"Honor all men; love the brotherhood, fear God, honor the king"
(1 Peter 2:17).

IF I could meet any man in history, there are several I would choose. One would be Albert Einstein, a born-again believer and one of the most brilliant men who ever lived. But, if I could meet only one person, outside of the Lord Himself, it would be Robert E. Lee.

I have read the diary of Robert E. Lee and many articles about him, and he was one of the most honest, moral men who ever graced the face of the earth.

Lee was a born-again believer, who put his commitment to the Lord and to his men above everything else. He was a gracious southern gentleman who had been thrust into a position he neither wanted nor desired: leading the southern forces during the Civil War.

Some might think it strange that I would want to meet a defeated general, but you only have to read his diary to see what a remarkable man he was.

Lee, unlike most of the generals throughout time, never slept in a building during the Civil War; he slept in a tent like his men. When his beloved daughter was dying, he refused to leave the battlefield, since he couldn't allow his men with family situations to leave.

After the war was over he could have made millions of dollars, based on his reputation, but he refused to profit from the misery of other people. When he allowed his name to be associated with Washington and Lee College, he did so only under the agreement that if the college ever stopped teaching the principles of Jesus, it would dissolve its charter.

Which honorable person would you most like to meet?

DAILY SCRIPTURE READING: John 9-10

MAGNIFICENCE

"Get yourself up on a high mountain,
O Zion, bearer of good news,
lift your voice mightily,
O Jerusalem, bearer of good news"
(Isaiah 40:9).

I LOVE mountains. I was born in Florida, in absolutely flatland. I knew I wasn't born for flatland; I just had never seen a mountain until I left Florida at age 19.

After I saw my first mountain, in North Carolina, I knew I was going to live in the mountains or at least in the mountainous terrain the rest of my life. And most of the time I have.

I marvel at how beautiful and majestic the mountains are and how insignificant we are when compared to God's creation.

When I'm standing on the top of a mountain and I look out over God's creation, I think of how amazing it is, how magnificent, and what a loving God He is to have created something this wonderful for us.

We have been given so much to appreciate, and we should spend more time being aware of God's creation, enjoying it, and praising God for it.

"The blessings of your father have surpassed the blessings of my ancestors up to the utmost bound of the everlasting hills" (Genesis 49:26).

Praise God from whom all blessings flow!

A JOYFUL HEART

"A joyful heart is good medicine,
but a broken spirit dries the bones"
(Proverbs 17:22).

THE name "Yahweh" is actually an American attempt to say a word that can't be pronounced. The word is "yhwh," with no vowels. So the closest we can come to pronouncing it is to say Yahweh.

Interestingly enough, when you say that over and over, it sounds like laughter. Laughter is universal, and it is the name of God. God is the God of Abraham, Isaac (which means laughter) and Jacob—the God of laughter!

There are many purposes for laughter, but the primary purpose would be to heal our souls, our spirits, and even to heal us physically. Science is now learning that when we laugh, we release endorphins, which help heal our bodies and stimulate our immune systems.

It's important for each of us to have a good sense of humor and be able to even laugh at ourselves sometimes. It makes it easier to go through difficult times.

I believe God gave us laughter to gladden our souls. If we are going to be "light" to the unsaved, we must act like we are happy with what we have.

"He will yet fill your mouth with laughter, and your lips with shouting" (Job 8:21).

DAILY SCRIPTURE READING: Luke 16:1-17:10; John 11:1-54

LEARN FROM CHILDREN

"Your wife shall be like a fruitful vine,
within your house, your children
like olive plants around your table"
(Psalm 128:3).

IF you never have children, you can pretty well do whatever you want with your money, your time, and your life. But when you have children, you no longer have that right. You give of your time and your resources.

With my own children, I think I've learned patience. I've also learned about love, because I find that they love me no matter what I do, and I love them no matter what. I've learned companionship.

I enjoyed my children when they were young, but now that they are adults I feel like they are my companions, more than my wards. I enjoy our conversations and just being around them.

I especially enjoy the fact that they have children; being a grandparent is the greatest. I can play with the grandchildren, have a wonderful time, and then give them back to their parents.

I've learned a lot about God through my children, as I have watched the glorious creation that starts so small and, despite the trips to the hospital's emergency room, grows to a mature adult.

I trust that, as a result of having children, when I leave this life I will have left a legacy to the next generation.

"I will put my trust in Him. . . . I and the children whom God has given Me" (Hebrews 2:13).

DAILY SCRIPTURE READING: Matthew 19:1-15;
Mark 10:1-16; Luke 17:11-18:17

BLESSED BY GOD

"All these blessings shall come upon you and overtake you,
if you will obey the Lord your God. . . .
Blessed shall be the offspring of your body"
(Deuteronomy 28:2, 4).

I'VE been blessed with nine grandchildren so far, and I've learned something from them that we all know academically, but I've seen it manifested physically and spiritually: Perfect love casts out fear.

Perfect love does conquer everything. I love my grandchildren unreservedly. I don't approve of everything they do, and that's okay; they are individuals.

But I love them and, because I do, they know that I love them, and we have a relationship unlike any other that I've had.

To me it is the nearest parallel to how our Heavenly Father feels about us, His children (He has no grandchildren, you know —just children).

My grandchildren absolutely trust me and want to be with me, and even when I correct them they accept that. They don't get mad at me and I don't get mad at them.

If all of us could love and accept one another the same way grandparents love and unconditionally accept their grandchildren, we would never have any problems with other human beings.

"Be like-minded, live in peace; and the God of love and peace shall be with you" (2 Corinthians 13:11).

DAILY SCRIPTURE READING: Matthew 19:16-20:28;
Mark 10:17-45; Luke 18:18-34

POOR IN SPIRIT

"Blessed are the poor in spirit,
for theirs is the kingdom of heaven"
(Matthew 5:3).

WHEN I think about the poor in spirit I think of the contrast between the humble and the haughty.

Jesus was not talking about the physically poor but those who were humble. Since He said, "Blessed are the poor in spirit," then He probably would have said, "Cursed are the haughty in spirit."

In fact, He did say that. He told us in His Word that to the extent you exalt yourself in this lifetime you will be humbled for all of eternity.

If we humble ourselves in true service to God, it will include being servants in the true sense of the word, not just to Him but to those around us.

I think the perfect example of being poor in spirit (humble) is when Jesus washed the disciples' feet.

Our humility can be shown in taking a less prominent position at church but giving it all we've got. It means being willing to sit back and let someone else take the credit for what we've done without being resentful.

I appreciate the verse in Proverbs that says, *"Before honor comes humility"* (Proverbs 15:33).

DAILY SCRIPTURE READING: Matthew 20:29-34, 26:6-13;
Mark 10:46-52, 14:3-9; Luke 18:35-19:28; John 11:55-12:11

OCTOBER 30

WRONG DECISION

"The word of the Lord came to Jonah. . .
saying, 'Arise, go to Nineveh the great city,
and cry against it,
for their wickedness has come up before Me' "
(Jonah 1:1–2).

WE are servants of the Most High God and He has the right to tell us what to do. When He told Jonah to go to Nineveh, He was saying, "Do what I tell you to."

When one of my sons didn't like something I told him to do, he said, "Dad, this isn't a very democratic way to run this family." Then I reminded him that in our home he didn't live in a democracy; he lived in a benevolent dictatorship.

I think God was teaching Jonah another lesson besides obedience: that God loves all of His creation, the good and the bad.

Jonah suspected when God sent him to Nineveh He was going to forgive the Ninevites, and Jonah didn't want to go. Instead, he chose another direction and suffered for it.

So, God taught Jonah two lessons: "Do what you are told." And "I get to decide who is forgiven and who isn't."

"When God saw their deeds, that they turned from their wicked way, then God relented concerning the calamity which He had declared He would bring upon them. And He did not do it" (Jonah 3:10).

DAILY SCRIPTURE READING: Matthew 21:1-22;
Mark 11:1-26; Luke 19:29-48; John 12:12-50

WHAT CONTROLS YOU?

"A man is a slave to whatever controls him"
(2 Peter 2:19 TLB).

THE things we value most usually reflect our spiritual condition, because in essence what we do is who we are and what we believe.

God's Word says, *"You are controlled by your new nature if you have the Spirit of God living in you"* (Romans 8:9 TLB).

I'm a very practical person and I try to live by the principles I teach: self-control, discipline, caring for other people, and being a good steward of my resources.

What we do is an outside manifestation of who we are inside.

I complained to my spiritual mentor one time, "Boy, can my wife make me angry!"

He said, "No, your wife doesn't make you angry. She only brings out the anger that's hidden inside."

God is more concerned with what you do than what you say.

James wrote, *"Prove yourselves doers of the word, and not merely hearers who delude themselves"* (James 1:22).

DAILY SCRIPTURE READING: Matthew 21:23-22:14;
Mark 11:27-12:12; Luke 20:1-19

DISCOURAGEMENT

"Be strong and courageous,
do not fear or be dismayed. . . .
With us is the Lord our God to help us
and to fight our battles"
(2 Chronicles 32:7, 8).

I AM sometimes discouraged, but because of my personality I rarely stay that way for a long period of time. I generally try to stop, take a look at whatever is happening, and then come up with a new approach.

I like challenges. I really do better when there is a specific problem I can address. And the bigger the problem, the better I do. I seem to respond better to pressure.

If I see something that bothers me, I try to get involved. For a long time I despaired over what was happening to our country politically. I could see it going downhill—especially the morality in Washington.

So, I decided to get involved and dedicate some time, which I still do every election year. I help by putting on fund-raisers and by doing whatever I can to get the godly candidates elected.

Although we may get discouraged, there's no excuse for staying that way. Read today's Scripture verses in 2 Chronicles again and you'll see what I mean.

DAILY SCRIPTURE READING: Matthew 22:15-46;
Mark 12:13-37; Luke 20:20-44

DEEPER RELATIONSHIP

*"Just tell me what to do and I will do it, Lord.
As long as I live, I'll wholeheartedly obey"*
(Psalm 119:33 TLB).

FROM the first day that I accepted Christ as my Savior, I made this commitment to the Lord: "God, You know that I'm an ignorant person; I don't know a lot about You, so I only ask that whatever You want me to do You will make it very clear. As of this day, I pledge that I will never again be willfully disobedient."

The way to know more about God is by reading and studying His Word. You can't possibly know about Him unless you know what His Word says.

The way you get to know God personally is by spending time in prayer (talking to God). As I've said before, I've never heard His voice audibly, but I have sensed His presence many times, and I have sensed His direction.

God never gives direction in contrast to what He has already said in His Word. That is His will for us: His Word.

Just accepting Christ doesn't develop a personal relationship with the Lord. That would be like getting married and the two of you moving to opposite sides of the U.S. and not seeing one another for the next 50 years. You'd still be married, but you wouldn't have much of a relationship.

To deepen your relationship with God, get immersed in His Word (God speaking to you) and spend time in prayer (you speaking to God). It must be done one-on-one if you want it to be personal relationship.

DAILY SCRIPTURE READING: Matthew 23;
Mark 12:38-44; Luke 20:45-21:4

NATIONAL MORALITY

*"Righteousness exalts a nation,
but sin is a disgrace to any people"*
(Proverbs 14:34).

THE only way we, as God's people, are ever going to restore morality to government is by demanding morality of our elected leaders.

That means we have to promote people to office who have good moral values and who have Christian ethics in their lives.

I've heard the definition of character is what somebody does when nobody else is watching. And that's precisely who we need to elect to public office: people who will do the right things when we aren't watching them.

We can reestablish morality in government by requiring certain values of our politicians and then holding them to those standards.

Until we are willing to stand up and vote against immorality and support those who share God's value systems, we are never going to change the direction of our country.

Morality is in the hands of the people, and we are the people!

"Blessed is the nation whose God is the Lord, the people whom He has chosen for His own inheritance" (Psalm 33:12).

DAILY SCRIPTURE READING: Matthew 24:1-31;
Mark 13:1-27; Luke 21:5-27

Powerful Prayer

"The prayer of the upright is His delight"
(Proverbs 15:8).

When Jesus' disciples attempted to cast out a demon, they couldn't. Then Jesus came along and cast it out, and the disciples asked, "Lord, why were we unable to do this?"

Jesus replied, *"Only by prayer and fasting can you do this."* Our Lord knew prayer and fasting were necessary in His own life in order to do His father's bidding on the earth (see Luke 6:12).

Prayer must be an integral part of a Christian's life; it is an intergalactic, ballistic missile that can span oceans, deserts, mountains, and galaxies.

Faster than the speed of light, prayer travels at the speed of God.

You don't even have to know what to say. As the apostle Paul wrote, *"We do not know how to pray as we should, but the Spirit Himself intercedes for us with groanings too deep for words"* (Romans 8:26).

Abraham Lincoln expressed his thoughts on prayer: "I have been driven many times to my knees by the overwhelming conviction that I had nowhere to go but prayer. My own wisdom and that of all about me seemed insufficient for the day."

How powerful is your prayer life?

Daily Scripture Reading: Matthew 24:32-26:5, 14-16; Mark 13:28-14:2, 10-11; Luke 21:28-22:6

QUIET TIMES

"O Thou who dost hear prayer, to Thee all men come"
(Psalm 65:2).

SOMETIMES my life is so hectic that it is difficult for me to schedule quiet times, but I believe it is absolutely imperative for a continued spiritual walk with the Lord that we have these quiet times.

It was necessary for Jesus to withdraw from the crowds and go out alone to pray. So, how much more important must it be for us, Jesus' followers, to do the same?

If you are reading this devotion book regularly, you probably already have a quiet time, and that's great.

Generally, my quiet time is when I first awake in the morning. I try to wake up at least an hour before I have to start getting ready to go to the office.

It's during that time that I go through my prayer list and ask God to bless the people who are doing His work and heal those who are sick. On behalf of my family and friends who are unsaved, I ask Him to intercede supernaturally.

It's during those quiet times that I get my inspiration from God and certainly it is when I get the majority of my answers.

As many people do, I also pray as I drive my car. Sometimes I pray as I am walking (for exercise).

Without those quiet times, I believe that my relationship with God would deteriorate, so I make time for the quiet communion with God.

"The Lord your God is in your midst. . . . He will be quiet in His love, He will rejoice over you with shouts of joy" (Zephaniah 3:17).

DAILY SCRIPTURE READING: Matthew 26:17-29;
Mark 14:12-25; Luke 22:7-38; John 13

WHAT TO DO WITH ANGER

"If you are only angry, even in your own home,
you are in danger of judgment"
(Matthew 5:22 TLB).

THERE are different kinds of anger. The apostle Paul tells us that anger will bring the wrath of God and we should *"put. . . aside; anger, wrath, malice, slander, and abusive speech from your mouth"* (Colossians 3:8). He was referring to personal relationships.

In Ephesians Paul said, *"Be angry, and yet do not sin; do not let the sun go down on your anger, and do not give the devil an opportunity"* (Ephesians 4:26–27). I believe he was saying that we should be careful not to give Satan room to work while we are angry.

However, I believe that not all anger is bad. When we see what's happening to our country because of the filth in movies and television and through politicians who care more about their own personal security than they do this county, that makes me angry (maybe I should just call it righteous indignation!).

When I'm angry I do three things: I let some time pass, which allows me to think rationally; I confess my anger to God and ask Him to forgive me; and I ask God to help me be totally honest, kind, and polite, which has to happen supernaturally.

If you are harboring anger, you need to pray and ask God to forgive you and help you to forgive. Remember, part of the Lord's prayer says, *"Forgive us our debts, as we also have forgiven our debtors"* (Matthew 6:12).

DAILY SCRIPTURE READING: John 14, 15, 16

RESTRAINED ANGER

*"A wise man restrains his anger
and overlook insults.
This is to his credit"*
(Proverbs 19:11 TLB).

SINCE I've been in ministry, I've received many angry letters. Fortunately I've gotten a lot more kind and loving letters from people who appreciate what I do.

Sometimes when we do our live broadcast I step on some toes, especially salespeople's. So then I'll get an angry letter or two. My normal action is to get irritated, but I find that if I wait and pray about it, my irritation passes.

I put the offense aside and then respond to the people in the kindest way I can. I often cushion what I say by adding, "This is only my opinion."

It is better never to react to anger with anger, because in God's Word we are told that *"A gentle answer turns away wrath, but a harsh word stirs up anger"* (Proverbs 15:1).

Remember, kindness begets kindness.

DAILY SCRIPTURE READING: Matthew 26:30-46;
Mark 14:26-42; Luke 22:39-46; John 17:1-18:1

CELEBRITIES

"Charm is deceitful and beauty is vain,
but [the one] *who fears the Lord. . .shall be praised"*
(Proverbs 31:30).

WE have a tendency to make celebrities of people and treat them as if they were superior. I have a real problem with "celebrities." Some people have even tried to make a celebrity of me because I have written books or have radio programs. No way!

First, there's no special reward in Heaven for teaching or writing any more than for the person who cleans the church or keeps the nursery.

Some Christian "celebrities" have allowed themselves to have their egos enlarged, which eventually will destroy their usefulness to God. Why? Because the Lord told us that if we exalt ourselves, He will humble us.

In the secular world we idolize professional athletes and actors. Amazingly, we allow them to speak on topics they have no knowledge of. Many times their value systems are so distorted they give the wrong signals to our young people.

The best thing we can do for celebrities is pray for them—that God would put them under conviction to accept salvation. Also, we should not promote celebrities in front of our young people. Instead, build up the pastor—one who is true to the Word. Or find heroes in the past who had good values in their lives: George Washington, Abraham Lincoln, and the like.

Remember, we are all equal in God's sight. All He desires is for our hearts to be completely His (see 2 Chronicles 16:9).

DAILY SCRIPTURE READING: Matthew 26:47-75;
Mark 14:43-72; Luke 22:47-65; John 18:2-27

PRAISING GOD

"I will bless the Lord at all times;
His praise shall continually be in my mouth"
(Psalm 34:1).

To me, praising God is an integral part of the Christian walk, because it is acknowledging God's ownership over my life.

I believe that one fundamental principle established all through God's Word is that as we praise Him; we acknowledge Him as the omnipotent, omniscient, and omnipresent Creator.

When I think about praising God, my mind always goes back to the psalms of David; he continually praised God in song, in word, and in spirit. And, of David, God said he was a man after His own heart. David's praise was an expression of his love for the Creator.

In David's day, when a subject entered a king's presence, that person bowed—an acknowledgment of authority. When we get on our knees before God we are doing the same thing: acknowledging His total dominion over our lives.

It's easy to praise God when things are going well, isn't it? But, we must continue to praise Him in all circumstances, realizing that He expects our "sacrifice of thanksgiving."

"Let them also offer sacrifices of thanksgiving, and tell of His works with joyful singing" (Psalm 107:22).

DAILY SCRIPTURE READING: Matthew 27:1–26; Mark 15:1–15; Luke 22:66-23:25

ABORTION'S SPIRITUAL IMPACT

*"I have set before you today life and prosperity,
and death and adversity"*
(Deuteronomy 30:15).

OBVIOUSLY abortion is an abomination before the Lord. In my mind, there's no difference between aborting babies and forcing children to walk through fire that consumes them. The only difference is that one is alive in the womb; the other is alive outside the womb.

When the sanctity of life is ignored and the most helpless are killed, it reduces society to the level of animals.

To allow people to believe that the unborn is not really a human being is a lie. God said that He formed us—our innermost, hidden parts—even while we were in the womb.

Until we are willing to stand up as a people and eliminate abortion, I believe the spiritual character of our nation will continue to degrade.

Some Christians are secret abortionists. Although they profess that they are pro-life, in their hearts they believe that abortion does benefit society by getting rid of the poor, the nonproductive, and the handicapped, because it reduces the burden on all of society. To harbor these thoughts is to be an abortionist, because God's Word says that as you think in your heart, that's who you are.

All fetuses should have a chance at life. The psalmist said, *"Children are a gift of the Lord; the fruit of the womb is a reward"* (Psalm 127:3).

DAILY SCRIPTURE READING: Matthew 27:27-56;
Mark 15:16-41; Luke 23:26-49; John 19:1-30

VETERANS' DAY

*"Thou hast been a refuge for me,
a tower of strength against the enemy"*
(Psalm 61:3).

ALL through the history of our nation, God has helped us battle the enemies of freedom and democracy. As we read the history books we learn about those who shed their blood and paid the supreme sacrifice in the wars against tyranny.

On Veterans' Day we honor the distinguished living heroes—those who carry the honored title of "veteran."

Andrew Jackson wrote, "Every good citizen makes his country's honor his own and cherishes it not only as precious but as sacred. He is willing to risk his life in its defense and is conscious that he gains protection while he gives it."

I invite you to join U.S. Senate Chaplain Dr. Lloyd Ogilvie in his prayer for this day: "Today, on Veteran's Day, I want to express my debt of gratitude for them and to make this a day of prayer for our nation. I commit myself anew to the battle for the realization of Your vision for this nation. . . . Make me and all Americans seasoned veterans in the daily struggle for righteousness in our land."

DAILY SCRIPTURE READING: Matthew 27:57-28:8;
Mark 15:42-16:8; Luke 23:50-24:12; John 19:31-20:10

THE LOCAL CHURCH

"Stimulate one another to love and good deeds,
not forsaking our own assembling together. . .
encouraging one another"
(Hebrews 10:24–25).

I WILL forever be indebted to the first church I attended after getting saved: Park Avenue Baptist Church. That's where I was baptized and joined as a member.

I immediately joined the new member's class, where I learned all the basics of Christianity. As soon as I finished it, the pastor put me back in it—to teach the next group. That forced me to get into the Word in a real way and to put some earnest time in study and prayer.

Even though that first church meant a great deal to me, I can say the same about every church where I've been a member. It's a blessing, a spiritual haven.

I go to church, not just to be fed the Word by a godly man, which is very important, but I also go there to fellowship with God's people, which the writer of Hebrews talks about in today's verse.

Going to church is a visible symbol that the Lord is first in my life.

Many blessed friendships have developed as a result of being a part of a local church, and it is something that none of us should ever take for granted, because in many places in the world being a church member will mark you for death.

Let us never forget that and praise God for the religious freedom we enjoy.

DAILY SCRIPTURE READING: Matthew 28:9-20;
Mark 16:9-20; Luke 24:13-53; John 20:11-21:25

CHANGING MY NAME

"You are Peter [the rock],
and upon this rock I will build My church"
(Matthew 16:18).

JESUS called Peter "The Rock" because he was solid. Yes, he fell short many times (including denying Christ three times), but God saw beyond that, knew his heart, and recognized his value.

What would my name be if Jesus was going to change it? Well, sometimes I feel like it might be "Stupid," but I guess we all have times like that.

If I had a choice of what he would call me, it would be "Larry, the Faithful." Even though I sometimes fail to measure up to God's best, I try never to do anything that is disobedient to God's Word.

We read about David in the Old Testament and the terrible things he did, including adultery and murder. And yet, God looked back on David and said that David was a man after His own heart.

God is able to look past our actions and see our hearts. I trust that is what He is doing with me, because I do want to serve Him faithfully.

"It is required of stewards that one be found trustworthy [faithful]" (1 Corinthians 4:2).

What name do you think Jesus would give to you?

November 14

Learning from Pets

*"In God I have put my trust;
I shall not be afraid"*
(Psalm 56:4).

THERE is absolutely no question that you can learn a great deal from pets. It is interesting that many studies show that people who get along well with animals will also get along well with people.

About ten years ago I inherited a tabby cat that we call Tigger. There's nothing special about her, though I think she's a pretty intelligent cat. I say inherited because she belonged to my daughter, but Tigger decided to adopt me. (Cats decide whether or not they like you.)

Tigger sleeps right next to me or on top of me, if I will allow her to. One of the things I've learned from her and from other animals is unconditional love. We have a great time together and even play a game of hide-and-seek from time to time.

I could pick Tigger up and dangle her out over the balcony, if I wanted to (but never would do), and she would be perfectly at peace, because she knows I would not drop her. She trusts me and knows that I love her.

Doesn't that make a perfect picture of our relationship with our Father in heaven? No matter what happens, we can rest in His love and trust His judgment because we know that He loves us, wants what is best for us, and will take care of us—unconditionally.

DAILY SCRIPTURE READING: Acts 3, 4, 5

HE WORKS IT OUT

*"God causes all things to work together for good
to those who love God,
to those who are called according to His purpose"*
(Romans 8:28).

IN the years that I've been in ministry, I've traveled all over the world and back and forth across our country many times. One of the experiences sticks out in my mind as being an inspirational experience.

I went to California to speak at Campus Crusade for Christ, and someone was to meet me at the Los Angeles airport. When I went to the appointed place to meet my ride, no one showed up. I waited for perhaps an hour, and I knew the trip to Arrowhead Springs would be at least another hour and a half. I was getting a little frantic and perhaps a little irritated. I bowed my head and said, "God, You know I've never missed a speaking engagement and I don't want to miss this one. I know it's in Your will to find me a way there. Please do whatever has to be done."

When I looked up there was a young man standing there. He asked, "Are you John Smith?" After I told him who I was, it turned out that the person he had come to pick up didn't show up. He wasn't looking for me, nor I for him, but guess where he was going? Arrowhead Springs. God provided me a ride to the front door of where I was to speak.

It was an uplifting experience that reaffirmed how much God cares about anything and everything that concerns me.

Can you think of a time He blessed you in that way?

DAILY SCRIPTURE READING: Acts 6:1-8:1

Favorite Book

*"Let the word of Christ richly dwell within you,
with all wisdom teaching and admonishing one another"*
(Colossians 3:16).

My favorite book of the Bible is Proverbs. This is probably because I'm a very pragmatic, practical, and objective person, and the proverbs are perfectly suited for me.

One good thing, the proverbs cover a whole variety of topics, most of which are totally functional. In other words, you can read them and apply them.

They have been especially helpful in my line of teaching about borrowing, lending, saving, investing, whom to trust and not to trust, the importance of seeking counsel, where to seek counsel, how to judge good counsel—just practical things.

Just because Proverbs is my favorite book (and the most applicable) doesn't mean that I don't love all of the other books.

The Bible is full of history and drama, miracles and promises, teachings and instructions. It is our handbook for living, and we should cherish it above all other possessions.

You'll enjoy your Bible more if you will get a modern translation, a good Bible dictionary, and a concordance. Then you can study it and learn what God has put in His Word.

"Man lives by everything that proceeds out of the mouth of the Lord" (Deuteronomy 8:3).

ACCEPTING CHRIST

*"With the heart man believes, resulting in righteousness,
and with the mouth he confesses, resulting in salvation"*
(Romans 10:10).

MANY years ago, 17-year-old Nuna and her husband were sitting in a revival service. Both were unsaved, but Nuna heard the Lord tell her to go to the front of the church and accept Him. She didn't dare move, because she knew her husband would object.

But she heard the voice again—this time more insistent: "Get up and go!" Nuna told her husband what she was going to do, and it made him so angry he said that if she did he would never talk to her again.

The Spirit of God was stronger, though, and she went forward, bowed before the altar, and prayed to receive Jesus. Nuna was three months pregnant at the time and, other than a very few words, her husband didn't speak to her again until after their son was born.

That lady was my mother, and she didn't tell me this story until she was in her 80s and only then because I asked her if she was a Christian and how it happened. You see, my mother had not gone to church for most of her life.

I was the fifth of her eight surviving children. My parents didn't have much time for us kids, and we weren't very close. One thing I learned from my mother, though, was not to judge anyone else.

Only God knows the heart of a person and knows who is saved and who isn't. It is not up to anyone else to decide.

I rest in the assurance that my mother is with the Lord now and I will see her again.

DAILY SCRIPTURE READING: Acts 10, 11

UNDER PERSECUTION

*"All who desire to live godly in
Christ Jesus will be persecuted"*
(2 Timothy 3:12).

IT is my firm belief that if this country continues to evolve in the way it is going, on an anti-spiritual basis, eventually we will face physical persecution.

We already are facing a kind of a mental or emotional persecution; Christianity has been ridiculed and blamed for all the ills of the world, or at least of this country. Certainly that is true politically.

If this country continues to stay on the secular slide it is now on, we will be physically persecuted for our faith.

There's no reason to believe that God will supernaturally intercede on behalf of Americans any more than He will on behalf of someone who is saved in Saudi Arabia or in China. They are just as precious to God as we are.

The only reason we haven't suffered that kind of persecution is that our foundation was so thoroughly based in Christian principle that we are still living off the legacy of our forefathers. We can be thankful that we don't have to face persecution for our beliefs.

We need to bear in mind the principle that Jesus Christ taught us: *"If they persecuted Me, they will also persecute you"* (John 15:20).

Have you ever thought of what you would do if you were threatened with torture or death if you did not renounce Jesus Christ? God's Word says that *"If we endure, we shall also reign with Him"* (2 Timothy 2:12).

DAILY SCRIPTURE READING: Acts 12, 13

1971

"Make my joy complete by being of the same mind, maintaining the same love, united in spirit, intent on one purpose"
(Philippians 2:2).

HAVE you ever wished you could go back and relive some period of your life? You often hear people talk about "the good ole days." The people living during that time probably were thinking the same thing about a prior time.

If I could relive any year of my life it would be 1971. That was the year I accepted the Lord Jesus Christ as my personal Savior.

That year might not be a meaningful one for some, but it was the most significant of my life. It was during that time that I first read the Bible from cover to cover and found it to be so alive and so refreshing.

Also, that was the year in which I attended my first couples' conference, where I heard somebody talk about the relationship between husband and wife as Christians. It was the first time I heard anybody describe how we, as God's people, were supposed to live our lives.

It was the most exciting, rewarding, fulfilling year in my entire life, and if I could go back and relive any particular year, it would be that one.

What year would you want to relive and why?

PREPARING FOR THANKSGIVING

"Enter His gates with thanksgiving, and His courts with praise.
Give thanks to Him; bless His name. For the Lord is good"
(Psalm 100:4–5).

As you think about Thanksgiving, what are you most thankful for? I think I'm most grateful for the freedom of worship. I've traveled all around the country, speaking to nearly every denomination, and I've been interested to see the various ways to worship the Lord. You can choose for yourself.

I choose to be a fundamental Christian: I believe that God's Word is infallible, inspired, and inerrant. But in this country we aren't forced to believe any certain way.

I own over a dozen Bibles of one kind of another and hundreds of Christian books. In many other countries if you even own one Bible it is grounds for imprisonment. If you have other Christian literature, that's considered to be subversive and you can lose your life.

I've heard of people in other countries, where Bibles are prohibited, who have no more than a page or two from a Bible, which they had to either memorize and destroy or take a chance on hiding it. Don't we take a lot for granted in this country?

With our religious freedom comes responsibility. We are responsible to show our gratitude by telling others about the Lord and helping them to know that their blessings come as a result of a loving God.

Think of what you are most thankful for so you'll be ready to celebrate Thanksgiving Day properly.

DAILY SCRIPTURE READING: Galatians 1, 2, 3

November 21

The Caring Business

*"I command you to be openhanded toward your brothers
and toward the poor and needy in your land"*
(Deuteronomy 15:11 NIV).

MANY years ago, when Davy Crockett was a congressman, a bill was brought before the Congress to help a widow of an American war hero because she was totally indigent.

Davy Crockett stood in that meeting and said, "I will, under no circumstances, vote money from the taxpayers of America to help this lady. It is not the role of the government to care for the needs of people. And when the people of this country begin to treat this government like it is their friend, we shall lose our freedoms."

He went on to say, "Though I will vote no money from the government treasury to help her, I will personally share from my bounty in her time of need, if others in this honored body will do the same."

What is the principle here? The government should not care for the needs of people; the people were always meant to do so.

This is the same principle we read in God's Word that says, "Share with others in your time of plenty so that when you have needs others will share from their plenty" (paraphrase of 2 Corinthians 8:14).

If the body of Christ doesn't voluntarily begin to accept the needs of other people and share with them, God may involuntarily involve us by letting us experience the same needs.

God wants to direct our attention back to the source of all material things: Himself. The only way people in need are ever going to sense that God is their source is by God's people becoming their source.

Is there someone you can help today?

DAILY SCRIPTURE READING: Galatians 4, 5, 6

PROBLEMS

"Consider it all joy, my brethren, when you encounter various trials,
knowing that the testing of your faith produces endurance"
(James 1:2–3).

I HAVE a good friend, an evangelist, who says, "There are only two kinds of Christians in this world: those who have problems and those who lie about it."

In 1 and 2 Corinthians, the apostle Paul laid to rest once and for all the idea that Christians don't have problems. Some of his best writing was done while sitting in a Roman jail with two guards—one chained to each arm. To Paul it was a golden opportunity to witness to the captive audience.

Some people like to think that problems are a result of sin. (Remember the story of Job and his "friends"?) We might experience problems as a result of sin, but all problems are not the result of sin. Think for a moment. Christ had problems in His life and He was without sin. He told his disciples, "If they have persecuted Me, how much more will they persecute those who come after Me?"

The moment you decide to turn everything over to God you probably will have more problems than you ever thought existed. Why? Because Satan is not going to give up easily.

God promises that if you will yield your rights to Him He will do whatever is best in your life to give you maximum fulfillment and spiritual maturity.

You can have joy in the midst of problems if you believe that God hears you. He knows your requests, He knows your needs, and He is listening to you.

"Cease striving and know that I am God" (Psalm 46:10).

DAILY SCRIPTURE READING: James

BAD EYESIGHT

"Having eyes, do you not see?"
(Mark 8:18).

THE only reason I can think of to explain my bad eyesight is that I didn't choose my parents carefully and they had some kind of genetic defect. Of course, I'm only kidding.

I do have pigmentary glaucoma, which has caused me to lose most of the sight in my left eye, and I only have partial sight in my right eye.

Why did God allow this to happen? I don't know, but I know it certainly has taught me to trust Him more.

For me, there is nothing much worse than the thought of going blind. It seems like it would be easier for a paraplegic or quadriplegic to get along in our society than for a blind person.

Of all the conditions I ever feared, blindness would be number one, because it is so debilitating, in terms of making you dependent on other people. That's not something I could handle easily.

Perhaps that's why God allowed this in my life: to teach me total dependence on Him and to affirm that He is sufficient in all things—even bad eyesight.

If you have a handicap of some kind, remember, *"The Lord is good, a stronghold in the day of trouble, and He knows those who take refuge in Him"* (Nahum 1:7).

DAILY SCRIPTURE READING: Acts 16:1-18:11

COMPASSION AND FORGIVENESS

*"Be kind to one another, tender-hearted, forgiving each other,
just as God in Christ also has forgiven you"*
(Ephesians 4:32).

WHEN I first started teaching, I was counseling two doctors who had the same specialty but lived in different towns. One of them saw in our newsletter that I was going to be speaking in a town near him, and he asked if Judy and I would come have dinner and spend the night with him. I said, "Sure, I'll be glad to."

The speaking engagement was over about 6:00, and Judy and I drove to his home. His wife answered the door and I could see through the house into the yard, where the doctor was barbecuing. She stood there looking at me until I introduced myself and said, "Your husband asked us to dinner." Then we were invited in.

She and her husband had a quick chat in the yard, and he added more meat to the grill. We had a good meal with them and talked until about 9:30. They didn't mention spending the night, and I didn't want to embarrass him (he seemed to have forgotten about his invitation for us to stay), so Judy and I left and drove the two and one-half hours home.

About a week later, I got a letter from the other doctor— very angry because I had not shown up at his house for dinner that night. I had gone to the wrong doctor's house! Because it was so embarrassing, I made it a point of staying in contact with him. We had a good laugh about it, became good friends, and we are still good friends.

If God can forgive you of all the mistakes you make, then can't you be forgiving to others?

DAILY SCRIPTURE READING: 1 Thessalonians

November 25

Where Are We?

"The mind of man plans his way, but the Lord directs his steps"
(Proverbs 16:9).

JUST to put a smile on your face, I must tell you another story.

In the early days of the ministry, I didn't have a staff, so I was doing my own scheduling. I had agreed to speak at a Presbyterian church on Peachtree in Atlanta.

Little did I know that there were a multitude of streets, avenues, boulevards, circles, lanes, and so forth—all named Peachtree. I drove until I found Peachtree and looked for the Presbyterian church. No problem. When I found it, I parked and went into the church.

I sat on the front row and no one seemed to notice me. Finally I whispered to the guy sitting next to me, "I'm Larry Burkett and I'm here to speak."

He went to the platform and spoke to the pastor, who came and sat down with me and asked, "Who did you say you are?"

I know I don't have to finish the story. I was at the wrong Presbyterian church. I found out there are lots of Presbyterian churches on lots of Peachtree streets (you have to know about Atlanta to understand that).

If we will allow ourselves to learn valuable lessons from these experiences—like learning to laugh at ourselves—we can benefit even from our failings.

We truly can benefit from everything that happens to us in life—in one way or another.

"In paths they do not know I will guide them" (Isaiah 42:16). Thank the Lord for that!

DAILY SCRIPTURE READING: Acts 18:12-19:22; 2 Thessalonians

A THANKFUL ATTITUDE

"If you have bitter jealousy and selfish ambition in your heart,
do not be arrogant and so lie against the truth.
This wisdom is not that which comes down from above,
but is earthly, natural, demonic"
(James 3:14–15).

IT is remarkable that in America we could ever think that God has failed us materially. It is only possible by comparison, which is one of Satan's primary tools.

The primary defense against this attitude is praise to God. Satan uses lavishness and waste to create discontent and selfish ambition. Why else would we drive ourselves to acquire more than we need or can logically use and, in the process, destroy our health, families, and usefulness to God?

Thankfulness is a state of mind, not an accumulation of assets. Until we can truly thank God for what we have and be willing to accept that as God's provision for our lives, contentment never will be possible.

Have everyone in your family make a list of all he or she has to be thankful for and then share your lists with one another. It may open your eyes to how much you've been blessed by God.

In your prayer of thanksgiving, ask God to help you continue to have a thankful attitude.

DAILY SCRIPTURE READING: 1 Corinthians 1, 2, 3, 4

GIVING THANKS

*"Every good thing bestowed and every perfect gift is from above,
coming down from the Father of lights,
with whom there is no variation, or shifting shadow"*
(James 1:17).

WHAT are you most thankful for? A visit from a loved one? Turkey and pumpkin pie? The sound of children laughing? Or your favorite team winning by a field goal?

Think about the first Thanksgiving—the day the forefathers set aside to give thanks. The early pilgrims gave thanks to the omnipotent Creator who provided their food. They were primarily concerned about having enough food to make it through the winters, because many of the early colonists died of starvation.

These people had no difficulty in believing in a Creator. They were simple people who lived off the land. They noticed that when acorns fell on the ground they grew into oak trees, and when pine cones fell pine trees grew. Not once did they see a pine tree come from an acorn, so they knew God had an orderly plan for everything.

They lived on the cutting edge of life and that's where they had their needs met by God.

In the excitement of Thanksgiving Day, it's easy to forget those who are less fortunate. We should always reach out to someone who is alone or hungry.

Above all, don't let your giving of thanks become a ritual. With your family and friends, either sing or recite the words to the Doxology (Praise God from whom all blessings flow. . .).

DAILY SCRIPTURE READING: 1 Corinthians 5, 6, 7, 8

WHOM TO HELP?

*"I was a father to the needy,
and I investigated the case which I did not know"*
(Job 29:16).

WHEN you have a surplus, how do you decide whom to help? Judy and I have faced that question, and we have a kind of pecking order that we go through.

First of all, we support our local church. The Bible says that we should support those who teach the Word.

Second, we support the organizations from which we benefit —the ones that minister to us. Our ministry is Christian Financial Concepts, which Judy and I started in 1976. I don't get an income from the ministry, but I do support it, because we benefit from it.

Then we support things like our Christian radio stations and other ministries that bless us.

Next, we try to meet the special needs of individuals. The first requirement is that we must know them personally, unless it's missionaries whose needs have been presented to us (of course we wouldn't know them).

If we hear of an individual in need and don't know him or her, we give through a trustworthy organization.

Even if you give to someone and find out later that the money was misspent, you will still be blessed for your heart attitude.

Giving to others should be made a matter of prayer and good stewardship.

"The wisdom from above is first pure, then peaceable, gentle, reasonable, full of mercy and good fruits, unwavering, without hypocrisy" (James 3:17).

DAILY SCRIPTURE READING: 1 Corinthians 9, 10, 11

ORGANIZATIONAL GIFTS

"Wealth adds many friends. . . .
And every man is a friend to him who gives gifts"
(Proverbs 19:4, 6).

I MENTIONED yesterday that Judy and I are sometimes faced with decisions about who we are to help financially. Often I'm asked about what political organizations I support. There also I follow a type of pecking order.

I'll support organizations that do the things I personally believe in. I believe that abortion is murder, so I'm going to support organizations that are pro-life, and that includes my local crisis pregnancy center. Obviously, since I'm not a woman I can't go there and help, but I do all I can.

I believe there are legitimately poor people and I try to find organizations that are discerning about helping them, like the Salvation Army and other help groups in the city in which we live. These groups do things I believe in but can't do myself, so we help them.

Judy and I believe that if we're going to keep good Christians on the mission field and in the pulpit, we've got to invest in them. So we regularly support several Bible college and seminary students.

Many of these young people come out of families who can't afford to pay for their education or don't approve of their chosen vocation, which is serving the Lord. If they are cut off from their families, it is up to those of who can to help them get an education.

"We have brought nothing into the world, so we cannot take any-thing out of it either" (1 Timothy 6:7).

DAILY SCRIPTURE READING: 1 Corinthians 12, 13, 14

November 30

Conversion

"Being found in appearance as a man,
He humbled Himself by becoming obedient to the point of death,
even death on a cross"
(Philippians 2:8).

At the heart of the Gospel is Christ's atonement and resurrection. Jesus came to the earth for one purpose: to die for our sins.

When we were created, God gave us the ability to make choices. One of those choices is whether or not to become a Christian.

I've been a Christian since age 32, but I have several members of my family who are unsaved. I don't have a great many unsaved friends anymore. Those that have been around me for a long period of time either accepted the Lord or moved on.

It's a fine balance that we walk sometimes, between sharing Christ and being obnoxious. Others must see consistency in our lives as we live for the Lord. That is what will attract them.

When I'm with the unsaved members of my family I don't hesitate to talk about the Lord—just as I would around my Christian family members. We are called to give an account for our faith. I'm believing God for the salvation of those who are unsaved.

If you have a close friend or family member who is not a believer, you are responsible to share the message: *"By grace you have been saved through faith; and that not of yourselves, it is the gift of God"* (Ephesians 2:8). So, you should share your gift.

The Bible asks, How will they hear unless someone tells them? Think of those you know who are unsaved and make it a practice to pray regularly for their salvation.

DECEMBER 1

CHRISTMAS GIFT GIVING

*"Instruct those who are rich in this present world not to be
conceited or to fix their hope on the uncertainty of riches,
but on God, who richly supplies us with all things to enjoy"*
(1 Timothy 6:17).

WE have become terribly imbalanced. We give a myriad of useless
gifts at Christmas because it's expected of us, and we feel guilty if
we don't. The commercialized world now makes a $100 toy seem
perfectly normal.

It's easy to observe the stress that our imbalanced society
places on family members. Christian parents who can't provide the
latest indulgences to their children are often depressed and dis-
traught. Obviously, no one person purposely makes them feel unworthy or insignificant, but the overwhelming emphasis we place on
giving at Christmas certainly does.

So great is this social pressure that the closer we get toward
Christmas Day, the more depressed and unworthy those who can't
indulge feel. Unfortunately, the pressures don't end after Christmas
is past either.

We must develop a plan for our families without the pressure
from the commercial world. To do so, we must first believe that
God's plan is different from the world's and is more, not less, fulfilling. More emphasis must be placed on the values taught in
God's Word.

The key is balance, which comes from following God's wisdom.

*"The Lord gives wisdom; from His mouth come knowledge and
understanding. He stores up wisdom for the upright; . . . and He pre-
serves the way of His godly ones"* (Proverbs 2:6–8).

DAILY SCRIPTURE READING:
Acts 19:23-20:1; 2 Corinthians 1, 2, 3, 4

"THE ESTABLISHMENT"

"We establish the Law"
(Romans 3:31).

THE apostle Paul gave a dissertation to some Jewish converts, telling them that the Law, established in the Old Testament, was not abolished as a result of salvation.

One common idea of that generation was that once someone was saved that person was no longer bound by the Law and could do anything he or she wanted to do.

Some even believed that if God's blessing was received as a result of forgiving sin, then the more they sinned the more blessings they received—a heresy commonly accepted at that time.

So, Paul made it very clear that they were not released from the Law; being a Christian does not nullify the Law. As Christians, we either confirm or complete the Law.

We know that the ritualistic practices of blood sacrifices were no longer necessary, because Jesus Christ, the Lamb of God, was sacrificed once and forever for all sins.

But God didn't change His mind about sin. The Ten Commandments remain just as applicable as they were in the time of Moses. The good news is that now we have the means to be forgiven if we stumble and violate God's laws.

It is only through the sacrifice of the Lord Jesus Christ and the fact that we stand before God cleansed by His blood that we are not judged by the Law.

DAILY SCRIPTURE READING: 2 Corinthians 5, 6, 7, 8, 9

SECOND COMING

*"In a moment, in the twinkling of an eye,
at the last trumpet; for the trumpet will sound,
and the dead will be raised imperishable, and we shall be changed"*
(1 Corinthians 15:52).

DURING the latter part of the twentieth century, there has been a Second Coming Movement, which consists of people who are convinced that Jesus is going to come again at the turn of the millennium.

However, the people who lived at the turn of the first millennium also believed that Christ's return was imminent. In fact, many of them were so convinced they sold their homes and spent the money or gave it away. They believed that God would come and rapture them.

And yet, here we are a thousand years later, and He still hasn't come. Those Christians were no less sincere in their generation than we are in ours.

I honestly don't know if the Lord is coming in our generation. I believe we should be ready for His imminent return, and the way to do that is to be about the work assigned to us. Jesus wants to find us alert and being good stewards of His resources when He comes again. That's the most important principle for our generation.

One thing I would not like to do is abandon the next generation to the clutches of Satan by throwing down our weapons and walking off the battlefield. We are here as ambassadors for Christ, and we are, in fact, engaged in spiritual warfare. We need to be about that warfare and about God's business.

If Christ is going to return soon, praise the Lord! If He isn't going to return soon, praise the Lord!

"Come, Lord Jesus" (Revelation 22:20).

DAILY SCRIPTURE READING: 2 Corinthians 10, 11, 12, 13

UFO OR USFO?

"Bless the Lord, you His angels,
mighty in strength, who perform His word"
(Psalm 103:20).

ONE of my employees asked me (tongue in cheek, I presume) if I believed in UFOs (unidentified flying objects). I said no; but I do believe in USFOs (unidentified spiritual flying objects): angels.

Clearly, God's Word tells us that angels were created to do God's bidding, and they're constantly going back and forth between the spiritual domain and our domain. They are carrying messages and ministering to us.

Billy Graham says, "Both angels and the Holy Spirit are at work in our world to accomplish God's perfect will. . . . Angels keep in close and vital contact with all that is happening on the earth."

I know one thing for certain: Angels are a reality. Are UFOs and creatures from other planets a reality? Probably not, but that's just my personal opinion.

Something I do know: If I were a creature from another planet, I would avoid this planet diligently. If I did land here, two things are certain: I wouldn't drink the water, and I'd probably wear a bulletproof vest.

Of course, I'm being facetious. That brings me back to the subject of angels. God's Word says, *"He will give His angels charge concerning you, to guard you in all your ways. They will bear you up in their hands"* (Psalm 91:11–12).

So, now when people start talking about UFOs, you can share with them about the USFOs.

DAILY SCRIPTURE READING: Romans 1, 2, 3

LESSONS LEARNED

"They cried out to the Lord in their trouble;
He saved them out of their distresses"
(Psalm 107:19).

WE can learn from all the experiences we have in life, especially the difficult times.

When I reflect on the years since I was diagnosed with cancer and underwent two major surgeries, I believe that God is teaching me how to trust Him day by day.

If somebody had asked me a few years ago if I were trusting the Lord daily, I would have said sincerely, "Yes, I am." But now I realize that I didn't understand what it meant to truly trust the Lord day by day—to wake up every day and accept that day as a true gift from God and praise Him for it and not anticipate anything long-term.

That doesn't mean that I don't do any planning. I do plan—for myself, my family, and the ministry—but I don't anticipate or take for granted a long life. I believe that has helped me learn to trust God more day by day.

"Behold, God is my salvation, I will trust and not be afraid; for the Lord God is my strength and song, and He has become my salvation" (Isaiah 12:2).

No matter what the circumstances, our sense of joy, satisfaction, and fulfillment in life will increase if we completely trust in the Lord.

Think of some difficulty you've experienced and how it has benefited your spiritual life; then praise God for it.

DAILY SCRIPTURE READING: Romans 4, 5, 6

CHANGING OPINIONS

*"Therefore I shall make the heavens tremble,
and the earth will be shaken from its place
at the fury of the Lord of hosts in the day of His burning anger"*
(Isaiah 13:13).

AFTER I received Christ I accepted many things I heard from others without questioning them. Then, as I matured in the Lord, I began to study for myself and developed my own conclusions.

Probably the most predominant in my mind is the position that I held on the Rapture. It was the opinion of many of the people I met that Christians would be raptured before the Tribulation. After studying the Scriptures for myself, I concluded that Christians may not be raptured before the Great Tribulation.

When people ask my position, I say, "I'm praying that I won't have to go through it and planning as if I will."

I do believe God will rapture Christians before He pours out His wrath upon the earth, but it's hard to imagine that God would equip this great army and then remove us from the earth just before the great battle occurs.

I don't look forward to going through the tribulation battle, but I surely would hate to miss it. I believe we're going to see miracles such as have not been seen on this earth since the Lord Jesus Christ and His apostles departed.

Instead of worrying about the Tribulation, we should be concerned with being prepared for eternity. The future is in God's hands.

"We have obtained our introduction by faith into this grace. . . and we exult in hope of the glory of God" (Romans 5:2).

DAILY SCRIPTURE READING: Romans 7, 8

POLITICAL CONVICTIONS

*"Such is the will of God that by doing right
you may silence the ignorance of foolish men"*
(1 Peter 2:15).

WHEN I first became a Christian, it was my conviction that politics was a corrupting influence and that Christianity and politics didn't mix.

However, as I look back over history, especially reading the early history of America, it's clear that Christianity and politics were intricately entwined—they were one and the same—and the religious convictions of our Founding Fathers are clear in everything they wrote: the Declaration of Independence, the Constitution, and the Bill of Rights.

So, now I'm more convinced that Christians must be involved in politics. I believe we have the responsibility to make our positions well-known. We have the right to vote for the candidates of our choice and to speak out against the candidates who don't stand for the value systems we hold dear.

If we don't get involved in politics, we will end up with exactly what we have today: a secular society. My spirit is grieved when I think of what we are leaving the generation of Americans who will follow us. Without the Christian foundation that was established in this country, we can easily become an evil society.

With a Christian foundation, we are God's unique creation and subject to God's unique blessings. So I would implore you to get involved. Pray about it and spend your money supporting candidates that best reflect your value system.

DAILY SCRIPTURE READING: Romans 9, 10, 11

YOUR CONSCIENCE, YOUR GUIDE

*"Fight the good fight, keeping faith and a good conscience,
which some have rejected and suffered shipwreck
in regard to their faith"*
(1 Timothy 1:18–19).

WE received a letter at the ministry from a woman who asked how we felt about a Christian using the telephone but not paying for the calls.

She said that when her husband travels he calls back home, person to person, and asks for himself, so she will know that he's okay. They use codes so that if she says one thing he will know to call back, but if the family's okay she uses another code.

She thought this was all right since, after all, she was paying a phone bill every month. But after listening to our radio broadcast she began to wonder if it was cheating.

The general principle you have to use is to let God guide your conscience. If you think something is wrong, it probably is.

The son of a friend of mine went off to college and he and some friends devised a system of sticking battery wires down into the telephone to make the operator think they were dropping coins in. Unfortunately, the phone company found out and his father ended up paying a $1,000 fine and got one year probation.

Sin is sin. Integrity is worth a lot more than what little can be saved by cheating someone. Always follow your conscience (your inner voice).

"If I regard wickedness in my heart, the Lord will not hear" (Psalm 66:18).

DAILY SCRIPTURE READING: Romans 12, 13, 14, 15

GETTING FIRED

"Put on a heart of compassion, kindness, humility, gentleness and
patience; bearing with one another, and forgiving each other. . .
just as the Lord forgave you, so also should you"
(Colossians 3:12–13).

I HAVE been fired only once in my life, and it was the best thing that could have happened to me—at least in the long run.

I had just graduated from high school and was trying to decide what to do with my life. I'd worked as an electrician for about four summers at that time, so I hired on as an apprentice electrician, working for a graduate electrical engineer.

I thought, because I had gone to electrician school, that I knew all there was to know about electricity. Twice I corrected the engineer when he was describing his power plant design to someone else, pointing out what I thought were a couple of flaws in his design.

The third time I did that, he was talking to a group of power executives for a plant he was designing. I was an 18-year-old kid— a kid who got fired as soon as that group left!

It made me so mad I could hardly stand it, but as I've grown older I've often looked back and chuckled. That was the best thing he could have done for me, because I never again corrected my superiors—certainly not in front of others.

If you ever have to dismiss someone because that person isn't doing the job or doesn't fit that particular task, be sure to use compassion and kindness. Or if it happens to you, try to believe that it is for the best and trust God for the future.

DAILY SCRIPTURE READING: Acts 20:2-21:16; Romans 16

HEARING GOD'S VOICE

"He fell to the ground, and heard a voice saying to him,
'Saul, Saul, why are you persecuting Me?'"
(Acts 9:4).

IN my travels as a lecturer, I've known many people who told me that God speaks audibly to them. I wish that were true in my life. I have never heard God speak to me audibly; but I know I will when I stand before Him one day.

In order to hear God speak in your spirit, you have to be in tune to God. It's kind of like turning on a radio to get your favorite program on FM 95. You aren't going to hear that program if your radio is tuned to AM 750.

Of course, being tuned to God's voice is not that simple, but I think it's a good analogy. Until your mind, your spirit, and your heart are tuned to God, you won't hear Him speak to you. (Sin will block your "reception.")

I believe I've heard God speak in my spirit and, almost without exception, He has spoken to me through His Word—through Scripture. He may speak to a particular situation or problem I'm facing, but I always hear Him speak inaudibly and with spiritual clarity.

If we want to be in tune with God and hear what He has to say to us, we have to be "tuned in" to His voice and receptive to His Word.

"He who is of God hears the words of God" (John 8:47).

DAILY SCRIPTURE READING: Acts 21:17-23:35

OBEYING GOD'S VOICE

"If you remain silent at this time,
relief and deliverance will arise for the Jews from
another place and you and your father's house will perish"
(Esther 14:4).

YESTERDAY I told you how I hear God speak to me in my spirit. I want to carry that thought further by giving you an example.

When I had been a Christian about two and a half years, I felt God calling me to do something different from what I was doing as a company vice president.

Often my pastor would take me on Wednesday visitation when he was going to visit hard cases, because he could use me as his example— "if God can save this guy He can save anybody."

This particular evening we had gone to three homes and nobody was home. So we were back at the church sitting in his car, half talking, half praying, and I mentioned that I believed God wanted me to do something different.

He asked what it was, but I had to admit that I didn't really know. At the time, I had been studying the area of biblical finances and had become the resident financial counselor for our church.

We prayed about it and during the prayer I heard God speak to me in that gentle, soft voice, and it was from His Word in Esther (our verse for today). Mordecai went on to say to Esther what I believe God was telling me, "Who knows but what you have been raised to this position for just such a time as this, but if you don't go another will be chosen."

I resigned my job and began the greatest adventure of my life—serving God's people in the area of finances.

Be careful to listen when God speaks to you.

DAILY SCRIPTURE READING: Acts 24, 25, 26

KNOWING SCRIPTURE

"Quietly trust yourself to Christ your Lord
and if anybody asks why you believe as you do,
be ready to tell him, and do it in a gentle and respectful way"
(1 Peter 3:15 TLB).

IF we are going to share Christ with others, and that is a requirement for all Christians, we need to know what to say to them and what Bible verses will confirm what we say. Since most of us don't usually carry a list of verses or a Bible with us, we must carry those verses in our memories.

In teaching, I often quote Scriptures dealing with finances. Friends ask me how I am able to remember so many verses. Through no credit of mine, I was given the ability to recall Scripture verses that deal with whatever question I am asked. This has to be a God-given ability, because I don't have to work at it. But, I have to stay in the Word and read the verses I need to recall. You can't remember what you have never read.

Often, when I go to bed, I spend the time until I fall asleep going back over Scripture verses so I'll remember them.

I encourage you to learn as much of God's Word as you can so you can keep it with you. Then, when given the opportunity, you will be able to share it with others. God's Word says that whatever is in your heart is going to come out of your mouth. And John 7:38 says, *"From his innermost being shall flow rivers of living water."*

Get a piece of paper and list all of the verses you can quote from memory. Which is your favorite? Now list the ones you want to learn and spend time each day working on that list.

DAILY SCRIPTURE READING: Acts 27, 28

DECEMBER 13

FASTING

"Whenever you fast,
do not put on a gloomy face as the hypocrites do,
for they neglect their appearance in order
to be seen fasting by men"
(Matthew 6:16).

IT is my personal conviction that any long-term relationship with the Lord is going to be accompanied by fasting and prayer.

The significance of fasting is twofold: spiritual and physical.

Physically, there are great benefits from fasting. It's a cleansing process for the body itself, because the body has the chance to rid itself of the toxins that are taken in on a daily basis through food.

Spiritually, fasting is the denial of something we need and literally surrendering that to God as a testimony that we love and trust Him. If our Lord considered fasting an essential part of His spiritual life, we certainly should.

I believe that fasting is a necessary element of any spiritual relationship with God and also a valuable part of good health.

"Having prayed with fasting, they commended them to the Lord in whom they had believed" (Acts 14:23).

DECEMBER 14

INVESTED LIVES

"It is the Lord Christ whom you serve"
(Colossians 3:24).

ONE of the blessings of running a ministry has been having the opportunity to see all the fine Christian employees who have invested their lives in the ministry.

Many took pay cuts to work with us, because they felt it was where God wanted them to be. And, I expect most of them could earn more money elsewhere. So, it has been an opportunity to witness sacrificial giving of self on the part of God's people.

As I walk through the ministry offices and talk to secretaries, receptionists, mail openers, and people in the shipping department, one of the things God has taught me through them is that these are all quality people and they are precious in God's eyes.

Just because I happen to be in charge of this organization in an administrative capacity does not in any way make me superior to them. They are godly, gracious people. As I sit in devotions with them and hear them pray I sense their spiritual depth and I praise God for sending them our way.

Working with our employees is a refreshing and rewarding experience for me. They love and serve the Lord and each other.

The apostle Paul wrote, *"For you were called to freedom, brethren; only do not turn your freedom into an opportunity for the flesh, but through love serve one another"* (Galatians 5:13).

Have you invested your life in service to the Lord? to your employer? to your family?

NAMES FOR GOD

*"The Lord is my **rock** and my **fortress** and my **deliverer**,*
my God, my rock; . . .
*my **shield** and the **horn of my salvation**, my **stronghold**"*
(Psalm 18:2, emphasis added).

IT is intriguing how many names there are for God. In today's Scripture verse, He is *Jehovah Eli*, my God.

He also is *Jehovah Ori*, my light (Psalm 27:1); *Jehovah Shalom*, my peace (Judges 6:24); *Jehovah Jireh*, my provider (Genesis 22:14); *Jehovah Machsi*, my refuge (Psalm 91:9). And there are others.

I suppose if I were asked which is my favorite name for God, it would be different from time to time, depending on the circumstances in my life. However, I think right now my favorite is *Jehovah Rapha*, the God who heals.

"If you will give earnest heed to the voice of the Lord your God, and do what is right in His sight. . .I will put none of the diseases on you which I have put on the Egyptians; for I, the Lord, am your healer" (Exodus 15:26).

God can heal supernaturally and sometimes He heals incrementally—by using people. God has healed me by using good doctors and by bringing people into my life who have the wisdom to know how to treat illnesses in alternative ways.

I believe the fact that I'm alive is a testimony of the fact that God does intercede and He does answer prayers. In my opinion, the greatest alternative treatment available is prayer.

So you can understand why my favorite name for God right now is *Jehovah Rapha*, my healer.

Think about which name for God is your favorite, and thank Him for being all-sufficient.

DAILY SCRIPTURE READING: Colossians

PICKIN' FRUIT

"The fruit of the Spirit is
love, joy, peace, patience,
kindness, goodness, faithfulness,
gentleness, self-control;
against such things there is no law"
(Galatians 5:22–23).

THE apostle Paul listed the fruit of the Spirit in Galatians, but I think the fruit that is most significant is the one he wrote about in 1 Corinthians 13: love.

We have all kinds of gifts—prophecy, evangelism, giving, speaking in tongues—but if they aren't based on love, they are ineffective. All those things are temporal and will pass away.

But love lasts forever, and one thing I pray for is that God would give me the ability to love more fully and much more deeply.

Some of my bad habits still haunt me from my secular life (remember I wasn't saved until I was 32 years old): irritation with people, driving too fast, and too much pride.

The only way to overcome ungodly characteristics is through love. Perfect love casts out not only fear but also anger, resentment, and pride.

All the fruit of the Spirit should be evident in our lives if we are going to be effective witnesses for the Lord. If you have love, all the other fruit will fall into place.

"Now abide faith, hope, love, these three; but the greatest of these is love" (1 Corinthians 13:13).

DAILY SCRIPTURE READING: Philippians

STAYED TUNED IN

"Thy word is a lamp to my feet,
and a light to my path"
(Psalm 119:105).

MY first pastor told me something about reading God's Word that I've tried to remember all these years: Don't promise God something you can't do.

When I was first saved, I would spend two to three hours a day doing nothing but reading and studying God's Word. But my pastor advised me not to promise that I'd always do that, because there would be times when it wouldn't be possible.

He started me on his "959" plan: Spend nine minutes and 59 seconds a day alone with God in study and in prayer. I try to do that every day. Sometimes I spend a lot more time than that, but sometimes I don't.

For me, on a day-in and day-out basis, that's how I stay tuned in to God.

Of course, when I have a big problem I adjust my time to God's time. When I was diagnosed with cancer, I spent long hours praying and asking God for wisdom and, most of all, for peace.

I have found from experience that God is ready to provide peace anytime we spend time with Him and ask for it.

"These things I have spoken to you, that in Me you may have peace. In the world you have tribulation, but take courage; I have overcome the world" (John 16:33).

If you want that peace, spend time with God and in His Word every day.

DAILY SCRIPTURE READING: 1 Timothy 1, 2, 3; Philemon

December 18

You Are Salt

"You are the salt of the earth"
(Matthew 5:13).

SALT has two major purposes: to season and to preserve.

Seasonings make things taste better and they become more palatable. When other people look at us, as Christians, they should see love, kindness, joy, and peace—pleasant things that make life more palatable.

Preservatives keep things from spoiling. When I was a boy, we raised hogs, and after butchering them we would smoke them and then cure them in salt. Since we didn't have much refrigeration then, the salt would preserve the meat.

We must preserve the truth by telling others about the Lord and by providing a light for those who are looking for the truth.

When things in our society start to "go bad," we must preserve life by making the Gospel message known. It will preserve life for all eternity.

I challenge you to be salt in your home, your church, and your community.

DAILY SCRIPTURE READING: 1 Timothy 4, 5, 6; Titus

December 19

My Temple

*"Do you not know that you are a temple of God,
and that the Spirit of God dwells in you?"*
(1 Corinthians 3:16).

SCRIPTURE is clear that, as a believer, when we put our faith in Jesus Christ the Holy Spirit comes to reside in us.

Therefore, whatever I do and wherever I go, the Holy Spirit is with me in my words and in my actions. That's a pretty sobering thought that should cause all Christians to stop and give thought to what we say and do. We are actual temples in which the Holy Spirit lives.

I have often regretted something I've just said or done and thought, *I just included the Holy Spirit in my pettiness* (or anger or resentment or irritation).

In the Old Testament He chose to make His presence known in the temple (the building). Now, living under the New Covenant, the Spirit lives within each born-again person.

When Scripture speaks of grieving the Holy Spirit, I think it means that the Spirit is emotionally, spiritually, and physically entwined in each and every believer. So we must bring our thoughts, actions, and deeds under God's control.

"To each one is given the manifestation of the Spirit for the common good" (1 Corinthians 12:7).

WILL IT BE MERRY?

"Be hospitable to one another. . . .
As each one has received a special gift,
employ it in serving one another, as good stewards
of the manifold grace of God"
(1 Peter 4:9–10).

CHRISTMAS is very close and I hope you are going to have a happy one—not because of the gifts you are going to get, but because you are celebrating the true meaning of Christmas. The saying has become almost trite; nevertheless, it is something to think about: "Jesus is the Reason for the season."

Christmas should be a joyful time, but for many people it becomes a depressing time—either because they can't afford to compete in the gift-giving activities or because they are away from their loved ones and feeling lonely.

Think of people you know who don't have much hope of having a happy Christmas—financially, physically, or emotionally. Call someone today, and tell that person that you love him or her and that God does too. See if there is anything that person needs.

The holidays can be a very lonely time for some people. If you can invite others into your home, that's great. But if not, at least call and give of yourself. The busier you are doing for others, the happier your Christmas will be.

"Commit your works to the Lord" (Proverbs 16:3).

GET INVOLVED

"Whoever in the name of a disciple gives to one
of these little ones even a cup of cold water to drink,
truly I say to you he shall not lose his reward"
(Matthew 10:42).

BE certain when you give that you are not using a gift of money to avoid a larger responsibility.

It may be that God desires your physical involvement as well. In other words, don't just give your money; give of yourself.

I know a Christian who helps to care for the poor in a major city. By caring, he not only gives money but also gives of himself by establishing thrift shops for the poor in the downtown ghetto areas.

Those shops supply clothing, furniture, food, and other necessities to the poor at prices they can afford. Although his time is limited, like everyone else's, he does it out of obedience to God and love for others.

He says that, often, when he contacts other Christians to help, the vast majority would rather give a little money to God's work than to get personally involved.

In today's Scripture verse, Jesus was saying that we must be involved in giving—including our time—if we don't want to lose our rewards.

MY EPITAPH

"Death is swallowed up in victory. . . .
victorious through Jesus Christ our Lord"
(1 Corinthians 15:54, 57 TLB).

AN epitaph is what is written on a tombstone in memory of the one buried there. My friend, James Dobson, mentioned on one of his radio programs that his father's gravestone says, "He Prayed."

When Judy and I were traveling through Europe, we visited some of the cemeteries and I found it interesting to read the gravestones.

One humorous one was on a woman's grave who was 102 at the time of her death. It read, "See, I told you I was sick."

Some epitaphs are funny and some are heartrending, but the ones I always appreciate the most speak of the spiritual lives of the people who are buried there.

I've given some thought to what my epitaph should be, and I think I'd like my tombstone to read, "Larry Burkett, a servant of the Most High God."

I just pray that at my death someone will be able to write that, legitimately.

I don't know if people use epitaphs anymore, but if you died suddenly and your family wanted to write an epitaph for your gravestone, what do you think it would be?

Remember, the greatest epitaph will be the one given by Christ. What will He be able to write about you?

DAILY SCRIPTURE READING: Hebrews 1:1-5:10

WHAT IS HELL LIKE?

*"In Hades he lifted up his eyes, being in torment. . . . He cried out and
said, 'Father Abraham, have mercy on me, and send Lazarus,
that he may dip the tip of his finger in water and cool off my tongue;
for I am in agony in this flame'"*
(Luke 16:23–24).

I READ a story once about a very evil man who had died. He woke
in a place that was totally dark—nothing around him. He had
always joked that since all his friends would be in hell that was
where he wanted to go.

He thought, *I'm alone. What happened? Well, this can't be forever; nothing is forever. God will come and get me.*

Time passed and he finally realized that no one was coming.
Then he began to feel the heat of the flames around him. He
looked down to see if he was burning, but there was no physical
body; yet he could feel the flames and the pain was real.

He cried out for mercy, but there was no one to hear him. He
realized he had died and gone to hell and would be there for eternity, which is forever and ever and ever. He would always be in
that lake of fire. No one was coming for him. He was completely
alone in his suffering.

I believe that's an accurate description of what hell probably
will be like. From what we read in Scripture (see today's verse) it
sounds frighteningly real.

Praise God that we don't have to fear that fate—not if we have
accepted the Lord Jesus Christ as Savior and Lord of our lives.

We do have to be concerned about those who have not
made that decision and do all we can to see that their eternity will
be joyful.

DAILY SCRIPTURE READING: Hebrews 5:11-9:28

WHAT WILL HEAVEN BE LIKE?

"Behold, I create new heavens and a new earth;
and the former things shall not be remembered or come to mind"
(Isaiah 65:17).

SHORTLY after Senator Harold Hughes became a Christian someone asked him, "Senator Hughes, what do you think is the advantage of being a Christian?" They thought he would say, "Well, God will make me the next president of the United States." But he didn't say that.

Senator Hughes replied, "The advantage of being a Christian is that this life is all of hell I shall ever experience. The disadvantage of being an unbeliever is that this life is all the Heaven some people will ever know."

I guess everybody has their own idea of what Heaven will be like. We are told in Revelation that God is going to bring New Jerusalem down out of Heaven—a city made of jasper, gold, onyx, and other precious stones, and the streets will be transparent gold. The city will be a 1500-mile cube.

God said there will be a new Heaven and a new Earth, and that's where His people will be. I'm looking forward to it, aren't you?

I don't care if I'm a street sweeper in Heaven. After all, the streets are made of gold!

The best part of Heaven is that we will be in the presence of God. And, there will be no more pain, fear, suffering, sickness, or sorrow, as well as no cancer, diabetes, heart trouble, overweight, gray hair, or wrinkles, so why wouldn't we look forward to getting to Heaven?

What are you looking forward to?

DAILY SCRIPTURE READING: Hebrews 10, 11

KEEPING CHRIST IN CHRISTMAS

"For all that is in the world, the lust of the flesh and
the lust of the eyes and the boastful pride of life,
is not from the Father, but is from the world"
(1 John 2:16).

IT irritates me to see Christ being taken out of Christmas. That's not limited to only non-Christians—even Christians have adjusted to the commercialism of the holiday season. Obviously, not all of it is bad; in fact, the holiday season provides opportunities for families to reunite and also provides a pleasant break from our routines.

I personally look forward to these days as an opportunity to visit with friends who are much too busy other times of the year to just stop and relax.

Gift-giving is a relatively new idea. Until a couple of centuries ago, Christmas was reserved as a religious holiday on a noncommercial basis. However, gift-giving became a generally accepted practice and was used primarily to show appreciation to loved ones.

As with most things that start out right, somewhere along the way the direction shifted. How did it happen? It seems apparent that Christians aren't as wise in the things of the Lord as non-Christians are.

The secular world is always looking for ways to shift attention from God to material things, and we've been naive enough to go along with it.

It's time for Christians to stop compromising with the enemy and put Christ back in the celebration of His birth.

"He who practices the truth comes to the light, that his deeds may be manifested as having been wrought in God" (John 3:21).

Have a wonderful day as you celebrate our Savior's birthday!

DAILY SCRIPTURE READING: Hebrews 12-13; 2 John; 3 John

AFTER CHRISTMAS

"The plans of the heart belong to man. . . .
Commit your works to the Lord,
and your plans will be established"
(Proverbs 16:1, 3).

WELL, Christmas is past. Praise the Lord! Right? That's what you may be thinking, especially if you went into debt. Now that Christmas is over, what are your goals for the coming year?

Let me make a suggestions for next year's Christmas that you can start right now. In fact, the first goal is to budget your Christmas gifts right now, while the memory of what you have done this year is fresh in your mind. Jot down some distinct spending goals and stick to them.

Next, set aside some money in your budget every month for Christmas shopping. If you are going to spend $600, save $50 every month; if it will be more like $1,200, save $100 every month. Then don't spend any more than you have saved.

Three, think about self-made gifts. You and your family could make gifts to exchange with one another, which will be some of your finest treasures.

Four, shop bargain sales throughout the year and don't wait until November or December, when you'll pay the higher prices.

Five, get your family members together and discuss drawing names. If you swap gifts with one or two people, that simplifies gift-giving.

Begin now to set some realistic goals for next Christmas. Make it a joyful Christmas—one that can be spent in the worship of our Lord, with less focus on material things.

DAILY SCRIPTURE READING: 1 John

CHOSEN TO INTERCEDE

"Esther was taken to the palace of the king. . . .
The king loved Esther more than any of the other girls. . . .
He set the royal crown on her head and declared her queen"
(Esther 2:16–17 TLB).

IF we are to be fulfilled Christians, we have to make the commitment to do what God has told us to do—no matter the outcome.

One of my favorite books in the Bible is Esther. Esther was a graphic example of obedience, timidity, and humility.

Esther's uncle, Mordecai, heard that the king (Esther's husband) had granted a request to issue an edict that all the Jews in the land could be killed and their property confiscated. When Mordecai heard this, he fasted and prayed; then he wrote to Esther and asked her to go to the king and intercede on behalf of her people.

Esther responded by saying that she couldn't go in to the king unless he summoned her—under penalty of death.

Mordecai wrote back to tell Esther that she could do nothing else (because Esther was also a Jew, although her husband, the king, didn't know it). He cautioned Esther that if she didn't go and intercede for her people, God would choose someone else.

Esther agreed and said, *"Fast for me. . .I will go in to see the king; and if I perish, I perish"* (Esther 4:16 TLB).

Esther made sure her husband, the king, and her people were saved, but the real point is that she was willing to face an uncertain fate to be obedient. All too often in our generation we choose the safe way and miss the blessing.

What would you do if being obedient risked your life?

DAILY SCRIPTURE READING: Revelation 1, 2, 3

I HEARD HIM SPEAK

"I will hear what God the Lord will say;
for He will speak peace to His people,
to His godly ones"
(Psalm 85:8).

GOD gives us clear and specific directions, if we are spiritually able to hear Him.

After my first cancer surgery (removal of my right kidney), I awoke during the middle of the night thinking, *One down and one to go.* I knew that in two weeks I would be returning to the hospital for the removal of my shoulder blade (more cancer).

I realized that I was full of fear, which I detest. I'm not afraid of dying, and I don't want to be fearful of anything. I want to be able to live my life in peace and do what God's called me to do here, without any debilitating fear.

That night I suddenly felt the presence of the Lord in that hospital room. Actually it could have been an angel; I just know it was from God.

I heard a voice, not audibly but in my spirit, saying, "Have no fear. This is not unto death. This is for the glory of God. Just do what God called you to do." From that point I have had no fear, either of the cancer or of dying.

The Holy Spirit resides within us for the purpose of giving peace and comfort and direction.

I say with the psalmist, *"I shall not die, but live, and tell of the works of the Lord"* (Psalm 118:17).

Jesus said, *"Do not be afraid, little flock, for your Father has chosen gladly to give you the kingdom"* (Luke 12:32).

DAILY SCRIPTURE READING: Revelation 4, 5, 6, 7, 8, 9

DECEMBER 29

A HANDICAPPED WOMAN

"When Jesus saw [a seriously handicapped woman
who had been bent double for eighteen years and
was unable to straighten herself]
*He called her over and said to her,
'Woman, you are freed from your sickness'. . . .
Immediately she was made erect again"*
(Luke 13:12–13).

THE verse for today is what happened when a seriously handicapped woman was blessed by Jesus. She immediately began glorifying God.

I've had many instances of Christ's blessings, but one I remember was when I had been a Christian for only about three months. Judy had a severe back problem and was in severe pain. We had four small children and she needed to be able to care for them—particularly because I was working all the time.

I can remember that while I was driving my car to work I felt a strong leading to stop and pray, so that's exactly what I did.

I asked that God's healing hand would reach out and touch Judy. When I returned home that evening, Judy told me that her pain had just gone away earlier that day. And it never came back again.

I believe God healed Judy of her physical problem as a confirmation to me, a new Christian.

Every day we experience answers to prayer, but how often do we remember to truly thank God for answered prayers?

We should follow the example of the woman in today's Scripture verse and immediately glorify God.

DAILY SCRIPTURE READING: Revelation 10, 11, 12, 13, 14

REFLECTION

*"The sorrow that is according to the will of God
produces a repentance without regret"*
(2 Corinthians 7:10).

AS I look back over the years, I have a few regrets; one, that I was not saved at an younger age so I would have had longer to serve the Lord. Also I regret that I didn't know more while my children were at home so I could have spent more time teaching them God's ways.

Obviously I can't do anything about the past, so I'm trying to pass along what I know to my grandchildren.

Other than those, I have no conscious regrets. For the last 25 years, God has allowed me to do exactly what He called me to do; and, I've never done anything in my life that I have enjoyed more. Of course, there were some parts I didn't enjoy, but that's true with anything, isn't it?

It is unfortunate that so few people can look back over their lives with few regrets.

It's a good idea to examine this past year, to see if there's anything you regret. You can correct it right now. It's never too late. Make up your mind that next year will be different.

We will all face judgment one day and should be prepared. You can't do anything about the past, but you don't have to continually live in it either.

"We shall all stand before the judgment seat of God" (Romans 14:10).

DAILY SCRIPTURE READING: Revelation 15, 16, 17, 18

NEW YEARS' EVE

*"First clean the inside of the cup and of the dish,
so that the outside of it may become clean also"*
(Matthew 23:26).

IN just a few hours the year will be over and another year will begin. By tomorrow thousands of New Year's resolutions already will be broken or forgotten. Intentions are good, but if the reform doesn't take place the resolutions are irrelevant.

This past year has been a difficult time for Christians as a minority group in America. Many of our Christian freedoms have been taken away to protect the freedoms of the most radical element in our society.

However frustrating and disheartening this may be from the outward appearance, we need to rejoice inwardly that God is working His plans to completion and these trials will actually cause God's people to look more to Him and less to other's efforts.

We are seeing more cooperation between ministries and God's people than I've seen in my lifetime. And I believe that unity is an important factor in riding through this time of change in America. God's people are ultimately going to be the victors.

No matter how good the intentions to change bad to good, we have to first be cleansed from within, as today's Scripture verse says. This applies to many areas of our lives. God's people must start trusting Him more.

As you welcome in the new year, get your eyes off of yourself and your circumstances and look forward with hope for God's mercy and grace. He is our ultimate resource.

DAILY SCRIPTURE READING: Revelation 19, 20, 21, 22

NOTES

NOTES

NOTES

NOTES

NOTES

NOTES

NOTES

NOTES